365 Yummy Easy Dessert Recipes

(365 Yummy Easy Dessert Recipes - Volume 1)

Wilma Walker

Published on December, 02 2020

Content

365 Awesome Easy Dessert Recipes

***

1. All Star Ice Cream Sandwiches

Serving: 4 servings. | Prep: 10mins | Cook: 5mins | Ready in:

Ingredients

- 1/2 cup chocolate chip cookie dough ice cream, softened
- 8 Oreo cookies
- 6 ounces milk chocolate candy coating, melted
- Red, white and blue sprinkles

Direction

- Scoop onto half of the cookies with 2 tbsp. of ice cream, then put leftover cookies on top. Scoop over tops with melted coating, then use sprinkles to garnish. Freeze on a baking sheet for a minimum of an hour.

Nutrition Information

- Calories:
- Cholesterol:
- Protein:
- Total Fat:
- Sodium:
- Fiber:
- Total Carbohydrate:

2. Almond Chocolate Torte

Serving: 10-12 servings. | Prep: 20mins | Cook: 0mins | Ready in:

Ingredients

- 2/3 cup sliced almonds, toasted
- 8 ounces semisweet chocolate, chopped
- 2 packages (8 ounces each) cream cheese, softened
- 1 cup sugar
- 1 envelope unflavored gelatin
- 1/4 cup cold water
- 2 cups heavy whipping cream, whipped

Direction

- Reserve 1 tablespoon of almonds for later garnish. Chop the remaining almonds; spread into a 9-in. springform pan coated with grease. Melt chocolate in a microwave; stir till smooth. Allow to cool slightly.
- Beat sugar and cream cheese in a large bowl till smooth. Meanwhile, sprinkle gelatin on top of cold water in a small saucepan; allow to sit for 1 minute. Cook while stirring over low heat till the gelatin is dissolved completely. Beat into the cream cheese mixture. Beat in the melted chocolate till smooth. Stir in whipped cream.
- Transfer to the prepared pan. Sprinkle the reserved almonds on top. Refrigerate with a cover for at least 3 hours.

Nutrition Information

- Calories:
- Total Fat:
- Sodium:
- Fiber:
- Total Carbohydrate:
- Cholesterol:
- Protein:

3. Ambrosia Tarts

Serving: 4 servings. | Prep: 10mins | Cook: 0mins | Ready in:

Ingredients

- 1 can (11 ounces) mandarin oranges, drained
- 1 can (8 ounces) crushed pineapple, drained
- 1/2 cup miniature marshmallows
- 1/4 cup sweetened shredded coconut
- 1 cup whipped topping
- 4 individual graham cracker shells

Direction

- Mix together coconut, marshmallows, pineapples and oranges in a small bowl. Stir in whipped topping. Transfer to shells. Chill until ready to serve.

Nutrition Information

- Calories: 303 calories
- Cholesterol: 0 cholesterol
- Protein: 2g protein.
- Total Fat: 11g fat (6g saturated fat)
- Sodium: 167mg sodium
- Fiber: 2g fiber)
- Total Carbohydrate: 51g carbohydrate (35g sugars

4. Angel Berry Tunnel Cake

Serving: 12 servings. | Prep: 30mins | Cook: 0mins | Ready in:

Ingredients

- 1 prepared angel food cake (8 to 10 ounces)
- 1-1/2 cups fresh or frozen raspberries, thawed and drained
- 1-1/2 cups fresh or frozen blueberries
- 8 cups whipped topping
- Additional berries, optional

Direction

- Slice off the top half inch of the cake with a serrated knife and set aside. Cut a 2-inch deep tunnel in the cake and leave a 3/4-inch shell. Remove the cake bits from the tunnel and cut into an inch cubes.
- Combine together cake chunks, half of the whipped topping, and berries and spoon the mixture into the tunnel. Substitute the cake top.
- Spread the rest of the whipped topping on top of the cake. Decorate with berries and refrigerate before serving.

Nutrition Information

- Calories:
- Protein:
- Total Fat:
- Sodium:
- Fiber:
- Total Carbohydrate:
- Cholesterol:

5. Angel Food Cake With Fruit

Serving: 8 servings. | Prep: 10mins | Cook: 0mins | Ready in:

Ingredients

- 1 can (21 ounces) peach pie filling
- 1 package (16 ounces) frozen unsweetened strawberries, thawed and drained or 1-1/2 cups fresh strawberries, halved
- 1 can (11 ounces) mandarin oranges, drained
- 2 medium apples, chopped
- 2 medium firm bananas, sliced
- 1 prepared angel food cake (8 to 10 ounces), cut into 8 slices

- Whipped topping, optional

Direction

- Combine apples, oranges, strawberries and pie filling in a large bowl. Fold in the bananas. Spoon onto each slice of the cake with a heaping half cupful. If desired, decorate with the whipped topping.

Nutrition Information

- Calories: 231 calories
- Sodium: 229mg sodium
- Fiber: 4g fiber)
- Total Carbohydrate: 56g carbohydrate (47g sugars
- Cholesterol: 0 cholesterol
- Protein: 3g protein.
- Total Fat: 1g fat (0 saturated fat)

6. Apple Cider Pie

Serving: 6-8 servings. | Prep: 15mins | Cook: 0mins | Ready in:

Ingredients

- 1 can (21 ounces) apple pie filling with cinnamon
- 1 graham cracker crust (10 inches)
- 1 package (8 ounces) cream cheese, softened
- 1/4 cup sour cream
- 4 envelopes (.74 ounce each) instant spiced cider mix
- 1-3/4 cups whipped topping
- 1 package (1.5 ounces) crunchy granola bars without raisins, crushed

Direction

- Pour the pie filling into the crust. Beat cream cheese in a small bowl until it becomes smooth. Beat in the cider mix and sour cream until it becomes fluffy and light. Fold in the whipped topping and pour over the pie filling, chill till set. Before serving, sprinkle with granola.

Nutrition Information

- Calories: 268 calories
- Cholesterol: 36mg cholesterol
- Protein: 3g protein.
- Total Fat: 15g fat (10g saturated fat)
- Sodium: 137mg sodium
- Fiber: 1g fiber)
- Total Carbohydrate: 30g carbohydrate (21g sugars

7. Apple Pie A La Mode

Serving: 8 servings. | Prep: 15mins | Cook: 0mins | Ready in:

Ingredients

- 1 can (21 ounces) apple pie filling
- 1 graham cracker crust (9 inches)
- 2 cups butter pecan ice cream, softened if necessary
- 1 jar (12 ounces) hot caramel ice cream topping
- 1/4 cup chopped pecans, toasted

Direction

- Spread 1/2 pie filling on crust. Put 1/2 ice cream on top. Freeze it for 30 minutes. Drizzle 1/2 caramel topping on top. Layer leftover pie filling on. Freeze it for 30 minutes. Scoop leftover ice cream on top. Freeze till firm, covered.
- Remove from freeze half an hour before you serve it. Warm leftover caramel topping in a microwave. Serve the pie with the warm caramel topping then sprinkle pecans on top.

Nutrition Information

- Calories: 398 calories
- Sodium: 357mg sodium
- Fiber: 2g fiber)
- Total Carbohydrate: 69g carbohydrate (59g sugars
- Cholesterol: 13mg cholesterol
- Protein: 3g protein.
- Total Fat: 14g fat (4g saturated fat)

8. Apple Rice Betty

Serving: 6 servings. | Prep: 10mins | Cook: 10mins | Ready in:

Ingredients

- 2 cups apple juice
- 1-1/2 cups chopped peeled tart apples (about 2 medium)
- 1 cup uncooked instant rice
- 1/2 cup raisins
- 1/2 teaspoon ground cinnamon
- 1/8 teaspoon salt
- Sugar substitute equivalent to 1/3 cup sugar
- 6 tablespoons reduced-fat whipped topping

Direction

- Mix the first 6 ingredients together in a big saucepan, then bring the mixture to a boil. Lower heat, then cook and stir until the liquid is mostly absorbed and rice soften, about 6 to 7 minutes. Take away from the heat, then stir in sugar substitute. Chill for an hour. Use 1 tablespoon of whipped topping to decorate each serving.

Nutrition Information

- Calories: 177 calories
- Protein: 2g protein. Diabetic Exchanges: 2 fruit
- Total Fat: 1g fat (1g saturated fat)
- Sodium: 56mg sodium
- Fiber: 3g fiber)
- Total Carbohydrate: 42g carbohydrate (0 sugars
- Cholesterol: 0 cholesterol

9. Apple Yogurt Parfaits

Serving: 4 servings. | Prep: 10mins | Cook: 0mins | Ready in:

Ingredients

- 1 cup sweetened applesauce
- Dash ground nutmeg
- 1/2 cup granola with raisins
- 1-1/3 cups vanilla yogurt

Direction

- Mix nutmeg and applesauce in a small bowl. In each of four parfait glasses, put 1 tablespoon granola. Then layer each with 1/3 cup yogurt and 1/4 cup applesauce; dust with remaining granola. Serve right away.

Nutrition Information

- Calories: 158 calories
- Total Fat: 2g fat (1g saturated fat)
- Sodium: 70mg sodium
- Fiber: 1g fiber)
- Total Carbohydrate: 30g carbohydrate (24g sugars
- Cholesterol: 4mg cholesterol
- Protein: 5g protein.

10. Apple Yogurt Parfaits For Two

Serving: 2 servings. | Prep: 5mins | Cook: 0mins | Ready in:

Ingredients

- 1/2 cup sweetened applesauce

- Dash ground nutmeg
- 1/4 cup granola with raisins
- 2/3 cup vanilla yogurt

Direction

- Mix in a small bowl the nutmeg and applesauce. Into each of two parfait glasses, put 1 tablespoon granola. Then layer each with 1/3 cup yogurt and 1/4 cup applesauce; dust with the leftover granola. Serve right away.

Nutrition Information

- Calories: 171 calories
- Protein: 5g protein. Diabetic Exchanges: 1 starch
- Total Fat: 4g fat (2g saturated fat)
- Sodium: 69mg sodium
- Fiber: 1g fiber)
- Total Carbohydrate: 30g carbohydrate (24g sugars
- Cholesterol: 8mg cholesterol

11. Apple Cinnamon Mini Pies

Serving: 1 dozen. | Prep: 20mins | Cook: 15mins | Ready in:

Ingredients

- 1 package (14.1 ounces) refrigerated pie pastry
- 1/2 cup chunky applesauce
- 3 teaspoons cinnamon sugar, divided
- 2 tablespoons butter, cut into 12 pieces
- 1 tablespoon 2% milk, divided

Direction

- Set oven to 350 degrees and start preheating. Roll out pastry sheets onto a surface lightly dusted with flour. Cut 6 circles out of each pastry sheet using a floured round cookie cutter of 3-1/2 inches.
- Combine 1-1/2 teaspoons cinnamon sugar and applesauce in a small bowl. Scoop 2 teaspoons of applesauce mixture onto each circle, covering half of each; dot each with butter. Make edges of the pastry wet with milk. Fold pastry to cover filling; use a fork to press edges to seal.
- Place on baking sheets without grease. Brush remaining milk on top; scatter with remaining cinnamon sugar. Bake in preheated oven until golden brown, about 12 to 15 minutes. Transfer to wire racks. Serve while still warm or cool to room temperature.

Nutrition Information

- Calories: 104 calories
- Fiber: 0 fiber)
- Total Carbohydrate: 11g carbohydrate (3g sugars
- Cholesterol: 8mg cholesterol
- Protein: 1g protein.
- Total Fat: 6g fat (3g saturated fat)
- Sodium: 77mg sodium

12. Apricot Cashew Clusters

Serving: 2-1/2 dozen. | Prep: 30mins | Cook: 0mins | Ready in:

Ingredients

- 1 package (11-1/2 ounces) milk chocolate chips
- 1 cup chopped dried apricots
- 1 cup chopped salted cashews

Direction

- Liquefy the chocolate chips in a double boiler or microwave; mix till smooth. Mix in cashews and apricots. On waxed paper-lined baking sheets, drop by rounded tablespoonfuls. Refrigerate for 15 minutes till set. Keep in an airtight container.

Nutrition Information

- Calories: 93 calories
- Protein: 2g protein.
- Total Fat: 5g fat (2g saturated fat)
- Sodium: 41mg sodium
- Fiber: 1g fiber)
- Total Carbohydrate: 11g carbohydrate (8g sugars
- Cholesterol: 2mg cholesterol

13. Apricot Sorbet

Serving: 4 servings. | Prep: 5mins | Cook: 0mins | Ready in:

Ingredients

- 1 can (15 ounces) apricot halves, undrained
- 1 to 2 tablespoons sugar
- 1 tablespoon lemon juice

Direction

- Freeze the apricots in a container that is freezer-proof. Put the frozen apricots in a blender or food processor and add the sugar and lemon juice. Cover the blender and process until well-combined. You can freeze it or serve it immediately.

Nutrition Information

- Calories: 101 calories
- Cholesterol: 0 cholesterol
- Protein: 1g protein.
- Total Fat: 0 fat (0 saturated fat)
- Sodium: 4mg sodium
- Fiber: 2g fiber)
- Total Carbohydrate: 26g carbohydrate (24g sugars

14. April Fools Berry Soda

Serving: 6 servings | Prep: 10mins | Cook: 0mins | Ready in:

Ingredients

- 2 packages (3 ounces each) strawberry gelatin
- 3/4 cup sliced fresh strawberries
- 3/4 cup fresh raspberries
- 3/4 cup fresh blueberries

Direction

- Follow the directions of the package to prepare gelatin. Put into a refrigerator for approximately 2 hrs until partially set. Whisk in berries. Add to 6 soda or tall drink glasses. Insert straws into the glasses, one for each glass. Put into a refrigerator until set.

Nutrition Information

- Calories: 76 calories
- Fiber: 2g fiber)
- Total Carbohydrate: 18g carbohydrate (16g sugars
- Cholesterol: 0 cholesterol
- Protein: 2g protein.
- Total Fat: 0 fat (0 saturated fat)
- Sodium: 33mg sodium

15. Asti & Strawberries Dessert

Serving: 4 servings. | Prep: 10mins | Cook: 0mins | Ready in:

Ingredients

- 1 envelope unflavored gelatin
- 3/4 cup cold Asti Spumante, divided
- 1/2 cup dark chocolate chips
- 3 ounces cream cheese, softened

- 1-1/2 cups whipped topping, divided
- 2-1/2 cups sliced fresh strawberries
- 1 tablespoon sugar
- 1/4 teaspoon vanilla extract
- 4 pizzelle cookies
- Additional whipped topping

Direction

- Sprinkle gelatin over 1/2 cup of Asti Spumante in a small microwavable bowl, then allow to stand for a minute. Heat in the microwave on high setting about a half minute, stirring until gelatin dissolves. Melt chocolate chips in a microwave and put aside to cool.
- Beat cream cheese in a big bowl until smooth. Put in 2/3 cup of whipped topping, melted chocolate and gelatin mixture, then beat until mixed. Fold in leftover whipped topping. Cover and chill about a half hour.
- In the meantime, mix together leftover Asti Spumante, vanilla, sugar and strawberries in a separate bowl, then beat the mousse until fluffy and light. Serve together with more whipped topping, cookies and strawberries.

Nutrition Information

- Calories: 402 calories
- Sodium: 77mg sodium
- Fiber: 2g fiber)
- Total Carbohydrate: 39g carbohydrate (27g sugars
- Cholesterol: 26mg cholesterol
- Protein: 6g protein.
- Total Fat: 23g fat (15g saturated fat)

16. Bacon Breakfast Cookies

Serving: 12 | Prep: 15mins | Cook: 15mins | Ready in:

Ingredients

- 1 cup whole wheat flour
- 3/4 cup white sugar
- 1/4 teaspoon baking soda
- 1/2 cup bacon bits
- 1/2 cup butter
- 1 egg, beaten
- 2 cups corn flake cereal
- 1/4 cup shredded Cheddar cheese

Direction

- Set the oven to 350°F or 175°C for preheating. Use a parchment paper to line the baking pan.
- In a bowl, combine baking soda, flour, and sugar. Mix in egg, butter, and bacon bits until well-combined. Fold in Cheddar cheese and corn flakes. Place spoonsful of the dough onto the prepared baking pan, arranging it 2-inches apart from each other.
- Let it bake inside the preheated oven for 13-15 minutes until it is golden brown.

Nutrition Information

- Calories: 199 calories;
- Total Fat: 10.1
- Sodium: 282
- Total Carbohydrate: 23.9
- Cholesterol: 42
- Protein: 4.9

17. Baked Apples On The Grill

Serving: 4 servings. | Prep: 10mins | Cook: 20mins | Ready in:

Ingredients

- 4 medium tart apples, cored
- 1/3 cup raisins
- 1/3 cup sweetened shredded coconut
- 1/4 cup packed brown sugar
- 1/2 teaspoon ground cinnamon

Direction

- Prepare a sheet of durable foil around 12 square inches. Put an apple on each piece. Mix the rest of the ingredients together and use it to fill up the centre of the apples with a spoon. Seal it up firmly after folding the foil on apples. At moderate heat, grill the apples with a cover on until they become tender. Cook for 20 to 25 minutes. Unravel the foil slowly to let the steam out.

Nutrition Information

- Calories: 209 calories
- Protein: 1g protein.
- Total Fat: 3g fat (3g saturated fat)
- Sodium: 27mg sodium
- Fiber: 5g fiber)
- Total Carbohydrate: 48g carbohydrate (40g sugars
- Cholesterol: 0 cholesterol

18. Baklava Tartlets

Serving: 45 tartlets. | Prep: 25mins | Cook: 0mins | Ready in:

Ingredients

- 3/4 cup honey
- 1/2 cup butter, melted
- 1 teaspoon ground cinnamon
- 1 teaspoon lemon juice
- 1/4 teaspoon ground cloves
- 2 cups finely chopped walnuts
- 3 packages (1.9 ounces each) frozen miniature phyllo tart shells

Direction

- Combine the first 5 ingredients in a small bowl until incorporated; mix in walnuts. Scoop 2 teaspoons of the mixture in each tart shell. Chill until ready to serve.

Nutrition Information

- Calories: 76 calories
- Protein: 2g protein.
- Total Fat: 5g fat (1g saturated fat)
- Sodium: 24mg sodium
- Fiber: 0 fiber)
- Total Carbohydrate: 6g carbohydrate (4g sugars
- Cholesterol: 5mg cholesterol

19. Banana Blueberry Pie

Serving: 12 | Prep: 20mins | Cook: | Ready in:

Ingredients

- 1 (8 ounce) package cream cheese, softened
- 1 cup white sugar
- 1 (1.3 ounce) envelope dry whipped topping mix
- 3 bananas, sliced
- 2 (9 inch) pie shells, baked
- 1 (21 ounce) can blueberry pie filling
- 1 (12 ounce) container frozen whipped topping, thawed

Direction

- In a large bowl, combine sugar and cream cheese until light. Based on the package instructions, prepare the whipped topping mix, and fold into the cream cheese mixture.
- Arrange a layer of sliced banana onto the bottom of each pie shell. Spoon 1/2 the cream cheese mixture into each pie, and spread evenly. Spoon 1/2 the blueberry pie filling over each pie in an even layer. Spread the tops of the pies with the thawed frozen whipped topping. Let chill until enjoying.

Nutrition Information

- Calories: 508 calories;
- Total Fat: 24.1
- Sodium: 231
- Total Carbohydrate: 69.6
- Cholesterol: 21
- Protein: 4.2

20. Banana Cheesecake Pie

Serving: 8 servings. | Prep: 25mins | Cook: 0mins | Ready in:

Ingredients

- 1 package (11.1 ounces) no-bake home-style cheesecake mix
- 1/2 cup crushed vanilla wafers (about 15 wafers)
- 2 tablespoons sugar
- 1/2 cup cold butter, cubed
- 1 cup 2% milk plus 1-1/2 cups 2% milk, divided
- 1 package (3.4 ounces) instant banana cream pudding mix
- 2 medium bananas, cut into 1/4-in. slices
- 1 cup whipped topping
- 1/4 cup chopped pecans, toasted

Direction

- Combine sugar, wafers and contents of the crust mix in large bowl; cut in butter until coarse crumbs resemble. Press up sides and onto bottom of an unoiled 9 inches deep-dish pie plate.
- Beat contents of the filling mix and one cup of milk in large bowl on low speed until they are blended. Beat for 3 mins on medium, until they become smooth (the filling should become thick). Transfer to crust by spoon. Let chill for half an hour.
- In the meantime, whisk pudding mix and remaining milk in small bowl for 2 mins. Allow to stand until soft-set, about 2 mins (the pudding should become stiff). Place banana slices onto filling. Spread pudding over, followed by the whipped topping. Top with the pecans. Let chill at least 60 mins. Then serve.

Nutrition Information

- Calories: 468 calories
- Sodium: 594mg sodium
- Fiber: 2g fiber)
- Total Carbohydrate: 64g carbohydrate (43g sugars
- Cholesterol: 38mg cholesterol
- Protein: 5g protein.
- Total Fat: 22g fat (12g saturated fat)

21. Banana Pudding Parfait

Serving: 10-12 servings. | Prep: 15mins | Cook: 0mins | Ready in:

Ingredients

- 1 package (8 ounces) cream cheese, softened
- 1 can (14 ounces) sweetened condensed milk
- 1 cup cold milk
- 1 package (3.4 ounces) instant vanilla pudding mix
- 1 carton (8 ounces) frozen whipped topping, thawed
- 52 vanilla wafers
- 4 medium firm bananas, sliced

Direction

- Whisk cream cheese in a bowl until smooth. Mix in condensed milk; put to side. Combine pudding mix and milk in another bowl; stir in cream cheese mixture. Add in whipped topping then fold. In a 2-1/2-qt. glass bowl put a third of the vanilla wafers. Place a third of the bananas and pudding mixture on top. Continue with 2 more layers. Keep in the refrigerator until ready to serve.

Nutrition Information

- Calories: 379 calories
- Sodium: 276mg sodium
- Fiber: 1g fiber)
- Total Carbohydrate: 53g carbohydrate (41g sugars
- Cholesterol: 36mg cholesterol
- Protein: 6g protein.
- Total Fat: 16g fat (10g saturated fat)

22. Banana Pudding Parfaits

Serving: 4 servings | Prep: 15mins | Cook: | Ready in:

Ingredients

- 24 vanilla wafers , divided
- 1 pkg. (3.4 oz.) JELL-O Banana Cream Flavor Instant Pudding
- 2 cups cold milk
- 3/4 cup thawed COOL WHIP Whipped Topping
- 1 banana , cut into 20 slices

Direction

- 1. Mash 20 wafers to make coarse crumbs. In a medium bowl, combine milk and pudding mix using a whisk for 2 minutes. Mix in COOL WHIP.
- 2. Set aside 4 slices of banana for decorating. Then layer half of the wafer crumbs and the rest of bananas evenly in 4 dessert dishes; continue layering.
- 3. Keep in the refrigerator for 15 minutes. Place the rest of the wafers and reserved banana slices on top just prior to serving.

Nutrition Information

- Calories: 320
- Saturated Fat: 5 g
- Cholesterol: 15 mg
- Protein: 6 g
- Total Fat: 9 g
- Sugar: 39 g
- Total Carbohydrate: 55 g
- Sodium: 510 mg
- Fiber: 1 g

23. Banana Split Brownie Cake

Serving: 14 servings. | Prep: 20mins | Cook: 0mins | Ready in:

Ingredients

- 2 packages (13 ounces each) fudge brownies
- 1 quart strawberry ice cream, softened
- 3 large firm bananas, halved lengthwise
- 1 cup hot fudge ice cream topping, warmed
- 1 quart vanilla ice cream, softened
- 3/4 cup chopped pecans

Direction

- In a 9-inch greased springform pan, place brownies, trimming to fit and filling in small holes. Use strawberry ice cream to spread over, then cover and freeze until firm, about 3 hours.
- Put on top of ice cream with bananas, trimming to fit if necessary. Use fudge topping and vanilla ice cream to spread over then sprinkle pecans over top. Cover tightly and freeze overnight. You can freeze it for a maximum of 2 months.
- Take out of the freezer 10 minutes prior to serving. Use a knife to run around the edge of pan carefully to loosen cake, then take off sides of pan.

Nutrition Information

- Calories: 487 calories
- Sodium: 231mg sodium
- Fiber: 3g fiber)

- Total Carbohydrate: 71g carbohydrate (42g sugars
- Cholesterol: 36mg cholesterol
- Protein: 7g protein.
- Total Fat: 21g fat (7g saturated fat)

24. Banana Split Freeze

Serving: 15-20 servings. | Prep: 30mins | Cook: 0mins | Ready in:

Ingredients

- 1 can (12 ounces) evaporated milk
- 1 cup (6 ounces) semisweet chocolate chips
- 1/2 cup plus 6 tablespoons butter, divided
- 2 cups confectioners' sugar
- 1-1/2 cups graham cracker crumbs
- 3 medium ripe bananas, cut into 1/4-inch slices
- 2 quarts strawberry ice cream, softened
- 2 cups chopped pecans
- 1 carton (8 ounces) frozen whipped topping, thawed

Direction

- Mix together the milk, chocolate chips and 1/2 cup butter in a small saucepan. Cook and stir on medium heat till smooth and melted. Stir confectioners' sugar into the mix. Heat until boiling. Lower the heat; simmer until thickened, uncovered, for about 12-15 minutes, stir regularly. Let it cool down to room temperature.
- In the meantime, melt the remaining butter; stir cracker crumbs into the butter. Pat the mixture into a greased 13-in. x 9-in. dish; freeze for about 10 minutes. Place bananas, ice cream and pecans on top. Spread the top with the cooled chocolate mixture. Freeze for about 1 hour.
- Spread the whipped topping on top. You can freeze it for up to 2 months. Take out of the freezer 15 minutes before serving.

Nutrition Information

- Calories:
- Sodium:
- Fiber:
- Total Carbohydrate:
- Cholesterol:
- Protein:
- Total Fat:

25. Banana Split Ice Cream Sandwiches

Serving: 12-15 servings. | Prep: 25mins | Cook: 10mins | Ready in:

Ingredients

- Brownie for Ice Cream Sandwiches
- 1/2 cup chopped pecans
- 1/2 cup hot fudge ice cream topping, warmed
- 4 cups strawberry ice cream, softened
- 1 medium firm banana, thinly sliced

Direction

- Make batter for Brownie for Ice Cream Sandwiches. Add to prepared pan; scatter with pecans. Bake and let cool following the recipe directions.
- Slice brownie widthwise in half. Put hot fudge topping evenly on top of 1 brownie half; spread ice cream over and layer with banana slices. Turn over leftover brownie half; put on top of bananas. Put in the freezer, covered, for 2 hours or until set.
- Slice into bars, desired shapes or squares. Cover in plastic. Put in the freezer until serving.

Nutrition Information

- Calories:

- Total Carbohydrate:
- Cholesterol:
- Protein:
- Total Fat:
- Sodium:
- Fiber:

26. Banana Yogurt Trifles

Serving: 4 servings. | Prep: 10mins | Cook: 0mins | Ready in:

Ingredients

- 2 medium ripe bananas, sliced
- 1/3 cup orange juice
- 6 slices angel food cake, cubed
- 2 cups (16 ounces) strawberry-banana yogurt

Direction

- Toss orange juice and bananas in small bowl; in 4 dessert dishes, layer 1/2 cake cubes. Top with 1/2 bananas then yogurt; repeat the layers.

Nutrition Information

- Calories: 229 calories
- Protein: 5g protein.
- Total Fat: 1g fat (1g saturated fat)
- Sodium: 349mg sodium
- Fiber: 2g fiber)
- Total Carbohydrate: 51g carbohydrate (43g sugars
- Cholesterol: 3mg cholesterol

27. Berries & Cream Desserts

Serving: 4 servings. | Prep: 15mins | Cook: 0mins | Ready in:

Ingredients

- 1 loaf (10-3/4 ounces) frozen pound cake, thawed
- 3 ounces cream cheese, softened
- 1 cup marshmallow creme
- 1 cup sliced fresh strawberries
- 1 cup fresh blueberries

Direction

- Slice pound cake to half; cut 1/2 to 1/2-in. cubes, keep leftover cake for another time. Beat marshmallow crème and cream cheese till smooth in small bowl.
- Layer cake cubes and fruit in 4 small serving dishes; put cream cheese mixture over. Chill till serving.

Nutrition Information

- Calories: 332 calories
- Total Carbohydrate: 48g carbohydrate (32g sugars
- Cholesterol: 78mg cholesterol
- Protein: 5g protein.
- Total Fat: 14g fat (8g saturated fat)
- Sodium: 222mg sodium
- Fiber: 2g fiber)

28. Berries 'N' Cream Brownies

Serving: 12-15 servings. | Prep: 15mins | Cook: 25mins | Ready in:

Ingredients

- 1 package fudge brownie mix (13-inch x 9-inch pan size)
- 1 carton (8 ounces) frozen whipped topping, thawed
- 4 cups quartered fresh strawberries
- 1/3 cup chocolate hard-shell ice cream topping

Direction

- Prepare and bake brownies as instructed on package, using a 13-in. x 9-in. greased baking pan. Allow to cool on a wire rack thoroughly.
- Over brownies, spread whipped topping. Layer strawberries on top, with the cut side down. Drizzle chocolate topping on top. Chill in refrigerator for no less than 30 minutes before serving.

Nutrition Information

- Calories:
- Total Fat:
- Sodium:
- Fiber:
- Total Carbohydrate:
- Cholesterol:
- Protein:

29. Berries With Vanilla Custard For Two

Serving: 2 servings. | Prep: 20mins | Cook: 0mins | Ready in:

Ingredients

- 1/2 cup half-and-half cream
- 1 large egg yolk
- 1 tablespoon sugar
- 1 teaspoon vanilla extract
- 1 cup fresh raspberries

Direction

- Mix together sugar, egg yolk and cream in a small saucepan. Cook and stir on moderate heat until the mixture is thick enough to coat the back of a spoon and registers 160 degrees. Take away from the heat and stir in vanilla. Refrigerate until ready to serve and serve together with raspberries.

Nutrition Information

- Calories: 166 calories
- Total Carbohydrate: 16g carbohydrate (11g sugars
- Cholesterol: 132mg cholesterol
- Protein: 4g protein. Diabetic Exchanges: 1-1/2 fat
- Total Fat: 9g fat (5g saturated fat)
- Sodium: 34mg sodium
- Fiber: 4g fiber)

30. Berry Applesauce Gelatin

Serving: 8 servings. | Prep: 10mins | Cook: 0mins | Ready in:

Ingredients

- 1 package (6 ounces) strawberry gelatin
- 1 cup boiling water
- 2 cups frozen unsweetened strawberries
- 2 cups applesauce
- 2 tablespoons lemon juice

Direction

- Dissolve gelatin in a bowl with boiling water. Stir in strawberries until separated and thawed. Put in lemon juice and applesauce, then blend well. Transfer into a 7-inch x11-inch pan and refrigerate until set.

Nutrition Information

- Calories: 48 calories
- Sodium: 48mg sodium
- Fiber: 0 fiber)
- Total Carbohydrate: 11g carbohydrate (0 sugars
- Cholesterol: 0 cholesterol
- Protein: 1g protein. Diabetic Exchanges: 1 fruit.
- Total Fat: 0 fat (0 saturated fat)

31. Berry Blue Pops

Serving: 18 pops. | Prep: 25mins | Cook: 0mins | Ready in:

Ingredients

- 6 tablespoons berry blue gelatin
- 1 cup sugar, divided
- 2 cups boiling water, divided
- 2 cups cold water, divided
- 6 tablespoons strawberry gelatin
- 18 freezer pop molds or 18 paper cups (3 ounces each) and wooden pop sticks

Direction

- Melt 1/2 cup sugar and berry blue gelatin powder in 1 cup boiling water in small bowl. Mix 1 cup cold water in. Melt leftover sugar and strawberry gelatin powder in leftover boiling water in a different bowl. Mix leftover cold water in.
- Mix 1/2 strawberry gelatin mixture and 1/2 berry blue gelatin mixture in small bowl. Put all in freezer till slushy or for 1 3/4-2 hours. Swirl 3 colors as desired in a big bowl. Fill each cup/mold with 1/4 cup gelatin mixture. Put holders on top. For cups (if used), top with foil then insert sticks through foil. Freeze till firm.

Nutrition Information

- Calories: 77 calories
- Sodium: 21mg sodium
- Fiber: 0 fiber)
- Total Carbohydrate: 19g carbohydrate (19g sugars
- Cholesterol: 0 cholesterol
- Protein: 1g protein. Diabetic Exchanges: 1 starch.
- Total Fat: 0 fat (0 saturated fat)

32. Berry Compote Topping

Serving: 6 cups. | Prep: 10mins | Cook: 10mins | Ready in:

Ingredients

- 1 cup sugar
- 1/3 cup cornstarch
- 1 cup cold water
- 1/2 cup lemon juice
- 1/2 cup maple syrup
- 4 cups fresh strawberries, halved
- 2 cups fresh raspberries
- 2 cups fresh blackberries

Direction

- Mix cornstarch with sugar in a big saucepan. Mix in syrup, lemon juice, and water. Mix in the berries. Boil it over medium heat, stir and cook until thickened, about 2 minutes.
- Enjoy immediately or move to freezer containers. You can freeze for a maximum of 3 months.
- To use the frozen sauce: Defrost in the fridge overnight. Put in a saucepan and heat through.

Nutrition Information

- Calories: 101 calories
- Fiber: 2g fiber)
- Total Carbohydrate: 25g carbohydrate (20g sugars
- Cholesterol: 0 cholesterol
- Protein: 1g protein.
- Total Fat: 0 fat (0 saturated fat)
- Sodium: 2mg sodium

33. Berry Gelatin Mold

Serving: 8 servings. | Prep: 15mins | Cook: 0mins | Ready in:

Ingredients

- 2 packages (3 ounces each) strawberry gelatin
- 2 cups boiling cranberry juice
- 1-1/2 cups club soda, chilled
- 1 teaspoon lemon juice
- 1 cup each fresh blueberries, raspberries and sliced strawberries
- Lettuce leaves
- Additional mixed fresh berries, optional

Direction

- Dissolve gelatin in boiling cranberry syrup in a large bowl. Allow to sit for 10 minutes. Pour lemon juice and club soda into the bowl, stir. Chill until partly firm for 45 minutes.
- Add berries and fold. Transfer the mixture into a 6-cup ring mold greased with cooking spray. Chill in the fridge until entirely firm for 4 hours. Remove the mold and place the jello onto a platter lined with lettuce leaves. Add more berries into the mold's center if desired.

Nutrition Information

- Calories: 131 calories
- Cholesterol: 0 cholesterol
- Protein: 3g protein. Diabetic Exchanges: 1 starch
- Total Fat: 0 fat (0 saturated fat)
- Sodium: 59mg sodium
- Fiber: 2g fiber)
- Total Carbohydrate: 32g carbohydrate (30g sugars

34. Birthday Cake Freezer Pops

Serving: 1-1/2 dozen. | Prep: 25mins | Cook: 0mins | Ready in:

Ingredients

- 2/3 cup sprinkles, divided
- 18 disposable plastic or paper cups (3 ounces each)
- 2 cups cold 2% milk
- 1 package (3.4 ounces) instant vanilla pudding mix
- 1 carton (8 ounces) frozen whipped topping, thawed
- 2 cups crushed vanilla wafers (about 60 wafers)
- 18 wooden pop sticks

Direction

- In each cup, spoon 1 teaspoon sprinkles.
- Whisk pudding mix and milk for 2 minutes in a big bowl. Let stand for 2 minutes till soft-set. Mix leftover sprinkles, crushed wafers and whipped topping in.
- Cut 1-in. hole in tip of pastry bag/corner of food-safe plastic bag. Use pudding mixture to fill bag. Pipe in prepped cups. Put foil on top of cups. Insert pop sticks through the foil.
- Freeze for 4 hours till firm. Let stand for 5 minutes at room temperature. Gently remove pops.

Nutrition Information

- Calories: 161 calories
- Protein: 1g protein. Diabetic Exchanges: 1-1/2 starch
- Total Fat: 7g fat (3g saturated fat)
- Sodium: 96mg sodium
- Fiber: 0 fiber)
- Total Carbohydrate: 23g carbohydrate (15g sugars
- Cholesterol: 4mg cholesterol

35. Biscuit Apple Cobbler

Serving: 4-6 servings. | Prep: 20mins | Cook: 0mins | Ready in:

Ingredients

- 1 can (21 ounces) apple pie filling
- 1/2 teaspoon ground cinnamon
- 1 tube (7-1/2 ounces) refrigerated flaky buttermilk biscuits
- Whipped topping and mint, optional

Direction

- In an ungreased 9-inch pie plate, position pie filling, then sprinkle cinnamon over. Divide each biscuit into 3 layers and place over apples.
- Bake at 400 degrees until the biscuits turn brown, about 12 to 14 minutes. Place whipped topping and mint on top, if you want.

Nutrition Information

- Calories: 186 calories
- Protein: 3g protein.
- Total Fat: 1g fat (0 saturated fat)
- Sodium: 347mg sodium
- Fiber: 1g fiber)
- Total Carbohydrate: 43g carbohydrate (20g sugars
- Cholesterol: 0 cholesterol

36. Bite Sized Apple Pies

Serving: 16 servings. | Prep: 20mins | Cook: 15mins | Ready in:

Ingredients

- 1/2 cup sugar
- 2 teaspoons ground cinnamon
- 1 package (14.1 ounces) refrigerated pie pastry
- 3 tablespoons butter, melted, divided
- 2 medium tart apples

Direction

- Set the oven to 425 degrees to preheat. Combine cinnamon and sugar together in a small bowl and save 1 tbsp. of mixture. Unroll pastry sheets on a surface coated lightly with grease, then roll and trim each to an 8-inch square. Use 2 tbsp. of butter to brush the sheets and sprinkle leftover sugar mixture over. Slice each square into 8 strips with 1 inch size.
- Cut each apple into 8 wedges and wrap each wedge with a strip of pastry, sugared-side of pastry against the apple.
- Put in a baking sheet lined with parchment paper. Use leftover butter to brush the tops and sprinkle reserved sugar mixture over. Bake until pastry turn golden brown, about 13 to 15 minutes. Serve warm.

Nutrition Information

- Calories: 163 calories
- Protein: 1g protein.
- Total Fat: 9g fat (4g saturated fat)
- Sodium: 108mg sodium
- Fiber: 0 fiber)
- Total Carbohydrate: 21g carbohydrate (9g sugars
- Cholesterol: 10mg cholesterol

37. Bittersweet Double Chocolate Truffles

Serving: 1-1/2 dozen. | Prep: 30mins | Cook: 0mins | Ready in:

Ingredients

- 1 cup 60% cacao bittersweet chocolate baking chips
- 3/4 cup whipped topping
- 1/4 teaspoon ground cinnamon
- 1 cup milk chocolate chips
- 1 teaspoon shortening
- Optional toppings: crushed peppermint candies, sprinkles and chopped nuts

Direction

- Heat bittersweet chips in a small saucepan over low heat until melted. Pour into a bowl and allow to cool for about 7 minutes until lukewarm.
- Beat cinnamon and whipped topping into the mixture. Freeze until firm enough to shape into balls, 15 minutes. Form into balls of an inch.
- Microwave shortening and milk chocolate chips until melted; stir until the mixture is smooth. Dunk truffles in chocolate and put on baking sheets lined with waxed paper. Add a sprinkle of preferred toppings immediately. Chill in the refrigerator to firm up. Keep refrigerated in an airtight container to store.

Nutrition Information

- Calories: 105 calories
- Cholesterol: 2mg cholesterol
- Protein: 1g protein.
- Total Fat: 6g fat (4g saturated fat)
- Sodium: 8mg sodium
- Fiber: 1g fiber)
- Total Carbohydrate: 12g carbohydrate (10g sugars

38. Black Forest Freezer Pie

Serving: 6-8 servings. | Prep: 20mins | Cook: 0mins | Ready in:

Ingredients

- 1 pint chocolate or vanilla ice cream, softened
- 1 extra-servings-size graham cracker crust (9 ounces)
- 4 ounces cream cheese, softened
- 1 cup confectioners' sugar
- 1 carton (8 ounces) frozen whipped topping, thawed
- 1 can (21 ounces) cherry pie filling, chilled
- 3 tablespoons chocolate syrup

Direction

- Scoop ice cream into the pie crust; freeze, covered, for 15 minutes.
- In the meantime, beat cream cheese with confectioners' sugar in a large bowl until smooth; add whipped topping and fold gently. Measure 1 1/2 cup cream cheese mixture and set aside for garnish.
- Spread the rest of cream cheese mixture over ice cream. Make an 8-inch well in the center of the pie for pie filling using the back of a spoon (do not add filling). Pipe the reserved cream cheese mixture around the pie.
- Freeze, covered, for 3 to 4 hours or until set. This pie can be stored for a maximum of 2 months in the freezer. Scoop pie filling into the well just before serving; drizzle chocolate syrup over the top. Serve right away.

Nutrition Information

- Calories: 520 calories
- Total Fat: 21g fat (12g saturated fat)
- Sodium: 266mg sodium
- Fiber: 2g fiber)
- Total Carbohydrate: 77g carbohydrate (63g sugars
- Cholesterol: 27mg cholesterol
- Protein: 4g protein.

39. Black Forest Icebox Cookies

Serving: 20 cookies. | Prep: 15mins | Cook: 5mins | Ready in:

Ingredients

- 3 tablespoons granulated sugar
- 4 teaspoons cornstarch
- Dash salt
- 3/4 cup fresh or frozen pitted tart cherries (thawed), coarsely chopped
- 3/4 cup cherry juice blend

- 1-1/2 teaspoons lemon juice
- 1 to 2 drops red food coloring, optional
- 1/2 cup mascarpone cheese
- 1 tablespoon confectioners' sugar
- 1 teaspoon cherry brandy
- 1 package (9 ounces) chocolate wafers
- 1/2 cup semisweet chocolate chips
- 1/4 cup heavy whipping cream

Direction

- Mix salt, cornstarch and granulated sugar together in a small saucepan. Add lemon juice, juice blend and cherries. Heat to a boil; cook, stirring, for 2 minutes or until mixture is thickened. Take off the heat and mix in food coloring (if using). Allow to cool to room temperature.
- Combine mascarpone cheese with brandy and confectioners' sugar in a small bowl. Spread approximately 1 teaspoon cheese mixture on top of 20 wafers. Add 2 teaspoons cherry mixture and the rest of wafer on top. Arrange on a baking pan lined with waxed paper.
- Put chocolate chips in a small bowl. Heat cream in a small saucepan just to a boil. Transfer on top of the chips; stir until smooth. Drizzle over cookies. Cover and chill for a maximum of 4 hours before serving.

Nutrition Information

- Calories: 139 calories
- Total Carbohydrate: 15g carbohydrate (9g sugars
- Cholesterol: 17mg cholesterol
- Protein: 2g protein.
- Total Fat: 9g fat (4g saturated fat)
- Sodium: 81mg sodium
- Fiber: 1g fiber)

40. Black Forest Sundaes

Serving: 4 servings. | Prep: 5mins | Cook: 0mins | Ready in:

Ingredients

- 1/2 cup crushed Oreo cookies
- 4 scoops vanilla ice cream
- 1 can (21 ounces) cherry pie filling
- Whipped cream in a can
- Chopped walnuts

Direction

- Distribute cookie crumbs between 4 dessert plates; put pie filling and ice cream on top of each. Use walnuts and whipped cream to garnish. Freeze until enjoying.

Nutrition Information

- Calories:
- Total Fat:
- Sodium:
- Fiber:
- Total Carbohydrate:
- Cholesterol:
- Protein:

41. Blackberry Brandy Sauce

Serving: 12 servings (1/4 cup each). | Prep: 10mins | Cook: 15mins | Ready in:

Ingredients

- 1 cup sugar
- 2 tablespoons cornstarch
- 1/4 cup cold water
- 4 cups fresh or frozen blackberries, thawed
- 1 tablespoon brandy or 1/2 teaspoon vanilla extract
- Vanilla ice cream, optional

Direction

- Blend sugar and cornstarch in a large saucepan; mix in water. Mix in blackberries; bring to a boil. Lower the heat; simmer without a cover until sauce is thickened for about 10-12 minutes, stirring occasionally. Take away from heat; mix in brandy. Let it cool slightly. If preferred, serve with ice cream.

Nutrition Information

- Calories: 93 calories
- Protein: 1g protein.
- Total Fat: 0 fat (0 saturated fat)
- Sodium: 1mg sodium
- Fiber: 2g fiber)
- Total Carbohydrate: 22g carbohydrate (19g sugars
- Cholesterol: 0 cholesterol

42. Blueberry Angel Dessert

Serving: 12 servings. | Prep: 10mins | Cook: 0mins | Ready in:

Ingredients

- 1 package (8 ounces) cream cheese, softened
- 1 cup confectioners' sugar
- 1 carton (8 ounces) frozen whipped topping, thawed
- 1 prepared angel food cake (8 to 10 ounces), cut into 1-inch cubes
- 2 cans (21 ounces each) blueberry pie filling

Direction

- In a large bowl make a smooth cream by beating confectioners' sugar with the cream cheese; fold in cake cubes and whipped topping. Spread equally over a 13x9-inch dish (no need to grease it) and top with the pie filling. Cover; refrigerate for at least two hours before serving.

Nutrition Information

- Calories: 384 calories
- Sodium: 223mg sodium
- Fiber: 3g fiber)
- Total Carbohydrate: 70g carbohydrate (50g sugars
- Cholesterol: 21mg cholesterol
- Protein: 3g protein.
- Total Fat: 10g fat (7g saturated fat)

43. Blueberry Cobbler

Serving: Serves 6 | Prep: | Cook: | Ready in:

Ingredients

- 1 stick butter
- 1 teaspoon lemon juice
- 4 cups fresh blueberries, rinsed and drained
- 1 cup sugar
- 1 cup self-rising flour
- 1 cup sugar
- 1 teaspoon vanilla
- 1/2 cup milk
- Accompaniment: Fresh whipped cream or vanilla ice cream

Direction

- To prepare the filling: Set the oven at 375°F and start preheating. Put butter into an 8x8-in. square glass baking dish (no substitutes); melt the butter in a microwave. Mix blueberries and lemon juice in a mixing bowl. Include in sugar; stir properly. Transfer the blueberry mixture into the prepared baking dish with the melted butter. Do not combine.
- To prepare the topping: In a small bowl, mix together all of the topping ingredients. Transfer this mixture over the blueberries; bake till brown, or for 45 minutes.

- This recipe also goes well with peaches, blackberries and apples.

Nutrition Information

- Calories: 538
- Protein: 4 g(7%)
- Total Fat: 16 g(25%)
- Saturated Fat: 10 g(51%)
- Sodium: 261 mg(11%)
- Fiber: 3 g(12%)
- Total Carbohydrate: 98 g(33%)
- Cholesterol: 43 mg(14%)

44. Blueberry Crumble

Serving: 15 | Prep: 10mins | Cook: 25mins | Ready in:

Ingredients

- 1 (21 ounce) can blueberry pie filling
- 1 teaspoon lemon juice
- 1 (18.25 ounce) package white cake mix
- 1/2 cup chopped pecans
- 1/2 cup butter, melted

Direction

- Set the oven to 350°F (175°C), and start preheating.
- In a baking dish of 9x13 inches, spread the pie filling. Sprinkle with lemon juice evenly.
- Mix melted butter, nuts and cake mix together in a large bowl until crumbly. Sprinkle on top of the pie filling.
- Bake in oven until the top is light brown, about 25 - 30 minutes.

Nutrition Information

- Calories: 296 calories;
- Protein: 2.1
- Total Fat: 12.5
- Sodium: 274
- Total Carbohydrate: 44.5
- Cholesterol: 16

45. Blueberry Fizz Pops

Serving: 16 pops. | Prep: 20mins | Cook: 0mins | Ready in:

Ingredients

- 2 cups fresh or frozen blueberries
- 1 medium ripe banana
- 3 to 4 drops neon purple food coloring, optional
- 2 cups sparkling Concord grape juice
- 16 freezer pop molds or 16 paper cups (3 ounces each) and wooden pop sticks

Direction

- In blender, put food coloring (optional), banana and blueberries. Cover. Process until smooth. Add grape juice; process until well blended.
- Fill cup or every mold with 1/4 cup of blueberry mixture. Put holders on molds. Top with foil and put sticks through foil for cups. Freeze until firm.

Nutrition Information

- Calories: 36 calories
- Total Carbohydrate: 9g carbohydrate (7g sugars
- Cholesterol: 0 cholesterol
- Protein: 0 protein. Diabetic Exchanges: 1/2 starch.
- Total Fat: 0 fat (0 saturated fat)
- Sodium: 10mg sodium
- Fiber: 1g fiber)

46. Blueberry Fluff Pie

Serving: 8 servings. | Prep: 25mins | Cook: 0mins | Ready in:

Ingredients

- 20 large marshmallows
- 1/4 cup milk
- 4 cups fresh blueberries, divided
- 1 carton (8 ounces) frozen whipped topping, thawed
- 1 pastry shell (9 inches), baked

Direction

- Combine marshmallows and milk in a heavy saucepan. Cook and stir over medium-low heat until marshmallows melts and mixture becomes smooth. Let it cool down for 8-10 minutes, stirring several times.
- Stir 3-1/2 cups blueberries into the mix. Put aside 1/2 cup whipped topping; fold remaining topping into blueberry mixture. Pour into crust. Refrigerate for no less than 2 hours. Garnish with remaining blueberries and reserved topping.

Nutrition Information

- Calories: 302 calories
- Fiber: 2g fiber)
- Total Carbohydrate: 45g carbohydrate (22g sugars
- Cholesterol: 6mg cholesterol
- Protein: 2g protein.
- Total Fat: 12g fat (8g saturated fat)
- Sodium: 113mg sodium

47. Blueberry Sherbet

Serving: 2 cups. | Prep: 10mins | Cook: 0mins | Ready in:

Ingredients

- 1 cup (8 ounces) sour cream
- 3/4 cup sugar
- 1 tablespoon lemon juice
- 1/2 teaspoon vanilla extract
- 3 cups fresh or frozen blueberries, thawed

Direction

- Mix all ingredients in a blender or food processor; blend, covered, until glossy. Press the mixture through a sieve, discarding the blueberry skin and seeds. Let freeze in the freezer for 8 hours or overnight. Take out from the freezer 30 minutes before serving.

Nutrition Information

- Calories: 323 calories
- Total Fat: 10g fat (7g saturated fat)
- Sodium: 30mg sodium
- Fiber: 3g fiber)
- Total Carbohydrate: 55g carbohydrate (49g sugars
- Cholesterol: 38mg cholesterol
- Protein: 3g protein.

48. Blueberry Shortcake Sundaes

Serving: 4 servings. | Prep: 10mins | Cook: 10mins | Ready in:

Ingredients

- 1/3 cup sugar
- 1-1/2 teaspoons cornstarch
- 1/4 teaspoon ground cinnamon
- 3 tablespoons water
- 1-1/2 cups fresh or frozen blueberries
- 4 slices pound cake
- 4 scoops vanilla ice cream

Direction

- Mix cinnamon, cornstarch and sugar in a small saucepan. Mix in blueberries and water till incorporated. Boil; cook and mix for 2 to 4 minutes till thickened.

- On 4 dessert plates, put the slices of cake. Put ice cream and blueberry sauce on top.

Nutrition Information

- Calories: 349 calories
- Total Carbohydrate: 56g carbohydrate (34g sugars
- Cholesterol: 95mg cholesterol
- Protein: 4g protein.
- Total Fat: 13g fat (8g saturated fat)
- Sodium: 173mg sodium
- Fiber: 2g fiber)

49. Blueberry Rhubarb Crisp

Serving: 6 servings. | Prep: 15mins | Cook: 10mins | Ready in:

Ingredients

- 2-1/2 cups diced fresh or frozen rhubarb, thawed
- 1/3 cup sugar
- 2 tablespoons all-purpose flour
- 1 can (21 ounces) blueberry pie filling
- TOPPING:
- 3/4 cup all-purpose flour
- 3/4 cup old-fashioned oats
- 1/3 cup packed brown sugar
- 3/4 teaspoon ground cinnamon
- 1/2 cup cold butter, cubed

Direction

- In a microwave-safe dish of 2 quarts, mix flour, sugar and rhubarb together. Cover up and microwave on high for 3 minutes; then stir. Put in pie filling.
- Mix cinnamon, brown sugar, oats and flour together in a small bowl. Cut in butter until crumbly; sprinkle atop the filling. Cover up and cook until bubbly while the rhubarb is tender, about 4 - 5 more minutes. Serve warm.

Nutrition Information

- Calories: 621 calories
- Cholesterol: 48mg cholesterol
- Protein: 5g protein.
- Total Fat: 20g fat (12g saturated fat)
- Sodium: 152mg sodium
- Fiber: 6g fiber)
- Total Carbohydrate: 108g carbohydrate (73g sugars

50. Breakfast Parfaits

Serving: 4 servings. | Prep: 10mins | Cook: 0mins | Ready in:

Ingredients

- 2 cups pineapple chunks
- 1 cup fresh or frozen raspberries
- 1 cup (8 ounces) vanilla yogurt
- 1 cup sliced ripe banana
- 1/2 cup chopped dates or raisins
- 1/4 cup sliced almonds

Direction

- Layer the dates, banana, yogurt, raspberries, and pineapple in 4 parfait glasses or serving dishes. Top with almonds. Serve right away.

Nutrition Information

- Calories: 0
- Cholesterol: 6 mg cholesterol
- Protein: 6 g protein.
- Total Fat: 5 g fat (2 g saturated fat)
- Sodium: 41 mg sodium
- Fiber: 7 g fiber
- Total Carbohydrate: 71 g carbohydrate

51. Brownie Affogato Sundaes

Serving: 6 servings. | Prep: 20mins | Cook: 0mins | Ready in:

Ingredients

- 1/2 cup heavy whipping cream
- 1/4 cup marshmallow creme
- 6 prepared brownies
- 6 tablespoons fudge ice cream topping
- 2 cups coffee ice cream
- 3/4 cup hot brewed espresso
- 6 tablespoons Kahlua (coffee liqueur), optional
- Chocolate-covered coffee beans
- Sea salt or smoked salt

Direction

- Whisk marshmallow crème and whipping cream in a small bowl until it forms soft peaks. Keep in the refrigerator until serving time.
- Put each brownie in a dessert dish to serve; place ice cream and fudge topping on top. Put espresso and, if wished, Kahlua over ice cream. Place cream mixture and coffee beans on top; dust with salt. Serve right away.

Nutrition Information

- Calories: 0
- Sodium: 62mg cholesterol
- Fiber: 38g carbohydrate (23g sugars
- Total Carbohydrate: 146mg sodium
- Cholesterol: 21g fat (10g saturated fat)
- Protein: 1g fiber)
- Total Fat: coffee beans and salt): 350 calories

52. Brownie Mix Snack Cake

Serving: 9 servings. | Prep: 10mins | Cook: 25mins | Ready in:

Ingredients

- 2 cups Brownie Mix
- 3 eggs, separated
- 3 tablespoons milk
- 1 teaspoon vanilla extract

Direction

- Mix together vanilla, milk, egg yolks and brownie mix in a big bowl. Whisk egg whites in a small bowl until it forms stiff peaks, then add to the batter and fold gently.
- Pour the batter into an 8" square baking pan coated with butter. Bake for 25-30 minutes at 350 degrees or until there is no crumbs clinging on a toothpick when inserted into the brownie. Let sit on a wire rack to cool down.

Nutrition Information

- Calories:
- Fiber:
- Total Carbohydrate:
- Cholesterol:
- Protein:
- Total Fat:
- Sodium:

53. Bunny In A Cup

Serving: 4 servings. | Prep: 20mins | Cook: 0mins | Ready in:

Ingredients

- 2 cups cold milk
- 1 package (3.4 ounces) instant vanilla pudding mix
- 2 twists black licorice
- 1/4 cup vanilla frosting
- Red liquid or paste food coloring
- 8 cream-filled oval vanilla sandwich cookies
- 8 green jelly beans
- 4 pink jelly beans

Direction

- Stir the pudding mix and milk in a small bowl for 2 minutes. Let it sit for 2 minutes until partially set. Distribute among 4 small bowls; cover and chill.
- At the same time, slice licorice widthwise into 4 portions, then lengthwise into 3 portions; put aside. Mix the red food coloring and the frosting, then spread over the top of the cookies to within half an inch of edge.
- Just before serving, add oval cookies into each pudding bowl for ears. Put in green jelly beans for eyes and pink jelly bean for nose. Arrange 3 pieces of licorice on each side of the nose for whiskers.

Nutrition Information

- Calories: 435 calories
- Total Fat: 13g fat (4g saturated fat)
- Sodium: 551mg sodium
- Fiber: 0 fiber)
- Total Carbohydrate: 73g carbohydrate (54g sugars
- Cholesterol: 17mg cholesterol
- Protein: 6g protein.

54. Butter Brickle Ice Cream Pie

Serving: 8 servings. | Prep: 20mins | Cook: 0mins | Ready in:

Ingredients

- 1/2 gallon vanilla ice cream, softened
- 1 graham cracker crust (9 inches)
- 1/2 cup English toffee bits or almond brickle chips
- SAUCE:
- 1 cup sugar
- 1 can (5 ounces) evaporated milk, divided
- 1/4 cup dark corn syrup
- 1/4 cup butter, cubed
- 1/8 teaspoon salt
- 1 tablespoon cornstarch
- 1/2 cup English toffee bits or almond brickle chips

Direction

- Into crust, spread 1/2 ice cream. Sprinkle toffee bits on. Spoon leftover ice cream on top. Freeze, covered, till firm.
- Put salt, butter, corn syrup, 3 tbsp. milk and sugar in a big saucepan. Boil on medium heat. Mix leftover milk and cornstarch till smooth. Add to sugar mixture gradually.
- Boil, constantly stirring. Stir and cook till thickened for 1-2 minutes. Cool, mixing a few times, to room temperature. Mix toffee bits in. Refrigerate till serving time.
- Prior to serving, put sauce into small microwave-safe bowl. Uncovered, microwave for 30-60 seconds on high till heated through, mixing once. Serve it with the pie.

Nutrition Information

- Calories: 733 calories
- Total Fat: 37g fat (19g saturated fat)
- Sodium: 507mg sodium
- Fiber: 0 fiber)
- Total Carbohydrate: 99g carbohydrate (81g sugars
- Cholesterol: 89mg cholesterol
- Protein: 7g protein.

55. Buttermilk Fruit Topping

Serving: about 4-1/2 cups. | Prep: 5mins | Cook: 0mins | Ready in:

Ingredients

- 1-1/2 cups cold buttermilk
- 1 package (3.4 ounces) instant vanilla pudding mix

- 1 carton (8 ounces) frozen whipped topping, thawed
- Fresh fruit

Direction

- Stir pudding mix and buttermilk together in a bowl. Beat for 2 minutes over low speed. Fold whipped topping into the mixture. Refrigerate for 60 minutes. Serve on top of the fruit.

Nutrition Information

- Calories: 22 calories
- Total Fat: 1g fat (0 saturated fat)
- Sodium: 43mg sodium
- Fiber: 0 fiber)
- Total Carbohydrate: 3g carbohydrate (0 sugars
- Cholesterol: 0 cholesterol
- Protein: 0 protein.

56. Butterscotch Angel Cake

Serving: 8 servings. | Prep: 20mins | Cook: 5mins | Ready in:

Ingredients

- 8 slices angel food cake
- 3/4 cup butter, melted, divided
- 1 cup packed brown sugar, divided
- 8 scoops butter brickle or butter pecan ice cream
- Butterscotch ice cream topping

Direction

- Put the slices of cake on a baking sheet that's been greased. Coat them with 6 tablespoons of butter. Press a tablespoon of brown sugar on the slices. Broil them for 1-2 minutes, 5-6 inches away from the heat source, until bubbly.
- Flip the slices. Brush the rest of the butter on them Top with the rest of the brown sugar. Broil for another minute or two, until bubbly. Let them cool for 2 to 3 minutes. Best served with ice cream. Top with butterscotch.

Nutrition Information

- Calories:
- Cholesterol:
- Protein:
- Total Fat:
- Sodium:
- Fiber:
- Total Carbohydrate:

57. Butterscotch Fruit Dip

Serving: about 3 cups. | Prep: 5mins | Cook: 45mins | Ready in:

Ingredients

- 2 packages (10 to 11 ounces each) butterscotch chips
- 2/3 cup evaporated milk
- 2/3 cup chopped pecans
- 1 tablespoon rum extract
- Apple and pear wedges

Direction

- Mix together the milk and butterscotch chips in one-and 1/2 quart size slow cooker. Cook with cover for 45 to 50 minutes over low heat or until the chips are softened. Stir until a smooth consistency is achieved. Pour in the extract and toss in the pecans. Serve while hot along with fruits.

Nutrition Information

- Calories: 197 calories
- Cholesterol: 6mg cholesterol
- Protein: 2g protein.
- Total Fat: 13g fat (7g saturated fat)

- Sodium: 32mg sodium
- Fiber: 1g fiber)
- Total Carbohydrate: 17g carbohydrate (16g sugars

58. Butterscotch Peanut Treats

Serving: about 2-1/2 dozen. | Prep: 30mins | Cook: 0mins | Ready in:

Ingredients

- 1/2 cup corn syrup
- 1/3 cup butter, cubed
- 1 package (3.5 ounces) cook-and-serve butterscotch pudding mix
- 4 cups cornflakes
- 1 cup coarsely chopped dry roasted peanuts

Direction

- Cook and mix the butter and corn syrup in a large heavy saucepan until butter is liquified. Stir in pudding mix until well combined. Cook, stir, until mixture comes to a boil. Cook and stir for another 1 minute.
- Remove from the heat. Allow to cool for 1 minute, stir a few times. Stir in peanuts and corn flakes until evenly coated.
- Drop onto waxed paper-lined baking sheets by rounded tablespoonfuls; cool.

Nutrition Information

- Calories: 173 calories
- Total Carbohydrate: 23g carbohydrate (11g sugars
- Cholesterol: 11mg cholesterol
- Protein: 3g protein.
- Total Fat: 9g fat (3g saturated fat)
- Sodium: 220mg sodium
- Fiber: 1g fiber)

59. Butterscotch Pudding Torte

Serving: 15 servings. | Prep: 15mins | Cook: 0mins | Ready in:

Ingredients

- 1 package (16 ounces) cream-filled vanilla sandwich cookies, crushed
- 1/2 cup butter, melted
- 1 package (8 ounces) cream cheese, softened
- 1 cup confectioners' sugar
- 1 carton (12 ounces) frozen whipped topping, thawed, divided
- 2-1/2 cups cold 2% milk
- 2 packages (3.4 ounces each) instant butterscotch pudding mix

Direction

- For topping, put 1 cup cookie crumbs aside. Mix butter and leftover cookie crumbs in a small bowl; press into 13x9-in. greased dish. Beat confectioners' sugar and cream cheese till smooth in a big bowl; fold in 1 1/2 cups of whipped topping. Spread on crust.
- Whisk pudding mix and milk for 2 minutes in a small bowl; stand till soft set for 2 minutes. Put over the cream cheese layer. Put leftover whipped toppings over; sprinkle reserved crumbs. Cover; refrigerate for a minimum of 2 hours.

Nutrition Information

- Calories: 413 calories
- Cholesterol: 36mg cholesterol
- Protein: 4g protein.
- Total Fat: 22g fat (12g saturated fat)
- Sodium: 414mg sodium
- Fiber: 0 fiber)
- Total Carbohydrate: 49g carbohydrate (33g sugars

60. Butterscotch Snack Cake

Serving: 12-16 servings. | Prep: 10mins | Cook: 35mins | Ready in:

Ingredients

- 1 package (3-1/2 ounces) cook-and-serve butterscotch pudding mix
- 2 cups milk
- 1 package yellow cake mix (regular size)
- 1 package (11 ounces) butterscotch chips
- 1/2 cup chopped pecans or walnuts

Direction

- Mix milk and pudding mix together in a big saucepan. Bring the mixture to a boil on medium heat while stirring continuously. Take away from the heat and stir in dry cake mix.
- Transfer into a 13"x9" baking pan that greased, then use nuts and butterscotch chips to sprinkle over top. Bake at 350 degrees until a toothpick inserted in the center exits clean, about 35 to 40 minutes. Allow to cool on wire rack.

Nutrition Information

- Calories: 307 calories
- Sodium: 264mg sodium
- Fiber: 1g fiber)
- Total Carbohydrate: 46g carbohydrate (32g sugars
- Cholesterol: 5mg cholesterol
- Protein: 4g protein.
- Total Fat: 13g fat (7g saturated fat)

61. Cake With Lemon Sauce

Serving: 4 servings. | Prep: 10mins | Cook: 0mins | Ready in:

Ingredients

- 3 ounces cream cheese, softened
- 1-3/4 cups cold whole milk
- 1 package (3.4 ounces) instant lemon pudding mix
- 4 slices pound cake or angel food cake
- Fresh raspberries, optional

Direction

- Beat the cream cheese in a small bowl until it has a smooth consistency. Mix in pudding mix and milk and continue beating until consistency is thickened and smooth. Consume with cake. Decorate with raspberries if preferred.

Nutrition Information

- Calories: 502 calories
- Fiber: 1g fiber)
- Total Carbohydrate: 66g carbohydrate (45g sugars
- Cholesterol: 79mg cholesterol
- Protein: 9g protein.
- Total Fat: 24g fat (10g saturated fat)
- Sodium: 688mg sodium

62. Calgary Nanaimo Bars

Serving: 3-1/2 dozen. | Prep: 20mins | Cook: 5mins | Ready in:

Ingredients

- 1/4 cup sugar
- 1/4 cup baking cocoa
- 3/4 cup butter, cubed
- 2 large eggs, beaten
- 2 cups graham cracker crumbs
- 1 cup sweetened shredded coconut
- 1/2 cup chopped almonds, optional
- FILLING:
- 2 cups confectioners' sugar
- 2 tablespoons instant vanilla pudding mix

- 1/4 cup butter, melted
- 3 tablespoons 2% milk
- GLAZE:
- 3 ounces semisweet chocolate, chopped
- 1 tablespoon butter

Direction

- Use foil to line an 8-inch baking pan that's square, allowing ends to overlap over sides by an inch. In a big, heavy saucepan, mix the cocoa and sugar; put butter. Stir and cook on medium-low heat until the butter melts. Beat a small amount of the hot mixture into the eggs. Put all back in the pan, beating constantly. Mix and cook until mixture achieves 160°F. Take off heat.
- Mix in coconut, cracker crumbs, and if you want, almonds. Then press in prepared pan. Keep in the refrigerator for 30 minutes or until it has set.
- To make filling, in a small bowl mix the milk, butter, pudding mix, and confectioner's sugar until it turns smooth; then spread on crust.
- Dissolve butter and chocolate in a microwave; whisk until smooth. Spread on top. Keep in the refrigerator until it has set. Take bars out of the pan using foil. Get rid of foil; slice into bars.

Nutrition Information

- Calories: 116 calories
- Total Carbohydrate: 14g carbohydrate (11g sugars
- Cholesterol: 21mg cholesterol
- Protein: 1g protein.
- Total Fat: 7g fat (4g saturated fat)
- Sodium: 72mg sodium
- Fiber: 0 fiber)

63. Candy Bar Fudge Reindeer

Serving: 2 dozen. | Prep: 15mins | Cook: 5mins | Ready in:

Ingredients

- 1 teaspoon butter
- 1 can (14 ounces) sweetened condensed milk
- 2 cups (12 ounces) butterscotch chips
- 1 cup (6 ounces) peanut butter chips
- 2 Snickers candy bars (2.07 ounces each), chopped
- 3/4 cup red and green milk chocolate M&M's
- 1 teaspoon vanilla extract
- M&M's minis and miniature pretzels

Direction

- Prepare a 9x9-inch baking pan with foil lining. Use butter to grease the foil then put aside.
- In a large microwavable bowl, mix together chips and milk. Put into the microwave and heat without covering on high for 60 seconds and whisk. Keep cooking for 30 to 60 seconds longer to melt chips, stirring every half a minute. Mix in vanilla, M&M's and candy bars. Pour into lined and greased pan. Chill while covered until firm, about 2 hours.
- Take out fudge by lifting with foil lining. Carefully remove foil and slice into bars of 3-inch width. Divide each piece into 8 triangles. Lightly press down M&M's minis to make eyes and mouth, attach pretzels to make antlers. Keep in a tightly closed container to store.

Nutrition Information

- Calories:
- Total Carbohydrate:
- Cholesterol:
- Protein:
- Total Fat:
- Sodium:
- Fiber:

64. Candy Bar Parfaits

Serving: 4 servings. | Prep: 10mins | Cook: 0mins | Ready in:

Ingredients

- 1/2 cup coarsely chopped unsalted peanuts
- 1/2 cup coarsely crushed pretzels
- 1 milk chocolate candy bar (1.55 ounces), chopped
- 1 pint vanilla ice cream, softened
- 1/3 cup chocolate syrup
- 2 tablespoons peanut butter

Direction

- Mix chopped candy bar, pretzels, and peanuts in a small bowl; into each of 4 parfait glasses, put 2 tablespoons. Place 1/4 cup ice cream, 2 tablespoons peanut mixture and another 1/4 cup ice cream on top.
- Mix peanut butter and chocolate syrup; pour over ice cream. Top with the rest of the peanut mixture.

Nutrition Information

- Calories: 443 calories
- Sodium: 276mg sodium
- Fiber: 3g fiber)
- Total Carbohydrate: 51g carbohydrate (33g sugars
- Cholesterol: 31mg cholesterol
- Protein: 11g protein.
- Total Fat: 24g fat (9g saturated fat)

65. Candy Cane Reindeer

Serving: 1 dozen. | Prep: 30mins | Cook: 0mins | Ready in:

Ingredients

- 8 ounces white candy coating, coarsely chopped
- 12 candy canes (6 inches)
- 12 to 20 pretzels
- 12 red-hot candies
- 24 black sugar pearls or miniature semisweet chocolate chips or black sprinkles

Direction

- Melt candy coating in a microwave; mix until smooth. Keep warm. Gripping the curved end of a candy cane, drizzle coating over the straight part of cane using a spoon. Shake off excess gently. Put on waxed paper to set. Keep coating the leftover candy canes. Crack pretzels into pieces to make them look like antlers; put 24 pieces aside.
- Dot a tiny amount of melted candy coating onto a red-hot for the reindeer's nose. Force onto the end of the curved part of the candy cane and hold for about 10 seconds. Put a tiny amount of coating on 2 sugar pearls to make the eyes and stick to candy cane above nose.
- Choose 2 pretzel pieces that look alike; on the candy cane where antlers will be stuck on, dot a tiny amount of coating. Force pretzel pieces into the coating and hold for about 30 seconds. Repeat with other reindeers. Put into mugs or drinking glasses; allow to dry for about 1 hour.

Nutrition Information

- Calories: 201 calories
- Sodium: 124mg sodium
- Fiber: 0 fiber)
- Total Carbohydrate: 37g carbohydrate (26g sugars
- Cholesterol: 0 cholesterol
- Protein: 1g protein.
- Total Fat: 6g fat (5g saturated fat)

66. Candy Store Pudding

Serving: 4 servings. | Prep: 10mins | Cook: 0mins | Ready in:

Ingredients

- 1 cup cold milk
- 1 package (3.9 ounces) instant chocolate pudding mix
- 1 cup heavy whipping cream, whipped
- 1/2 to 1 cup miniature marshmallows
- 1/4 to 1/2 cup chopped salted peanuts

Direction

- Whisk pudding mix and milk together in a big bowl about 2 minutes, the mixture will become thick. Fold in peanuts, marshmallows and whipped cream, then scoop into separate dessert dishes. Chill until ready to serve.

Nutrition Information

- Calories: 413 calories
- Sodium: 503mg sodium
- Fiber: 1g fiber)
- Total Carbohydrate: 36g carbohydrate (27g sugars
- Cholesterol: 90mg cholesterol
- Protein: 6g protein.
- Total Fat: 29g fat (16g saturated fat)

67. Cappuccino Chocolate Pie

Serving: 6-8 servings. | Prep: 15mins | Cook: 10mins | Ready in:

Ingredients

- 1 cup (6 ounces) semisweet chocolate chips
- 1/3 cup heavy whipping cream
- 1 tablespoon light corn syrup
- 1/2 teaspoon vanilla extract
- Dash salt
- 1 graham cracker crust (10 inches)
- 1 cup chopped pecans
- 4 ounces cream cheese, softened
- 1-1/2 cups milk
- 2 tablespoons brewed coffee
- 2 packages (3.4 ounces each) instant vanilla pudding mix
- 2 tablespoons instant coffee granules
- 1 carton (8 ounces) frozen whipped topping, thawed, divided

Direction

- Melt together the salt, cream, corn syrup, vanilla and chocolate chips in a saucepan on low heat; stir till smooth. Spoon the mixture into the crust. Sprinkle pecans on top.
- Beat cream cheese in a large bowl till smooth. Add milk and brewed coffee into the mixture slowly; combine thoroughly. Add pudding mixes and instant coffee into this mixture; beat till smooth. Fold 1-1/2 cups whipped topping into the mixture. Spoon it onto the pecans. Spread the rest of the whipped topping over the filling. Chill in the refrigerator for no less than 3 hours before serving.

Nutrition Information

- Calories: 554 calories
- Total Carbohydrate: 52g carbohydrate (39g sugars
- Cholesterol: 35mg cholesterol
- Protein: 6g protein.
- Total Fat: 37g fat (17g saturated fat)
- Sodium: 384mg sodium
- Fiber: 3g fiber)

68. Caramel Chocolate Sauce

Serving: 2 cups. | Prep: 10mins | Cook: 0mins | Ready in:

Ingredients

- 30 caramels
- 1 cup (6 ounces) semisweet chocolate chips
- 1 can (5 ounces) evaporated milk
- 1/2 cup butter, cubed
- Ice cream

Direction

- Mix the butter, chocolate chips, milk and caramels in a 1-quart microwave-safe bowl. Heat in the microwave on high for 1 to 2 minutes, uncovered; stir. Microwave for 30-60 seconds more or until the caramels are nearly melted; mix until smooth. Serve warm, if you like, over ice cream (sauce will thicken upon standing). Chill leftovers.

Nutrition Information

- Calories: 185 calories
- Sodium: 115mg sodium
- Fiber: 1g fiber)
- Total Carbohydrate: 22g carbohydrate (19g sugars
- Cholesterol: 20mg cholesterol
- Protein: 2g protein.
- Total Fat: 11g fat (7g saturated fat)

69. Caramel Corn Chocolate Bars

Serving: 2 dozen. | Prep: 10mins | Cook: 35mins | Ready in:

Ingredients

- 5 cups caramel corn
- 1 cup chopped pecans
- 1 package (10-1/2 ounces) miniature marshmallows, divided
- 1/4 cup butter, cubed
- 1/2 cup semisweet chocolate chips

Direction

- Mix 1 cup marshmallows, pecans and caramel corn in big bowl. Melt butter in small heavy saucepan on low heat. Add leftover marshmallows and chips; mix and cook till smooth.
- Put on caramel corn mixture; toss till coated. Press into 13x9-in. greased pan using buttered hands; cool then use a serrated knife to cut.

Nutrition Information

- Calories: 143 calories
- Fiber: 1g fiber)
- Total Carbohydrate: 20g carbohydrate (13g sugars
- Cholesterol: 5mg cholesterol
- Protein: 1g protein.
- Total Fat: 7g fat (2g saturated fat)
- Sodium: 52mg sodium

70. Caramel Toffee Bombe

Serving: 4-6 servings. | Prep: 15mins | Cook: 0mins | Ready in:

Ingredients

- 3/4 cup crushed gingersnaps (about 14 cookies)
- 3 tablespoons butter, melted
- 1 pint vanilla ice cream, softened
- 2 Heath candy bars (1.4 ounces each), chopped
- 1/3 cup caramel ice cream topping, warmed

Direction

- Line plastic wrap on 3-cup bowl. Mix butter and cookie crumbs; press up the sides and on bottom of prepped bowl. Beat chopped candy bars and ice cream till blended in a big bowl; scoop into crust. Cover; freeze till firm.
- If needed, trim crust's edge even with ice cream. Invert onto serving platter then remove plastic wrap. Allow to stand before cutting for 10 minutes; drizzle using caramel topping.

Nutrition Information

- Calories:
- Fiber:
- Total Carbohydrate:
- Cholesterol:
- Protein:
- Total Fat:
- Sodium:

71. Caramel Pecan Ice Cream Sandwiches

Serving: 4 servings. | Prep: 10mins | Cook: 5mins | Ready in:

Ingredients

- 8 pretzel crisps
- 2 ounces milk chocolate candy coating, melted
- 8 teaspoons marshmallow creme
- 1/2 cup chocolate ice cream, softened
- 2 teaspoons hot caramel ice cream topping, warmed
- 4 teaspoons chopped pecans

Direction

- Dunk the pretzel crisps into the melted chocolate, letting the excess drip off. Arrange on the waxed paper; allow to stand until they have set.
- Spread each pretzel crisp bottom with marshmallow creme. Spread half of pretzel crisps with 2 tablespoons of the ice cream. Drizzle ice cream topping over top; add the remaining pretzel crisps over top. Press the pecans into the sides. Cover with the plastic. Place in the freezer at least 60 mins.

Nutrition Information

- Calories: 155 calories
- Total Fat: 8g fat (4g saturated fat)
- Sodium: 55mg sodium
- Fiber: 1g fiber)
- Total Carbohydrate: 20g carbohydrate (15g sugars
- Cholesterol: 6mg cholesterol
- Protein: 2g protein.

72. Caramelized Angel Food Cake Sundaes

Serving: 6 servings. | Prep: 15mins | Cook: 5mins | Ready in:

Ingredients

- 3 ounces cream cheese, softened
- 1/4 cup sour cream
- 2 tablespoons confectioners' sugar
- 1/4 cup butter, softened
- 1/4 cup packed brown sugar
- 1/8 teaspoon ground cinnamon
- 6 slices angel food cake
- 6 scoops fudge ripple ice cream

Direction

- Place a cream cheese in a small bowl and whisk it with confectioner's sugar and sour cream until the mixture is smooth. In a separate bowl, cream the butter with cinnamon and brown sugar, making a fluffy and light mixture.
- Coat each cake slice with the butter mixture, spreading it over the sides and top of the cake. Transfer onto an ungreased baking sheet. Broil the cake for 1-2 minutes, four to six inches from the heat source, until bubbly. Allow it to cool slightly. Serve with sour cream mixture and ice cream.

Nutrition Information

- Calories: 404 calories

- Protein: 6g protein.
- Total Fat: 22g fat (14g saturated fat)
- Sodium: 360mg sodium
- Fiber: 1g fiber)
- Total Carbohydrate: 47g carbohydrate (27g sugars
- Cholesterol: 62mg cholesterol

73. Card Club Dessert

Serving: 12-15 servings. | Prep: 15mins | Cook: 5mins | Ready in:

Ingredients

- 30 Oreo cookies, finely crushed (about 2-1/4 cups)
- 1/3 cup butter, melted
- 1-3/4 cups cold milk
- 1 package (3.4 ounces) instant vanilla pudding mix
- 1 cup peanut butter
- 4 ounces German sweet chocolate, chopped
- 1 carton (12 ounces) frozen whipped topping, thawed

Direction

- Mix together butter and cookie crumbs in a bowl, then put aside 1/4 cup of mixture for topping. Press into an ungreased 13″x9″ baking pan with the rest of crumb mixture. Bake at 375 degrees about 5 minutes to fully cool.
- Whisk pudding mix and milk in a bowl until thickened, about 2 minutes. Stir in chocolate and peanut butter immediately, then fold in whipped topping. Spread the mixture over cooled crust and use reserved crumb mixture to sprinkle over top.
- Place a cover and chill about 4 hours to overnight.

Nutrition Information

- Calories: 383 calories
- Sodium: 372mg sodium
- Fiber: 2g fiber)
- Total Carbohydrate: 36g carbohydrate (23g sugars
- Cholesterol: 15mg cholesterol
- Protein: 7g protein.
- Total Fat: 24g fat (11g saturated fat)

74. Cherry Almond Bark

Serving: about 1 pound. | Prep: 25mins | Cook: 0mins | Ready in:

Ingredients

- 1 pound white candy coating, coarsely chopped
- 3/4 cup chopped candied cherries
- 1/2 cup unblanched whole almonds

Direction

- Melt coating in a microwave-safe bowl, stir until smooth. Add almonds and cherries. Spread the mixture on top of a baking sheet lined with foil. Chill in refrigerator until firm. Smash into pieces.

Nutrition Information

- Calories: 201 calories
- Total Fat: 10g fat (7g saturated fat)
- Sodium: 7mg sodium
- Fiber: 0 fiber)
- Total Carbohydrate: 27g carbohydrate (25g sugars
- Cholesterol: 0 cholesterol
- Protein: 1g protein.

75. Cherry Cheese Danish

Serving: 4 servings. | Prep: 15mins | Cook: 12mins | Ready in:

Ingredients

- 1 tube (8 ounces) refrigerated crescent rolls
- 4 tablespoons cream cheese, softened
- 1 cup cherry pie filling
- 1/2 cup vanilla frosting

Direction

- Divide the crescent dough into four rectangles. Then put on a baking sheet that is not greased; secure the perforations. Onto each rectangle, scatter 1 tablespoon cream cheese. Put 1/4 cup cherry pie filling on top. Place inside the oven and bake for 10-12 minutes at 375 degrees F or until edges are golden brown in color. Let it cool for 5 minutes. In a small microwave-safe bowl, put the frosting; then heat on high temperature for 15-20 seconds. Sprinkle over hot pastries. Serve hot. Store the leftovers inside the refrigerator.

Nutrition Information

- Calories: 499 calories
- Cholesterol: 16mg cholesterol
- Protein: 5g protein.
- Total Fat: 23g fat (8g saturated fat)
- Sodium: 570mg sodium
- Fiber: 0 fiber)
- Total Carbohydrate: 64g carbohydrate (41g sugars

76. Cherry Cream Dessert

Serving: 10 servings. | Prep: 15mins | Cook: 0mins | Ready in:

Ingredients

- 1 package (8 ounces) cream cheese, softened
- 1 can (20 ounces) crushed pineapple, undrained
- 1 can (21 ounces) cherry pie filling
- 1/2 cup chopped pecans
- 1 carton (8 ounces) frozen whipped topping, thawed
- Additional whipped topping and cherries, optional

Direction

- Beat pineapple and cream cheese in a big bowl, then mix in pecans and pie filling. Fold in whipped topping, then scoop into separate dessert dishes. Use additional whipped topping and cherry to decorate each, if you want. Place a cover and chill until ready to serve.

Nutrition Information

- Calories: 296 calories
- Sodium: 78mg sodium
- Fiber: 1g fiber)
- Total Carbohydrate: 35g carbohydrate (28g sugars
- Cholesterol: 25mg cholesterol
- Protein: 3g protein.
- Total Fat: 16g fat (9g saturated fat)

77. Cherry Mallow Dessert

Serving: 9 servings. | Prep: 25mins | Cook: 0mins | Ready in:

Ingredients

- 1-1/2 cups graham cracker crumbs
- 1/3 cup butter, melted
- 1 can (21 ounces) cherry pie filling
- 3 cups miniature marshmallows
- 1 cup heavy whipping cream, whipped

Direction

- Reserve a tablespoon of graham cracker crumbs to use as topping. Put the rest of crumbs in a bowl; mix in butter until combined. Press the mixture into a 9-inch square baking pan coated with grease. Put in an oven and bake at 350° until light brown, about 10-12 minutes. Let cool completely.
- Spread the pie filling over crust. Fold marshmallows into the whipped cream; spread on the filling. Scatter with the reserved crumbs. Put in refrigerator for at least 6 hours.

Nutrition Information

- Calories: 339 calories
- Protein: 2g protein.
- Total Fat: 18g fat (11g saturated fat)
- Sodium: 183mg sodium
- Fiber: 1g fiber)
- Total Carbohydrate: 44g carbohydrate (29g sugars
- Cholesterol: 54mg cholesterol

78. Cherry Oatmeal Wedges

Serving: 12 servings. | Prep: 10mins | Cook: 15mins | Ready in:

Ingredients

- 1 tube (16-1/2 ounces) refrigerated chocolate chip cookie dough
- 3/4 cup old-fashioned oats
- 1 can (21 ounces) cherry pie filling

Direction

- Mix together oats and cookie dough in a large bowl. Pat into an ungreased pizza pan.
- Bake in 350-oven until golden browned, about 14 to 16 minutes. Let cool for 5 minutes on a wire rack. Slice into wedges and put pie filling on top.

Nutrition Information

- Calories: 264 calories
- Fiber: 1g fiber)
- Total Carbohydrate: 43g carbohydrate (29g sugars
- Cholesterol: 10mg cholesterol
- Protein: 3g protein.
- Total Fat: 9g fat (3g saturated fat)
- Sodium: 98mg sodium

79. Cherry Surprise Cookies

Serving: 36-40 cookies. | Prep: 10mins | Cook: 10mins | Ready in:

Ingredients

- 2 cups Basic Cookie Dough
- 36 to 40 chocolate stars or chocolate kisses
- 36 to 40 candied cherry halves

Direction

- By heaping teaspoonfuls, drop cookie dough onto greased baking sheets, 2-in. apart. Put a chocolate star on top of each; wrap dough around it. Put candied cherry half over each; bake at 375° till bottoms are lightly browned or for 10-12 minutes. Transfer to wire racks; cool.

Nutrition Information

- Calories:
- Cholesterol:
- Protein:
- Total Fat:
- Sodium:
- Fiber:
- Total Carbohydrate:

80. Cherry Nut Chocolate Pie

Serving: 6-8 servings. | Prep: 10mins | Cook: 0mins | Ready in:

Ingredients

- 2 pints dark chocolate ice cream, softened
- 1 jar (10 ounces) maraschino cherries, drained and coarsely chopped
- 3/4 cup slivered almonds
- 1 chocolate crumb crust (8 inches)
- Whipped topping

Direction

- Mix almonds, cherries and ice cream in a big bowl. Spoon onto crust. Freeze, covered, overnight. 10 minutes before cutting, remove from freezer. Put whipped topping on top.

Nutrition Information

- Calories: 350 calories
- Fiber: 3g fiber)
- Total Carbohydrate: 48g carbohydrate (38g sugars
- Cholesterol: 23mg cholesterol
- Protein: 6g protein.
- Total Fat: 17g fat (6g saturated fat)
- Sodium: 152mg sodium

81. Chewy Peanut Bars

Serving: 2 dozen. | Prep: 15mins | Cook: 0mins | Ready in:

Ingredients

- 5 cups cornflakes
- 3 cups crisp rice cereal
- 1 cup dry roasted peanuts
- 1 cup sweetened shredded coconut
- 1 cup light corn syrup
- 1/4 cup butter, cubed
- 1/2 cup half-and-half cream
- 1/2 cup sugar

Direction

- Mix the first 4 ingredients in a large bowl and put aside. Mix sugar, cream, butter and corn syrup; cook and stir over medium heat in a heavy pan until sugar melts and the mixture reaches 234 degrees on candy thermometer (soft-ball stage).
- Stir into cereal mixture until evenly coated. Grease a 13x9-inch pan and press mixture in the prepared pan. Let cool then cut.

Nutrition Information

- Calories: 166 calories
- Sodium: 171mg sodium
- Fiber: 1g fiber)
- Total Carbohydrate: 26g carbohydrate (13g sugars
- Cholesterol: 8mg cholesterol
- Protein: 2g protein.
- Total Fat: 7g fat (3g saturated fat)

82. Chewy Peanut Butter Cookies

Serving: 18 | Prep: | Cook: | Ready in:

Ingredients

- 1 cup packed brown sugar
- 1 cup white sugar
- 1 cup peanut butter
- 1 cup shortening
- 1 teaspoon baking soda
- 2 tablespoons hot water
- 2 1/2 cups all-purpose flour
- 2 eggs

Direction

- Mix shortening, peanut butter and sugars. Put baking soda into hot water; add to mixture. Mix well.
- Mix eggs in; add flour then roll dough to balls.
- On ungreased cookie sheets, put balls. Use fork dipped in water to press to create crisscross design. Bake for 8-10 minutes at 175-190°C/350-375°F.

Nutrition Information

- Calories: 346 calories;
- Total Carbohydrate: 39.2
- Cholesterol: 21
- Protein: 6.1
- Total Fat: 19.3
- Sodium: 147

83. Chocolate Almond Crescents

Serving: 6 dozen. | Prep: 20mins | Cook: 10mins | Ready in:

Ingredients

- 1-1/4 cups butter, softened
- 2/3 cup sugar
- 2 cups finely chopped almonds
- 1-1/2 teaspoons vanilla extract
- 2 cups all-purpose flour
- 1/2 cup baking cocoa
- 1/8 teaspoon salt
- 1-1/4 cups semisweet chocolate chips, melted
- 1 to 2 tablespoons confectioners' sugar
- Sweetened shredded coconut, optional

Direction

- Cream sugar and butter together in a big bowl until fluffy and light. Beat in vanilla and almonds. Whisk together salt, cocoa and flour in a separate bowl, then beat into the creamed mixture gradually. Chill with a cover until firm enough to shape, about 2 hours.
- Set the oven to 350 degrees to preheat. Form 2 tsp. of dough into logs with the length of 2 inches, then shape each into a crescent. Put on ungreased baking sheets with 2 inches apart. Bake until set, about 10 to 12 minutes. Transfer from pans to wire rack to completely cool.
- Dip into the melted chocolate with halfway of cookies, the let excess chocolate drip off. Arrange coated cookies on waxed paper. Sprinkle coconut over top if you want. Allow to stand until set, then use waxed paper to cover the dipped sides of cookies. Use confectioners' sugar to sprinkle over the undipped sides. Keep between pieces of waxed paper in airtight containers.

Nutrition Information

- Calories: 85 calories
- Total Carbohydrate: 7g carbohydrate (4g sugars
- Cholesterol: 8mg cholesterol
- Protein: 1g protein.
- Total Fat: 6g fat (3g saturated fat)
- Sodium: 27mg sodium
- Fiber: 1g fiber)

84. Chocolate Almond Dessert

Serving: 15 servings. | Prep: 20mins | Cook: 10mins | Ready in:

Ingredients

- 1 prepared angel food cake (8 to 10 ounces), cut into 1-inch cubes
- 4 cups cold 2% milk
- 2 packages (3.4 ounces each) cook-and-serve chocolate pudding mix
- 1 milk chocolate candy bar (1.55 ounces), chopped
- 3/4 cup sliced almonds, toasted, divided
- 1 cup heavy whipping cream, whipped

Direction

- Spread half of the cake cubes onto an ungreased 13x9-in. sheet; set aside. Whisk pudding mixes and milk together in a large saucepan. Put in candy bar. Cook while stirring over medium heat till the mixture comes to a boil. Cook while stirring till thickened, 1-2 more minutes.
- Spread 1/2 of the pudding over the cake cubes. Sprinkle 1/2 of the almonds over top; refrigerate with a cover. Put the remaining pudding into a small bowl; refrigerate with a cover till chilled.
- Spread the remaining cake cubes over the dessert. Whisk the chilled pudding; mix in whipped cream. Spread over the top; sprinkle the remaining almonds over all. Refrigerate with a cover for at least 1 hour. To serve, cut into squares.

Nutrition Information

- Calories: 215 calories
- Fiber: 1g fiber)
- Total Carbohydrate: 26g carbohydrate (13g sugars
- Cholesterol: 27mg cholesterol
- Protein: 5g protein.
- Total Fat: 11g fat (5g saturated fat)
- Sodium: 211mg sodium

85. Chocolate Berry Parfaits

Serving: 4-6 servings. | Prep: 15mins | Cook: 0mins | Ready in:

Ingredients

- 2 cups cold 2% milk
- 1 package (3.9 ounces) instant chocolate pudding mix
- 1 package (10 ounces) frozen sweetened strawberries, thawed
- 1 cup heavy whipping cream
- 1/4 cup confectioners' sugar
- Sliced fresh strawberries, optional

Direction

- Combine pudding mix and milk for 2 minutes in a large bowl. Allow it to stand for 2 minutes or until set to soft; reserve. Strain strawberries (discard the juice or keep for another use); transfer berries in a blender. Then cover and pulse until smooth; reserve.
- Whisk sugar and cream in a large bowl until stiff peaks form. Slightly fold in strawberry puree. Split half of the chocolate pudding among four or six parfait glasses. Put half of the strawberry mixture on top. Continue layers. Decorate with a slice of strawberry if preferred.

Nutrition Information

- Calories: 317 calories
- Sodium: 329mg sodium
- Fiber: 1g fiber)
- Total Carbohydrate: 39g carbohydrate (33g sugars
- Cholesterol: 65mg cholesterol
- Protein: 4g protein.
- Total Fat: 18g fat (11g saturated fat)

86. Chocolate Cake Mix Cookies

Serving: 4 dozen. | Prep: 15mins | Cook: 10mins | Ready in:

Ingredients

- 1 package (8 ounces) cream cheese, softened
- 1/2 cup butter, softened
- 1 egg
- 1 teaspoon vanilla extract
- 1 package chocolate cake mix (regular size)
- 1 cup semisweet chocolate chips

- 1 cup peanut butter chips

Direction

- Set oven to preheat at 375°. Beat together butter and cream cheese till smooth in a large bowl. Beat in vanilla and egg. Add the cake mix into the mixture; beat until incorporated on low speed. Stir in peanut butter chips and chocolate.
- On the greased baking sheets, drop rounded tablespoonfuls of the dough 2 in. apart. Bake until set, or 10-12 minutes. Allow to cool for 3 minutes, then take out and transfer to wire racks. Keep in an airtight container.

Nutrition Information

- Calories: 113 calories
- Fiber: 1g fiber)
- Total Carbohydrate: 13g carbohydrate (9g sugars
- Cholesterol: 15mg cholesterol
- Protein: 2g protein. Diabetic Exchanges: 1 starch
- Total Fat: 7g fat (4g saturated fat)
- Sodium: 111mg sodium

87. Chocolate Cake In A Mug

Serving: 1 | Prep: 10mins | Cook: 3mins | Ready in:

Ingredients

- 1/4 cup all-purpose flour
- 1/4 cup brown sugar
- 3 1/2 tablespoons cocoa powder
- 1 teaspoon hot cocoa mix
- 1/2 egg, beaten
- 3 tablespoons chocolate milk
- 3 tablespoons vegetable oil
- 2 tablespoons chocolate chips (optional)
- 1 splash vanilla extract

Direction

- In a large microwave-safe mug, put flour, cocoa powder, hot cocoa mix, and brown sugar and mix together. Add egg and stir. Add vegetable oil and chocolate milk into the flour mixture and mix until the batter turns smooth; add vanilla extract and chocolate chips, then stir.
- Place mug inside the microwave and cook for 3 minutes on high power, or until a toothpick poked in middle comes out clean.

Nutrition Information

- Calories: 841 calories;
- Total Carbohydrate: 90.8
- Cholesterol: 96
- Protein: 12.5
- Total Fat: 53.5
- Sodium: 94

88. Chocolate Caramel Corn

Serving: 40 | Prep: | Cook: 1hours | Ready in:

Ingredients

- 5 quarts popped popcorn
- 1 1/3 cups brown sugar
- 1 1/2 cups butter, divided
- 2 1/2 cups light corn syrup, divided
- 1 teaspoon vanilla extract
- 4 cups milk chocolate chips

Direction

- Set the oven to 120°C (250°F) then begin preheating. Spread cooking spray on a large roasting pan. Transfer the popcorn to the roasting pan and keep warm in the oven.
- Mix together half a cup of corn syrup, a cup of butter and brown sugar in a heavy saucepan over medium heat. Heat up to 121°C to 129°C (250°F to 265°F) without blending, or until a

tiny quantity of syrup dropped into cold water shapes a stiff ball. Expel from heat and mix in vanilla. Pour over popcorn with syrup and toss to coat. Put popcorn back to the oven.

- Mix together 2 cups corn syrup with the rest of half cup butter and chocolate chips in the same saucepan. Cook over medium heat, whisking, until chocolate melts. Remove from heat and immediately pour over popcorn, blending to coat.
- Put popcorn back to the oven, mixing occasionally, for 30 to 40 minutes. To cool entirely, remove and pour over waxed paper lined sheets.

Nutrition Information

- Calories: 269 calories;
- Sodium: 150
- Total Carbohydrate: 35.5
- Cholesterol: 24
- Protein: 1.6
- Total Fat: 14.9

89. Chocolate Caramel Hazelnut Pie

Serving: 8 servings | Prep: 25mins | Cook: 0mins | Ready in:

Ingredients

- 1-1/2 cups salted caramel pretzel pieces
- 12 Lorna Doone shortbread cookies
- 1/4 cup sugar
- 6 tablespoons butter, melted
- 5 tablespoons caramel topping, divided
- FILLING:
- 1 package (8 ounces) cream cheese, softened
- 1/2 cup Nutella
- 1 jar (7 ounces) marshmallow creme
- 1 carton (8 ounces) frozen whipped topping, thawed
- 1 cup miniature marshmallows
- 1 Snickers candy bar (1.86 ounces), chopped

Direction

- In a food processor, put cookies and pretzel pieces; pulse until forming fine crumbs. Put in melted butter and sugar; pulse until just combined. Press the mixture onto the bottom and sides of a 9-inch pie plate. Drizzle 3 tablespoons caramel topping over the surface. Freeze when making filling.
- To make filling, beat Nutella and cream cheese until smooth. Slowly whisk in marshmallow crème. Fold in marshmallows and whipped topping gently. Scoop into crust.
- Chill in the fridge 3-4 hours until set. Add the rest of caramel topping and chopped candy over top; serve.

Nutrition Information

- Calories: 663 calories
- Sodium: 327mg sodium
- Fiber: 1g fiber)
- Total Carbohydrate: 74g carbohydrate (57g sugars
- Cholesterol: 60mg cholesterol
- Protein: 6g protein.
- Total Fat: 35g fat (19g saturated fat)

90. Chocolate Cherry Trifle

Serving: 18 servings. | Prep: 20mins | Cook: 0mins | Ready in:

Ingredients

- 3 cups cold fat-free milk
- 2 packages (1.4 ounces each) sugar-free instant chocolate fudge pudding mix
- 1 prepared angel food cake (8 to 10 ounces), cut into 1-inch cubes
- 2 cans (20 ounces each) reduced-sugar cherry pie filling

- 2 cans (20 ounces each) unsweetened crushed pineapple, drained
- 1 carton (16 ounces) frozen reduced-fat whipped topping, thawed
- 1/4 cup chopped pecans

Direction

- Whisk pudding mixes and milk for 2 minutes in big bowl; stand till soft set or for 2 minutes.
- Put 1/2 cake cubes in glass bowl/4-qt. trifle bowl; top with 1/2 each of: pudding, the pie filling, the pineapple then whipped topping. Repeat the layers; sprinkle pecans then refrigerate leftovers.

Nutrition Information

- Calories: 221 calories
- Fiber: 1g fiber)
- Total Carbohydrate: 41g carbohydrate (29g sugars
- Cholesterol: 1mg cholesterol
- Protein: 3g protein.
- Total Fat: 5g fat (3g saturated fat)
- Sodium: 266mg sodium

91. Chocolate Chip Bars

Serving: 36 | Prep: | Cook: | Ready in:

Ingredients

- 2 cups all-purpose flour
- 1 teaspoon baking powder
- 1/4 teaspoon baking soda
- 1 cup shortening
- 1/4 teaspoon salt
- 1 1/2 cups packed brown sugar
- 2 eggs
- 2 tablespoons milk
- 1 teaspoon vanilla extract
- 1 cup semisweet chocolate chips

Direction

- Preheat the oven to 175 degrees C (350 degrees F). Coat a 9x13 inch baking pan with grease.
- Cream brown sugar, shortening and eggs in a large bowl. Pour in vanilla extract and milk and combine well. Slowly add in baking soda, salt, flour and baking powder. Combine until blended well.
- Fold in chocolate chips and mix until the chips are distributed evenly in the dough. Spread the dough into the pan and bake for 25 to 30 minutes. Allow to cool before slicing into bars.

Nutrition Information

- Calories: 138 calories;
- Total Fat: 7.5
- Sodium: 46
- Total Carbohydrate: 17.3
- Cholesterol: 10
- Protein: 1.3

92. Chocolate Chip Cookies Small Batch

Serving: 4 dozen. | Prep: 15mins | Cook: 10mins | Ready in:

Ingredients

- 1/2 cup reduced-fat margarine
- 3/4 cup sugar
- 3/4 cup packed brown sugar
- 2 eggs
- 1/4 cup fat-free plain yogurt
- 2 teaspoons vanilla extract
- 2-1/2 cups all-purpose flour
- 1 teaspoon baking soda
- 1 teaspoon salt
- 1-1/2 cups miniature semisweet chocolate chips
- 1/2 cup chopped walnuts, toasted

Direction

- Cream the margarine and sugars lightly in a large bowl. Add eggs into the mixture, one by one, beat thoroughly after each time you add. Beat yogurt and vanilla into the mixture. Mix together the salt, baking soda and flour; add them into the creamed mixture slowly. Stir chocolate chips and walnuts into the mixture.
- Drop heaping tablespoonfuls of the dough 2 in. apart onto baking sheets sprayed using cooking spray. Bake to a golden brown at 375° or for 8-10 minutes. Transfer to wire racks.

Nutrition Information

- Calories: 190 calories
- Sodium: 187mg sodium
- Fiber: 1g fiber)
- Total Carbohydrate: 30g carbohydrate (19g sugars
- Cholesterol: 18mg cholesterol
- Protein: 3g protein. Diabetic Exchanges: 2 starch
- Total Fat: 7g fat (2g saturated fat)

93. Chocolate Chip Mallow Pie

Serving: 8 servings. | *Prep: 10mins* | *Cook: 0mins* | *Ready in:*

Ingredients

- 2 pints chocolate chip ice cream, softened
- 1 graham cracker crust (9 inches)
- 1 cup marshmallow creme
- 1/3 cup hot fudge ice cream topping, warmed

Direction

- In crust, spoon ice cream in. Freeze, covered, till set for 3 hours minimum. Remove from freezer. Spread on marshmallow crème. Before cutting, let stand for about 15 minutes. Drizzle warm fudge topping on.

Nutrition Information

- Calories: 358 calories
- Total Carbohydrate: 49g carbohydrate (39g sugars
- Cholesterol: 25mg cholesterol
- Protein: 4g protein.
- Total Fat: 16g fat (7g saturated fat)
- Sodium: 183mg sodium
- Fiber: 1g fiber)

94. Chocolate Cookie Mousse

Serving: 16 servings. | *Prep: 25mins* | *Cook: 0mins* | *Ready in:*

Ingredients

- 1 package (15-1/2 ounces) Oreo cookies, divided
- 2 tablespoons milk
- 2 cups heavy whipping cream, divided
- 2 cups (12 ounces) semisweet chocolate chips

Direction

- Crush 16 cookies; sprinkle in 8-in. square dish. Drizzle milk. Microwave chocolate chips and 2/3 cup cream in microwave-safe bowl, uncovered, for 45 seconds on high. Mix; microwave till chips melt for 20-40 seconds more. Mix till smooth then cool down to room temperature.
- Meanwhile, beat leftover cream till soft peaks form in bowl; fold into chocolate mixture. Spread 1/3 chocolate mixture on crushed cookies. Separate 8 cookies; put on chocolate mixture then repeat. Put leftover chocolate mixture on top; use leftover whole cookies to garnish. Cover; freeze for 2 months maximum. Thaw for 3 hours minimum in the fridge; serve.

Nutrition Information

- Calories: 343 calories
- Sodium: 170mg sodium
- Fiber: 2g fiber)
- Total Carbohydrate: 35g carbohydrate (23g sugars
- Cholesterol: 41mg cholesterol
- Protein: 2g protein.
- Total Fat: 23g fat (12g saturated fat)

95. Chocolate Hazelnut Mousse Cups

Serving: 6 servings. | Prep: 30mins | Cook: 0mins | Ready in:

Ingredients

- 1 package (10 ounces) frozen puff pastry shells, thawed
- 1/2 cup heavy whipping cream
- 1 to 2 tablespoons confectioners' sugar
- 1/4 teaspoon vanilla extract
- 1/2 cup mascarpone cheese
- 1/2 cup Nutella
- 1/4 teaspoon ground cinnamon
- 2 tablespoons miniature semisweet chocolate chips
- Additional miniature semisweet chocolate chips, melted, optional
- 2 tablespoons chopped hazelnuts, toasted

Direction

- Follow package directions to bake pastry shells; completely cool.
- Beat cream till it starts to thicken in small bowl. Add vanilla and confectioners' sugar; beat till soft peaks form.
- Beat cinnamon, Nutella and mascarpone cheese till blended in another bowl. Fold chocolate chips and whipped cream in; put in pastry shells. Drizzle melted chocolate (optional). Sprinkle hazelnuts; refrigerate till serving.

Nutrition Information

- Calories: 581 calories
- Total Fat: 48g fat (19g saturated fat)
- Sodium: 269mg sodium
- Fiber: 2g fiber)
- Total Carbohydrate: 36g carbohydrate (19g sugars
- Cholesterol: 74mg cholesterol
- Protein: 9g protein.

96. Chocolate Ice Cream Dessert

Serving: 16-20 servings. | Prep: 25mins | Cook: 0mins | Ready in:

Ingredients

- 2 ounces unsweetened chocolate
- 1 cup sugar
- 1 can (5 ounces) evaporated milk
- 1 package (15-1/2 ounces) Oreo cookies, crushed
- 1/2 cup butter, melted
- 1 quart vanilla ice cream, softened
- 1 quart chocolate ice cream, softened
- Whipped topping, optional

Direction

- Mix milk, sugar and chocolate in saucepan on low heat. Boil, mixing continuously; let boil for a minute. Take off from heat; let cool for ten minutes.
- Meantime, mix butter and cookie crumbs; reserve 2 cups. Force the rest of the crumb mixture into an oiled 13x9-inch pan. On top of crust, cautiously scoop the vanilla ice cream; evenly spread. Over the top, scoop chocolate sauce. Scatter reserved mixture of crumb over. Cautiously scatter chocolate ice cream on top of crumbs. Put cover and place in freezer

overnight. Serve together with whipped topping if wished. Can be place in freezer for up to 2 months.

Nutrition Information

- Calories: 323 calories
- Fiber: 1g fiber)
- Total Carbohydrate: 42g carbohydrate (31g sugars
- Cholesterol: 35mg cholesterol
- Protein: 3g protein.
- Total Fat: 17g fat (9g saturated fat)
- Sodium: 205mg sodium

97. Chocolate Marshmallow Peanut Butter Squares

Serving: 5 dozen | Prep: 15mins | Cook: 5mins | Ready in:

Ingredients

- 1 can (14 ounces) sweetened condensed milk
- 1 package (11 ounces) peanut butter and milk chocolate chips
- 1/2 cup milk chocolate chips
- 1/2 cup creamy peanut butter
- 1 teaspoon vanilla extract
- 1-1/2 cups miniature marshmallows
- 1 cup broken miniature pretzels
- 1 cup Rice Krispies

Direction

- Put the first 5 ingredients in a large heavy saucepan; cook, stirring, over low heat for about 5 minutes or until smooth, and blended. The mixture is expected to be very thick. Put off the heat; mix in remaining ingredients. Spread mixture all over the bottom of an oiled 13x9-inch pan.
- Cover and chill for about 4 hours until firm. Divide into squares. Keep in an airtight container in the fridge.

Nutrition Information

- Calories: 85 calories
- Total Carbohydrate: 12g carbohydrate (8g sugars
- Cholesterol: 3mg cholesterol
- Protein: 1g protein.
- Total Fat: 4g fat (2g saturated fat)
- Sodium: 50mg sodium
- Fiber: 0 fiber)

98. Chocolate Mint Parfaits

Serving: 4 servings. | Prep: 15mins | Cook: 0mins | Ready in:

Ingredients

- 2 cups plus 1 tablespoon cold 2% milk, divided
- 1 package (3.9 ounces) instant chocolate pudding mix
- 4 ounces cream cheese, softened
- 1 tablespoon sugar
- 1/4 teaspoon peppermint extract
- 1 cup whipped topping
- Mint Andes candies, optional

Direction

- Beat pudding mix and 2 cups of milk for 2 minutes in a large bowl; reserve. Whisk the rest of the milk, extract, sugar, and cream cheese in a small bowl. Add in whipped topping then fold.
- Into four glasses of parfait, put half of the pudding. Place half of the cream cheese mixture on top. Continue layers. Decorate with candies if preferred.

Nutrition Information

- Calories: 323 calories
- Total Fat: 16g fat (11g saturated fat)
- Sodium: 555mg sodium
- Fiber: 1g fiber)
- Total Carbohydrate: 39g carbohydrate (30g sugars
- Cholesterol: 41mg cholesterol
- Protein: 7g protein.

99. Chocolate Mousse Frosting

Serving: 3-1/2 cups. | Prep: 10mins | Cook: 0mins | Ready in:

Ingredients

- 1 cup cold fat-free milk
- 1 package (1.4 ounces) sugar-free instant chocolate fudge pudding mix
- 1 carton (8 ounces) frozen reduced-fat whipped topping, thawed
- 1 prepared angel food cake

Direction

- Beat in a bowl the pudding mix and milk for 2 minutes on low speed. Add whipped topping and fold. Then frost the cake.

Nutrition Information

- Calories: 56 calories
- Fiber: 0 fiber)
- Total Carbohydrate: 7g carbohydrate (0 sugars
- Cholesterol: 0 cholesterol
- Protein: 1g protein. Diabetic Exchanges: 1/2 starch
- Total Fat: 2g fat (0 saturated fat)
- Sodium: 94mg sodium

100. Chocolate Peanut Butter Bites

Serving: 14 cookies. | Prep: 10mins | Cook: 10mins | Ready in:

Ingredients

- 2/3 cup sweetened condensed milk
- 1/3 cup creamy peanut butter
- 1/2 teaspoon vanilla extract
- 1 cup biscuit/baking mix
- 1/3 cup semisweet chocolate chips

Direction

- Beat vanilla, peanut butter and milk till smooth in small bowl; add biscuit mix till just blended. Fold chocolate chips in.
- By rounded tablespoonfuls, drop on ungreased baking sheets, 2-in. apart; bake for 10-12 minutes at 375° till edges are browned lightly. Cool for 2 minutes; transfer to wire racks.

Nutrition Information

- Calories: 137 calories
- Sodium: 155mg sodium
- Fiber: 1g fiber)
- Total Carbohydrate: 17g carbohydrate (11g sugars
- Cholesterol: 5mg cholesterol
- Protein: 3g protein. Diabetic Exchanges: 1 starch
- Total Fat: 7g fat (2g saturated fat)

101. Chocolate Peanut Butter Cake

Serving: 12-15 servings. | Prep: 15mins | Cook: 35mins | Ready in:

Ingredients

- 1 package devil's food cake mix (regular size)
- 1 cup creamy peanut butter
- 1 tablespoon canola oil
- 1 can (16 ounces) chocolate frosting

Direction

- Prepare and bake cake following package directions, using a greased 13x9-in. baking pan.
- Mix together oil and peanut butter in a small bowl until smooth and spread onto warm cake. Place on a wire rack to cool fully.
- Microwave frosting on high power until achieving a pouring consistency, 25 to 30 seconds; stir to smoothen. Carefully pour on the peanut butter layer and spread out. Allow to sit until set.

Nutrition Information

- Calories:
- Total Carbohydrate:
- Cholesterol:
- Protein:
- Total Fat:
- Sodium:
- Fiber:

102. Chocolate Peanut Crunch Ice Cream Cake

Serving: 14 servings. | Prep: 30mins | Cook: 0mins | Ready in:

Ingredients

- 1 cup milk chocolate chips
- 2 cups crushed Nutter Butter cookies (about 18 cookies)
- 1 quart vanilla ice cream, softened
- 1 quart chocolate ice cream, softened
- 1 cup heavy whipping cream
- 1 tablespoon confectioners' sugar
- 1 teaspoon vanilla extract

Direction

- Melt chocolate chips in a small saucepan on low heat. Stir in crushed cookies until coated, then spread on waxed paper to cool. Chop the mixture coarsely.
- Spread into a 9-inch springform pan with vanilla ice cream and use 2 cups of cookie mixture to sprinkle over. Freeze the ice cream for a half hour. Spread over with chocolate ice cream, then place a cover and chill until firm, about 4 hours.
- Beat cream in a small bowl until starts to thicken. Put in vanilla and confectioners' sugar, then beat until stiff peaks form. Run round edges of pan carefully with a knife to loosen. Take off sides of pan.
- Spread over top and sides of the dessert with whipped cream, then press into sides with leftover cookie mixture. Freeze until whipped cream is set, about an hour. Take out of the freezer about 15 minutes, then server.

Nutrition Information

- Calories: 369 calories
- Protein: 6g protein.
- Total Fat: 22g fat (12g saturated fat)
- Sodium: 141mg sodium
- Fiber: 1g fiber)
- Total Carbohydrate: 39g carbohydrate (30g sugars
- Cholesterol: 55mg cholesterol

103. Chocolate Peanut Sundaes

Serving: about 1-2/3 cups sauce. | Prep: 5mins | Cook: 10mins | Ready in:

Ingredients

- 1 package (3.4 ounces) cook-and-serve chocolate pudding mix
- 3/4 cup water
- 3/4 cup corn syrup
- 1/4 teaspoon salt
- 1/3 cup peanut butter
- 1 tablespoon butter
- 1/2 teaspoon vanilla extract
- Vanilla ice cream
- Chopped peanuts, optional

Direction

- Mix the salt, corn syrup, water and pudding mix in a big saucepan. Cook and mix until mixture heats up to a boil. Take it off from the heat; mix in the vanilla, butter and peanut butter until smooth. Serve while still warm with ice cream. Scatter with peanuts (optional).

Nutrition Information

- Calories: 165 calories
- Sodium: 183mg sodium
- Fiber: 1g fiber)
- Total Carbohydrate: 29g carbohydrate (19g sugars
- Cholesterol: 3mg cholesterol
- Protein: 3g protein.
- Total Fat: 5g fat (2g saturated fat)

104. Chocolate Rum Balls

Serving: 42 servings, 2 balls each | Prep: 20mins | Cook: | Ready in:

Ingredients

- 6 pkg. (4 oz. each) BAKER'S Semi-Sweet Chocolate, broken into small pieces
- 1 can (14 oz.) sweetened condensed milk
- 1 Tbsp. rum extract
- 2/3 cup finely chopped PLANTERS Pecans

Direction

- Follow the packaging direction to melt the chocolate. Mix in rum extract and milk. The mixture will become extremely thick. Rest for about 5 minutes.
- Roll approximately 1 teaspoon of chocolate mixture into a ball to make 84 balls. Roll into the nuts.
- Arrange on tray covered in waxed paper in one layer.
- Chill till firm, about an hour.

Nutrition Information

- Calories: 140
- Total Fat: 8 g
- Saturated Fat: 4 g
- Sugar: 12 g
- Protein: 2 g
- Sodium: 10 mg
- Fiber: 2 g
- Total Carbohydrate: 15 g
- Cholesterol: 2.423 mg

105. Chocolate Sundae Pie

Serving: 6-8 servings. | Prep: 20mins | Cook: 0mins | Ready in:

Ingredients

- 4 ounces cream cheese, softened
- 1/2 cup sweetened condensed milk
- 4 teaspoons baking cocoa
- 1 carton (8 ounces) frozen whipped topping, thawed
- 1 chocolate crumb crust (9 inches)
- 1/2 cup chocolate syrup
- 1/2 cup chopped pecans

Direction

- Beat cream cheese in a bowl till smooth. Add milk and cocoa into the mix; beat till smooth.

Fold whipped topping into the mixture. Spoon it into the crust. Drizzle chocolate syrup and pecans on top. Freeze, covered, overnight.

Nutrition Information

- Calories: 398 calories
- Sodium: 178mg sodium
- Fiber: 2g fiber)
- Total Carbohydrate: 45g carbohydrate (31g sugars
- Cholesterol: 22mg cholesterol
- Protein: 5g protein.
- Total Fat: 22g fat (11g saturated fat)

106. Chocolate Swirl Delight

Serving: 12 servings. | Prep: 25mins | Cook: 0mins | Ready in:

Ingredients

- 1-1/2 packages (13 ounces each) Swiss cake rolls
- 2-3/4 cups 2% milk
- 2 packages (3.9 ounces each) instant chocolate fudge pudding mix
- 2 cups whipped topping

Direction

- Cut every cake roll to 6 slices; keep broken chocolate coating for topping. Line cake slices on sides and bottom of 9-in. springform pan, completely covering.
- Whisk pudding mixes and milk for 2 minutes; it will be thick. Spread on bottom cake rolls layers; use whipped topping to cover. Sprinkle leftover chocolate pieces; refrigerate for minimum of 2 hours, covered. Serve.

Nutrition Information

- Calories: 331 calories
- Total Fat: 12g fat (5g saturated fat)
- Sodium: 382mg sodium
- Fiber: 1g fiber)
- Total Carbohydrate: 46g carbohydrate (35g sugars
- Cholesterol: 16mg cholesterol
- Protein: 4g protein.

107. Chocolate Yummies

Serving: 12 | Prep: 20mins | Cook: 1hours | Ready in:

Ingredients

- 7 Keebler® Grahams Original Crackers
- 2 1/2 cups miniature marshmallows
- 1 (12 ounce) package semi-sweet chocolate morsels
- 2/3 cup light corn syrup
- 3 tablespoons butter or margarine
- 1/2 cup crunchy peanut butter
- 3 cups Kellogg's® Rice Krispies®

Direction

- Use cooking spray to grease a 13x9x2-in. microwaveable dish. Line one layer of Keebler(R) Grahams Original crackers in the dish, fit with broken crackers if needed. Evenly scatter marshmallows on top.
- Put in microwave for a minute on high power, or until marshmallows are puffed. Take out of the microwave. Wait until fully cool.
- Mix together butter, corn syrup and chocolate morsels in a 2-qt microwaveable bowl. Put in the microwave on high power to melt chocolate for 1-1/2 minutes, whisking after each 30-second interval. Mix in peanut butter. Pour in Kellogg's(R) Rice Krispies(R) cereal, stirring until incorporated.
- Pour evenly over marshmallows. Chill while covered till firm, about an hour. Slice and keep refrigerated in a tightly sealed container to store.

Nutrition Information

- Calories: 367 calories;
- Total Fat: 16.6
- Sodium: 226
- Total Carbohydrate: 55.7
- Cholesterol: 8
- Protein: 4.5

108. Chocolate Covered Pomegranate Seeds

Serving: about 1 pound (2 dozen) | Prep: 5mins | Cook: 5mins | Ready in:

Ingredients

- 1 package (12 ounces) dark chocolate chips
- 1 cup pomegranate seeds, patted dry

Direction

- Melt chocolate chips in a microwave; mix until smooth. Mix in pomegranate seeds.
- Drop the mixture onto the baking sheets that are lined with a waxed paper by tablespoonfuls. Chill in the refrigerator until firm, about 1 hour. Keep in between layers of waxed paper that are placed in an airtight container and store inside the fridge.

Nutrition Information

- Calories: 70 calories
- Protein: 1g protein.
- Total Fat: 4g fat (3g saturated fat)
- Sodium: 5mg sodium
- Fiber: 1g fiber)
- Total Carbohydrate: 10g carbohydrate (9g sugars
- Cholesterol: 0 cholesterol

109. Chocolate Oat Toffee Bars

Serving: 15 servings. | Prep: 30mins | Cook: 0mins | Ready in:

Ingredients

- 6 tablespoons butter, cubed
- 1 cup all-purpose flour
- 1 cup quick-cooking oats
- 1/3 cup packed brown sugar
- 3 tablespoons corn syrup
- 1 cup (6 ounces) semisweet chocolate chips
- 1/3 cup English toffee bits or almond brickle chips
- 1/3 cup chopped pecans

Direction

- Melt butter in big microwave-safe bowl; mix corn syrup, brown sugar, oats and flour in. Press in 9-in. square greased baking pan.
- Bake for 8-12 minutes till golden brown at 450°. Put on wire rack; sprinkle chocolate chips. Let stand for 5 minutes then spread chocolate on crust. Sprinkle pecans and toffee bits; refrigerate till chocolate sets.

Nutrition Information

- Calories: 221 calories
- Protein: 2g protein.
- Total Fat: 12g fat (6g saturated fat)
- Sodium: 85mg sodium
- Fiber: 2g fiber)
- Total Carbohydrate: 28g carbohydrate (17g sugars
- Cholesterol: 14mg cholesterol

110. Citrus Cookies

Serving: 24 | Prep: | Cook: | Ready in:

Ingredients

- 1/2 cup butter
- 2/3 cup white sugar
- 1/8 teaspoon salt
- 1 tablespoon lemon juice
- 2 teaspoons lemon zest
- 6 drops yellow food coloring
- 1 1/2 cups all-purpose flour

Direction

- Cream sugar and margarine or butter together. Put in food coloring, zest, juice and salt. Mix the mixture until well combined.
- Put in 1/2 cup of flour at a time and mix well together. Dough should be ball up once completed. Form into a cylinder with a diameter of 2 1/2 inches. Refrigerate for about 4 hours.
- Set the oven to 180°C or 350°F to preheat.
- Cut into 24 cookies and bake on cookie sheet about 6-8 minutes.

Nutrition Information

- Calories: 84 calories;
- Protein: 0.9
- Total Fat: 3.9
- Sodium: 40
- Total Carbohydrate: 11.6
- Cholesterol: 10

111. Citrus Shortcake

Serving: 4 servings. | Prep: 10mins | Cook: 0mins | Ready in:

Ingredients

- 1 cup (8 ounces) lemon yogurt
- 1 cup whipped topping
- 4 individual round sponge cakes
- 1/4 cup orange juice
- 2-2/3 cups sliced fresh strawberries

Direction

- Mix yogurt and whipped topping in a bowl. Serve sponge cakes on plates. Drizzle orange juice on top. Apply half the yogurt mix on the cakes. Garnish with strawberries and the rest of the yogurt mix.

Nutrition Information

- Calories: 238 calories
- Protein: 5g protein.
- Total Fat: 6g fat (4g saturated fat)
- Sodium: 214mg sodium
- Fiber: 2g fiber)
- Total Carbohydrate: 40g carbohydrate (29g sugars
- Cholesterol: 31mg cholesterol

112. Citrus Torte

Serving: 10 servings. | Prep: 20mins | Cook: 0mins | Ready in:

Ingredients

- 1 jar (10 ounces) lemon curd
- 1 carton (8 ounces) frozen whipped topping, thawed, divided
- 1 loaf (10-3/4 ounces) frozen pound cake, thawed
- 1 can (15 ounces) mandarin oranges, drained

Direction

- Put lemon curd in a bowl. Fold half of the whipped topping in until mixed well. Slice cake into 3 horizontal layers. Put the bottom layer on a plate. Apply half cup of lemon curd mix. Repeat layering. Place the cake top.
- Use the rest of the lemon curd mix. Apply frosting on the sides using the rest of the whipped topping. Top with mandarin oranges. Chill before serving.

Nutrition Information

- Calories: 303 calories
- Protein: 2g protein.
- Total Fat: 10g fat (7g saturated fat)
- Sodium: 135mg sodium
- Fiber: 1g fiber)
- Total Carbohydrate: 47g carbohydrate (36g sugars
- Cholesterol: 65mg cholesterol

113. Cocoa Mint Truffles

Serving: 16 truffles. | Prep: 25mins | Cook: 5mins | Ready in:

Ingredients

- 3/4 cup semisweet chocolate chips
- 6 mint Andes candies
- 3/4 cup whipped topping
- 2 tablespoons baking cocoa
- 1/8 teaspoon instant coffee granules

Direction

- Melt candies and chocolate chips in small saucepan on low heat; put in small bowl. Cool for 7 minutes to lukewarm. Beat whipped topping in; put in freezer till firm enough to shape to balls for 15 minutes.
- Mix coffee granules and cocoa in small bowl. Form chocolate mixture to 1-in. balls then roll into cocoa mixture. Keep in airtight container in the fridge.

Nutrition Information

- Calories: 58 calories
- Protein: 1g protein.
- Total Fat: 4g fat (2g saturated fat)
- Sodium: 2mg sodium
- Fiber: 1g fiber)
- Total Carbohydrate: 7g carbohydrate (6g sugars
- Cholesterol: 0 cholesterol

114. Coconut Caramel Oat Cookies

Serving: 4-1/2 dozen. | Prep: 10mins | Cook: 0mins | Ready in:

Ingredients

- 1/2 cup butter, cubed
- 1/2 cup milk
- 1 cup sugar
- 1 teaspoon vanilla extract
- 1/2 teaspoon salt
- 25 caramels
- 3 cups quick-cooking oats
- 1 cup sweetened shredded coconut

Direction

- In the heavy saucepan, boil the milk and butter; put in the salt, vanilla and sugar. Cook for 60 seconds. Put in the caramels and stir for roughly 4 minutes till melted. Stir in the coconut and oats.
- Drop by heaping tablespoonfuls onto the waxed paper. Allow it to stand till set.

Nutrition Information

- Calories: 149 calories
- Sodium: 112mg sodium
- Fiber: 1g fiber)
- Total Carbohydrate: 22g carbohydrate (15g sugars
- Cholesterol: 10mg cholesterol
- Protein: 2g protein.
- Total Fat: 6g fat (4g saturated fat)

115. Coconut Chocolate Cake

Serving: 16-20 servings. | Prep: 10mins | Cook: 20mins | Ready in:

Ingredients

- 1 package chocolate cake mix (regular size)
- 1-1/2 cups evaporated milk, divided
- 1-1/2 cups sugar, divided
- 24 large marshmallows
- 1 package (14 ounces) sweetened shredded coconut
- 1/2 cup butter, cubed
- 2 cups (12 ounces) semisweet chocolate chips
- 1/2 cup slivered almonds, toasted

Direction

- In a 15x10x1-inch baking pan, follow package instructions to mix cake. Bake at 350 degrees until a toothpick slid into the middle comes out with no streaks of batter, about 20 minutes.
- In the meantime, mix together 1 cup of sugar and 1 cup of milk in a big saucepan; boil and stir from time to time. Turn off the heat. Put in marshmallows; whisk until melted. Mix in coconut. Scatter onto the cake right after baking. Let cool for half an hour.
- Mix together the rest of the milk, sugar and butter in a small saucepan, then boil. Turn off the heat and whisk in chocolate chips until melted. Smear on top of coconut layer and sprinkle almonds over.

Nutrition Information

- Calories: 454 calories
- Total Fat: 22g fat (14g saturated fat)
- Sodium: 285mg sodium
- Fiber: 3g fiber)
- Total Carbohydrate: 66g carbohydrate (50g sugars
- Cholesterol: 18mg cholesterol
- Protein: 4g protein.

116. Coconut Chocolate Trifle

Serving: 10-14 servings. | Prep: 15mins | Cook: 0mins | Ready in:

Ingredients

- 1 loaf (10-3/4 ounces) frozen pound cake, thawed
- 1/3 cup apricot preserves
- 1/3 cup plus 2 tablespoons orange juice, divided
- 4 ounces German sweet chocolate
- 1-1/4 cups sweetened shredded coconut, toasted, divided
- 1-3/4 cups cold 2% milk
- 1 cup half-and-half cream
- 1 package (5.9 ounces) instant chocolate pudding mix

Direction

- Trim crust from bottom, sides and top of cake; cut cake into 16 slices. On 8 slices, spread preserves; top with leftover cake then cut into 1-in. cubes.
- Put in a 2-qt. serving bowl then drizzle with 1/3 cup orange juice. Chop the chocolate; put 2 tbsp. aside for garnish. Sprinkle 1 cup coconut and leftover chocolate on cake.
- Beat leftover orange juice, dry pudding mix, cream and milk for 2 minutes on low in a big bowl; put on cake. Sprinkle with reserved chocolate and leftover coconut; refrigerate before serving for at least 4 hours.

Nutrition Information

- Calories: 267 calories
- Protein: 4g protein.
- Total Fat: 12g fat (8g saturated fat)
- Sodium: 304mg sodium
- Fiber: 1g fiber)
- Total Carbohydrate: 38g carbohydrate (29g sugars

- Cholesterol: 44mg cholesterol

117. Coconut Cream Torte

Serving: 12-16 servings. | Prep: 20mins | Cook: 20mins | Ready in:

Ingredients

- 1 package butter recipe golden cake mix (regular size)
- 2 cups (16 ounces) sour cream
- 3-1/2 cups sweetened shredded coconut (about 10 ounces)
- 1 cup chopped pecans, toasted
- 1/2 cup sugar

Direction

- Follow package directions to prep cake batter; put in 3 9-in. round greased and floured baking pans.
- Bake for 20-25 minutes at 350° or till inserted toothpick in middle exits clean; cool for 10 minutes. Transfer from pan onto wire racks; completely cool.
- Mix sugar, pecans, coconut and sour cream in big bowl.
- Put 1 cake on serving platter; spread 1/3 sour cream mixture. Repeat the layers twice; keep in fridge.

Nutrition Information

- Calories:
- Cholesterol:
- Protein:
- Total Fat:
- Sodium:
- Fiber:
- Total Carbohydrate:

118. Coconut Gingerbread Cake

Serving: 9 servings. | Prep: 15mins | Cook: 25mins | Ready in:

Ingredients

- 1 package (14-1/2 ounces) gingerbread cake/cookie mix
- 1 large navel orange
- 1-1/3 cups sweetened shredded coconut
- 1/2 cup packed brown sugar
- 2 tablespoons orange juice

Direction

- Following package direction to prepare and bake cake using an 8-inch square baking pan coated with grease. Allow to cool a bit on wire rack.
- Grate from the orange 1 tbsp. of peel, then put aside. Peel orange and section it, eliminating white pith. Dice the orange.
- Mix together reserved peel, diced orange, orange juice, brown sugar and coconut in a small bowl, then spread the mixture over warm cake. Broil 4 inches away from heat source until top is browned slightly, about 2 to 3 minutes. Allow to cool on wire rack.

Nutrition Information

- Calories: 323 calories
- Total Fat: 11g fat (6g saturated fat)
- Sodium: 341mg sodium
- Fiber: 2g fiber)
- Total Carbohydrate: 55g carbohydrate (35g sugars
- Cholesterol: 0 cholesterol
- Protein: 3g protein.

119. Coconut Ice Cream Squares

Serving: 12-15 servings. | Prep: 15mins | Cook: 0mins | Ready in:

Ingredients

- 3-1/2 cups crushed Cinnamon Life cereal
- 1 cup sweetened shredded coconut
- 3/4 cup packed brown sugar
- 1/2 cup chopped pecans
- 1/2 cup butter, melted
- 1/2 gallon vanilla ice cream, softened

Direction

- Mix together pecans, brown sugar, coconut and cereal in a big bowl. Drizzle butter over top and stir until mixed. Press into a grease-free 13″x9″ dish with 1/2 of the pecan mixture. Spread ice cream on top carefully. Use leftover cereal mixture to spread over and press down gently. Cover and freeze until firm. Take out of the freezer 10 minutes prior to cutting. You can freeze it for a maximum of 2 months.

Nutrition Information

- Calories: 332 calories
- Cholesterol: 47mg cholesterol
- Protein: 4g protein.
- Total Fat: 19g fat (11g saturated fat)
- Sodium: 190mg sodium
- Fiber: 1g fiber)
- Total Carbohydrate: 39g carbohydrate (27g sugars

120. Coconut Macadamia Bars

Serving: 16 servings. | Prep: 20mins | Cook: 0mins | Ready in:

Ingredients

- 1/3 cup butter
- 1 cup graham cracker crumbs
- 1 teaspoon sugar
- 1-1/4 cups sweetened shredded coconut, divided
- 2/3 cup sweetened condensed milk
- 1/2 cup chopped macadamia nuts
- 1 cup vanilla or white chips
- 1 teaspoon shortening

Direction

- Place butter in an 8-inch square microwaveable dish. Microwave, covered, for about 30 seconds on high power until butter is melted. Mix in sugar and cracker crumbs; pour mixture into the dish and press firmly onto the bottom. Uncover and microwave for 1 minute on high power. Allow to cool for 5 minutes.
- Combine nuts, milk, and 1 cup coconut in a small mixing bowl; ladle over the crust. Microwave without a cover on high power until heated through, about 1 and 1/2 minutes.
- Melt shortening and chips together in microwave; stir until no lumps remain. Instantly pour over coconut mixture, spread evenly.
- If desired, toast remaining coconut; sprinkle toasted coconut over the top. Place on a wire rack to cool; divide into bars to serve.

Nutrition Information

- Calories: 224 calories
- Sodium: 126mg sodium
- Fiber: 1g fiber)
- Total Carbohydrate: 22g carbohydrate (11g sugars
- Cholesterol: 17mg cholesterol
- Protein: 3g protein.
- Total Fat: 15g fat (8g saturated fat)

121. Coconut Peach Pie

Serving: 8 servings. | Prep: 10mins | Cook: 0mins | Ready in:

Ingredients

- 4 cups sliced fresh or frozen peaches, thawed, divided
- 1-3/4 cups cold milk
- 1/2 teaspoon coconut extract
- 1 package (3.4 ounces) instant vanilla pudding mix
- 1/2 cup sweetened shredded coconut
- 1 graham cracker crust (9 inches)
- 1 cup whipped topping
- Additional sliced peaches, optional

Direction

- Use paper towels to pat dry frozen peaches, if using. In a big bowl, whisk the pudding mix, extract and milk for 2 minutes. Allow to stand for 2 minutes or till soft-set. Fold in coconut.
- Line 1/3 of the peaches in crust; add half of the pudding on top. Redo the layers one more time. Refrigerate for a minimum of 3 hours or till serving.
- Top with the rest of peaches. If wished, garnish with extra peaches and whipped topping.

Nutrition Information

- Calories: 0
- Sodium: 273 mg sodium
- Fiber: 2 g fiber
- Total Carbohydrate: 38 g carbohydrate
- Cholesterol: 7 mg cholesterol
- Protein: 3 g protein.
- Total Fat: 10 g fat (5 g saturated fat)

122. Coconut Shortbread

Serving: 16 servings | Prep: 15mins | Cook: | Ready in:

Ingredients

- 3/4 cup butter , softened
- 1/2 cup sugar
- 1 tsp. vanilla
- 1-1/2 cups flour
- 1 pkg. (7 oz.) BAKER'S ANGEL FLAKE Coconut (2-2/3 cups), lightly toasted

Direction

- Use foil to line a 13"x9" pan with extended ends of foil over sides, then use cooking spray to coat.
- In a medium bowl, beat sugar and butter using a mixer until fluffy and light, then blend in vanilla. Put in flour slowly while beating between additions. Stir in coconut.
- Press on the bottom of prepped pan the coconut mixture. Use a fork to pierce at 1-in. intervals entire the way through to bottom of pan.
- Bake until browned slightly, about 20-25 minutes, then allow to cool 5 minutes.
- Run around edges of pan to loosen shortbread using a small knife. Use foil handles to take shortbread out of pan. Cut warm shortbread into sixteen bars, then allow to cool thoroughly.

Nutrition Information

- Calories: 200
- Saturated Fat: 9 g
- Cholesterol: 25 mg
- Protein: 2 g
- Total Fat: 13 g
- Sugar: 10 g
- Total Carbohydrate: 20 g
- Sodium: 105 mg
- Fiber: 1 g

123. Colorful Easter Cake

Serving: 12 servings. | Prep: 30mins | Cook: 25mins | Ready in:

Ingredients

- 1 package white cake mix (regular size)
- 1 can (16 ounces) vanilla frosting
- Fruit Roll-Ups
- Jelly beans
- Decorating icing of your choice

Direction

- Following package directions to prepare and bake cake with 2 9-inch round baking pans that greased. Allow to cool about 10 minutes before transferring from pan to wire rack to fully cool.
- Spread between layers as well as over top and sides of cake with frosting. Cut the Fruit Roll-Ups into strips of your preferred widths. Press the mixture lightly onto sides of cake then place around edges of cake with jelly beans. Use icing to garnish as wanted.

Nutrition Information

- Calories: 391 calories
- Protein: 3g protein.
- Total Fat: 16g fat (3g saturated fat)
- Sodium: 389mg sodium
- Fiber: 0 fiber)
- Total Carbohydrate: 60g carbohydrate (40g sugars
- Cholesterol: 0 cholesterol

124. Contest Winning Chocolate Mint Cookies

Serving: 32 sandwich cookies. | Prep: 15mins | Cook: 10mins | Ready in:

Ingredients

- 1-1/4 cups butter, softened
- 2 cups sugar
- 2 large eggs
- 2 teaspoons vanilla extract
- 2 cups all-purpose flour
- 3/4 cup baking cocoa
- 1 teaspoon baking soda
- 1/2 teaspoon salt
- 32 round thin chocolate-covered mint patties

Direction

- Cream sugar and butter together in a bowl. Put in one egg at a time while beating well between additions. Beat in vanilla. Mix together salt, baking soda, cocoa and flour, then put into the creamed mixture gradually while beating until well-blended.
- Drop on ungreased baking sheets by tablespoonfuls of batter, 2 inches apart. Bake at 350 degrees until puffy and tops become cracked, about 8 to 9 minutes. Invert on wire racks half of the cookies. Instantly put on each cookie the mint patty, then place leftover cookies on top and press slightly to seal. Allow to cool thoroughly.

Nutrition Information

- Calories: 179 calories
- Cholesterol: 32mg cholesterol
- Protein: 2g protein.
- Total Fat: 8g fat (5g saturated fat)
- Sodium: 154mg sodium
- Fiber: 1g fiber)
- Total Carbohydrate: 25g carbohydrate (18g sugars

125. Cool & Creamy Ice Cream Sandwiches

Serving: 4 servings. | Prep: 15mins | Cook: 5mins | Ready in:

Ingredients

- 6 tablespoons chopped seeded jalapeno peppers
- 4 teaspoons butter
- 1/4 cup jalapeno pepper jelly
- 8 soft snickerdoodle cookies
- 4 scoops strawberry ice cream
- 4 fresh strawberries, hulled and sliced

Direction

- Sauté peppers in butter in a small skillet until soft. Put in jelly and put aside to cool.
- For ice cream sandwiches, put on the bottom of 1/2 of the cookies with a scoop of ice cream. Put jalapeno mixture, strawberries and leftover cookies on top. Use plastic wrap to wrap each and freeze on baking sheet overnight.

Nutrition Information

- Calories: 497 calories
- Protein: 6g protein.
- Total Fat: 19g fat (10g saturated fat)
- Sodium: 272mg sodium
- Fiber: 3g fiber)
- Total Carbohydrate: 77g carbohydrate (29g sugars
- Cholesterol: 49mg cholesterol

126. Countdown Cheesecake

Serving: 8-10 servings. | Prep: 20mins | Cook: 10mins | Ready in:

Ingredients

- 1-1/2 cups graham cracker crumbs (about 24 squares)
- 3 tablespoons sugar
- 1/3 cup butter, melted
- FILLING:
- 2 cartons (8 ounces each) spreadable strawberry cream cheese
- 1/2 cup sugar
- 1 carton (8 ounces) frozen whipped topping, thawed
- 1-1/2 cups sliced fresh strawberries
- Red decorating gel
- 1 fresh strawberry, halved

Direction

- Mix butter, sugar and cracker crumbs in a bowl. Press 1-in. up sides and on the bottom of a greased 9-in. springform pan. Bake for 10 minutes at 325°; cool.
- Beat sugar and cream cheese till smooth in a bowl. Fold in whipped topping. Spread 1/3 filling on top of the crust gently. Put strawberries over. Put leftover filling on berries; smoothen the top. Refrigerate it overnight.
- Pipe numerals and the hour and minute hands for the clock dial on the cheesecake with decorating gel. Put strawberry halves at the tips of the clock hands.

Nutrition Information

- Calories: 301 calories
- Sodium: 209mg sodium
- Fiber: 1g fiber)
- Total Carbohydrate: 34g carbohydrate (23g sugars
- Cholesterol: 34mg cholesterol
- Protein: 2g protein.
- Total Fat: 18g fat (12g saturated fat)

127. Cranberry Crispies

Serving: 2-1/2 dozen. | Prep: 10mins | Cook: 10mins | Ready in:

Ingredients

- 1 package (15.6 ounces) cranberry-orange quick bread mix
- 1/2 cup butter, melted
- 1/2 cup finely chopped walnuts
- 1 egg
- 1/2 cup dried cranberries

Direction

- Combine egg, walnuts, butter, and bread mix in a large bowl. Mix in cranberries. Shape mixture into 1 1/4-inch balls. Arrange them 3 inches apart on unoiled baking sheets. Press the balls to a thickness of 1/8 inch thick using a glass dipped in sugar.
- Bake for 10 to 12 minutes at 350° until top turns light golden brown. Transfer to wire racks to cool.

Nutrition Information

- Calories: 223 calories
- Cholesterol: 36mg cholesterol
- Protein: 3g protein.
- Total Fat: 12g fat (5g saturated fat)
- Sodium: 205mg sodium
- Fiber: 1g fiber)
- Total Carbohydrate: 26g carbohydrate (16g sugars

128. Cranberry Ice Cream Pie

Serving: 8 servings. | Prep: 25mins | Cook: 0mins | Ready in:

Ingredients

- Pastry for single-crust pie (9 inches)
- 3/4 cup cold 2% milk
- 1 package (3.4 ounces) instant vanilla pudding mix
- 3 cups vanilla ice cream, softened
- 1 can (14 ounces) jellied cranberry sauce, cut into slices
- 2 cups whipped topping
- Red food coloring, optional

Direction

- Line pastry on a 9-in. pie plate. Trim then flute edges. Line a double thickness of heavy-duty foil onto unpricked pastry. Bake for 8 minutes at 450°F. Remove foil. Bake till golden brown for 5-7 more minutes. On a wire rack, cool.
- Whisk pudding mix and milk for 2 minutes in a big bowl. Let stand till soft set for 2 minutes. Fold ice cream in. In the crust, put 1/2 cranberry slices. Spread 1/2 ice cream mixture on top. Repeat the layers.
- Freeze, covered, till firm for 2 hours minimum. Tint whipped topping, if desired, with red food coloring in a small bowl. Prior to serving, spread it on the pie.

Nutrition Information

- Calories: 397 calories
- Total Carbohydrate: 59g carbohydrate (34g sugars
- Cholesterol: 28mg cholesterol
- Protein: 4g protein.
- Total Fat: 16g fat (10g saturated fat)
- Sodium: 332mg sodium
- Fiber: 1g fiber)

129. Cranberry Icebox Cookies

Serving: 5-1/2 dozen. | Prep: 15mins | Cook: 10mins | Ready in:

Ingredients

- 1-1/4 cups butter, softened

- 1 cup packed brown sugar
- 2/3 cup sugar
- 2 large eggs
- 1 teaspoon vanilla extract
- 1/4 teaspoon almond extract
- 3-1/4 cups all-purpose flour
- 1 teaspoon baking powder
- 1/2 teaspoon salt
- 1/4 teaspoon baking soda
- 1 cup chopped walnuts
- 2 cups chopped fresh or frozen cranberries

Direction

- Cream sugars and butter in a bowl. Put in eggs, one by one, beating thoroughly after each adding. Beat in extracts. Combine baking soda, salt, baking powder, and flour; gently put into the creamed mixture. Mix in walnuts. Gently mix in cranberries. Form into three 7-inch rolls; use plastic wrap to wrap each roll and refrigerate for 4 hours up to overnight.
- Remove wrap and cut into 1/4-inch slices. Arrange on ungreased baking sheets 1 inch apart. Bake at 375° until golden brown, about 10-12 minutes. Allow to cool on wire racks.

Nutrition Information

- Calories: 178 calories
- Cholesterol: 31mg cholesterol
- Protein: 3g protein.
- Total Fat: 9g fat (5g saturated fat)
- Sodium: 134mg sodium
- Fiber: 1g fiber)
- Total Carbohydrate: 21g carbohydrate (11g sugars

130. Cranberry Nut Fudge

Serving: about 2 pounds. | Prep: 15mins | Cook: 0mins | Ready in:

Ingredients

- 1 teaspoon butter
- 1 can (16 ounces) milk chocolate frosting
- 1 package (11-1/2 ounces) milk chocolate chips
- 1 package (5 ounces) dried cranberries
- 1/2 cup chopped pecans

Direction

- Use the foil to line the 8-inch square plate and use the butter to grease foil; put aside.
- In the heavy saucepan, mix the chocolate chips and frosting. Cook and whisk on medium low heat till the chips melt. Whisk in the nuts and cranberries. Add to the prepped pan.
- Chill for roughly 2 hours or till firm. With foil, lift the fudge from the pan. Get rid of the foil; chop fudge into 1-inch square pieces. Keep in fridge.

Nutrition Information

- Calories: 278 calories
- Total Carbohydrate: 38g carbohydrate (32g sugars
- Cholesterol: 5mg cholesterol
- Protein: 2g protein.
- Total Fat: 14g fat (5g saturated fat)
- Sodium: 84mg sodium
- Fiber: 2g fiber)

131. Cranberry Ribbon Loaf

Serving: 8 servings. | Prep: 10mins | Cook: 0mins | Ready in:

Ingredients

- 3 ounces cream cheese, softened
- 1/4 cup sugar
- Dash salt
- 1 can (14 ounces) whole-berry cranberry sauce
- 1 cup heavy whipping cream, whipped
- 6 slices angel food cake (1/2 inch thick)

Direction

- Prepare a 9x5″ loaf pan lined with heavy-duty foil on the bottom and up the sides; put aside. Beat salt, sugar and cream cheese until smooth in a large bowl. Mix in cranberry sauce. Fold whipped cream into the mixture.
- Spread on the lined pan with 1/3 of the mixture; add 3 slices of cake on top (if necessary, trim cake to fit). Make more layers. Add the rest of cranberry mixture on top. Leave in the freezer with a cover.
- Take out of the freezer 15 minutes prior to serving. Use foil to take loaf out of pan; put foil away. Slice into slices.

Nutrition Information

- Calories: 300 calories
- Protein: 3g protein.
- Total Fat: 15g fat (9g saturated fat)
- Sodium: 233mg sodium
- Fiber: 1g fiber)
- Total Carbohydrate: 41g carbohydrate (31g sugars
- Cholesterol: 52mg cholesterol

132. Cream Cheese Candies

Serving: 72 | Prep: 20mins | Cook: | Ready in:

Ingredients

- 1 (3 ounce) package cream cheese, softened
- 1/4 teaspoon peppermint extract
- 3 cups confectioners' sugar

Direction

- In the small-sized mixing bowl, whip the cream cheese with the peppermint extract. Whip in 1/2 of confectioners' sugar till smooth. Knead in the rest of the confectioners' sugar till incorporated completely. Form the dough into half-inch balls, add onto the baking sheets, flatten using the fork, and let rest for 60 minutes to harden. Keep it stored in the airtight containers in the fridge.

Nutrition Information

- Calories: 24 calories;
- Cholesterol: 1
- Protein: 0.1
- Total Fat: 0.4
- Sodium: 4
- Total Carbohydrate: 5

133. Cream Puff Pyramids

Serving: 8 servings. | Prep: 15mins | Cook: 0mins | Ready in:

Ingredients

- 2 cans (21 ounces each) cherry pie filling
- 24 to 32 frozen cream-filled miniature cream puffs, thawed
- 1 cup (6 ounces) semisweet chocolate chips, melted
- 3 tablespoons confectioners' sugar
- Whipped cream in a can

Direction

- Warm cherry pie filling in a small saucepan on medium low heat until just heated through. Put on each dessert plate with 3-4 cream puffs.
- In a small resealable plastic bag, add melted chocolate, then cut in the corner of bag with a small hole. Scoop over cream puffs with approximately 1/4 cup of warm pie filling, then use chocolate to drizzle over. Use confectioners' sugar to sprinkle over and decorate with whipped cream.

Nutrition Information

- Calories: 314 calories

- Sodium: 169mg sodium
- Fiber: 2g fiber)
- Total Carbohydrate: 47g carbohydrate (33g sugars
- Cholesterol: 60mg cholesterol
- Protein: 4g protein.
- Total Fat: 13g fat (5g saturated fat)

134. Creamy Chocolate Mousse

Serving: 6 servings. | Prep: 10mins | Cook: 0mins | Ready in:

Ingredients

- 1-1/2 cups heavy whipping cream
- 3 tablespoons sugar
- 1-1/2 teaspoons vanilla extract
- 1/3 cup chocolate syrup
- 3 tablespoons baking cocoa
- Maraschino cherries and fresh mint, optional

Direction

- Beat cream till soft peaks form in chilled small bowl; add vanilla and sugar slowly, beating till stiff peaks form then fold cocoa and chocolate syrup in.
- Put in dessert dishes with spoon; refrigerate till serving. If desired, garnish with mint and cherries.

Nutrition Information

- Calories: 285 calories
- Total Carbohydrate: 20g carbohydrate (17g sugars
- Cholesterol: 82mg cholesterol
- Protein: 2g protein.
- Total Fat: 22g fat (14g saturated fat)
- Sodium: 31mg sodium
- Fiber: 1g fiber)

135. Creamy Cranberry Gelatin

Serving: 10 servings. | Prep: 20mins | Cook: 0mins | Ready in:

Ingredients

- 1 package (12 ounces) fresh or frozen cranberries, chopped
- 1 to 1-1/4 cups sugar
- 2 packages (3 ounces each) cherry gelatin
- 2 cups (16 ounces) plain yogurt
- 1 carton (8 ounces) frozen whipped topping, thawed
- 1/3 cup chopped pecans

Direction

- Mix sugar and cranberries in a bowl; keep it covered and let chill in refrigerator for 8 hours or overnight.
- Mix gelatin and cranberry mixture in a big saucepan. Cook and stir till gelatin dissolves totally; let it cool down. Mix in whipped topping and yogurt. Add to a 2-qt. serving bowl. Drizzle with pecans. Keep chilled in the refrigerator till firm, about 2 hours.

Nutrition Information

- Calories: 204 calories
- Total Fat: 6g fat (3g saturated fat)
- Sodium: 83mg sodium
- Fiber: 2g fiber)
- Total Carbohydrate: 33g carbohydrate (0 sugars
- Cholesterol: 1mg cholesterol
- Protein: 4g protein. Diabetic Exchanges: 2 fruit

136. Creamy Peach Pudding

Serving: 9 servings. | Prep: 20mins | Cook: 0mins | Ready in:

Ingredients

- 1 cup uncooked acini di pepe or orzo pasta
- 1 can (29 ounces) sliced peaches
- 1-3/4 cups cold milk
- 1 package (3.4 ounces) instant vanilla pudding mix
- 1/4 cup sugar
- 3 cups miniature marshmallows
- 2 cups whipped topping

Direction

- Following package directions to cook pasta, then drain and rinse under cold water. Drain peaches and save 1/4 cup of syrup, then put peaches aside.
- Whisk together reserved syrup, sugar, pudding mix and milk in a big bowl about 2 minutes. Allow to stand until soft-set, about 2 minutes, then stir in pasta and peaches. Fold in whipped topping and marshmallows, then cover and chill until ready to serve.

Nutrition Information

- Calories:
- Total Carbohydrate:
- Cholesterol:
- Protein:
- Total Fat:
- Sodium:
- Fiber:

137. Creamy Raspberry Pie

Serving: 8 servings. | Prep: 15mins | Cook: 0mins | Ready in:

Ingredients

- 1 package (3 ounces) raspberry gelatin
- 1/2 cup boiling water
- 1 cup low-fat vanilla frozen yogurt
- 1 cup fresh or frozen unsweetened raspberries
- 1/4 cup lime juice
- 2 cups whipped topping
- 1 graham cracker crust (9 inches)
- Lime slices and additional raspberries and whipped topping, optional

Direction

- Dissolve gelatin in a bowl with boiling water. Use frozen yogurt to stir in until melted. Put in the lime juice and raspberries. Fold in the whipped topping. Put into crust using spoon.
- Put in refrigerator for 3 hours, or until firm. If preferred, garnish with whipped topping, raspberries and lime.

Nutrition Information

- Calories: 233 calories
- Fiber: 1g fiber)
- Total Carbohydrate: 35g carbohydrate (27g sugars
- Cholesterol: 3mg cholesterol
- Protein: 3g protein.
- Total Fat: 9g fat (4g saturated fat)
- Sodium: 156mg sodium

138. Crisp Butter Pecan Cookies

Serving: about 2 dozen. | Prep: 20mins | Cook: 10mins | Ready in:

Ingredients

- 3/4 cup butter, softened
- 1 package (3.4 ounces) instant butterscotch pudding mix
- 1-1/4 cups all-purpose flour
- 1/2 cup chopped pecans

Direction

- Beat the pudding mix with butter in a small bowl until smooth. Slowly whisk in flour. Fold in pecans. Roll the dough into one and a half-inch balls.
- Arrange the balls 2 inches apart on the greased baking sheets; flatten the balls to half an inch using the bottom of a glass greased with cooking spray.
- Bake for 10-13 min. at 375° until light golden brown. Transfer from pans to wire racks.

Nutrition Information

- Calories: 211 calories
- Protein: 2g protein.
- Total Fat: 15g fat (7g saturated fat)
- Sodium: 241mg sodium
- Fiber: 1g fiber)
- Total Carbohydrate: 18g carbohydrate (6g sugars
- Cholesterol: 31mg cholesterol

139. Crispy Kiss Squares

Serving: 2 dozen. | Prep: 20mins | Cook: 0mins | Ready in:

Ingredients

- 6 cups Cocoa Puffs
- 1/4 cup butter
- 40 large marshmallows
- 1 package (11-1/2 ounces) milk chocolate chips
- 24 striped chocolate or milk chocolate kisses

Direction

- In a big bowl, add cereal and put aside. Mix together marshmallows and butter in a microwavable bowl. Microwave on high setting without a cover for about 2 minutes, then stir. Keep on cooking until smooth while stirring every minute. Put in chocolate chips and stir well until melted.
- Pour the mixture over cereal and stir until coated well. Spread the mixture evenly in a 13"x9" pan that greased. Arrange over top with rows of kisses, then allow to cool before cutting.

Nutrition Information

- Calories: 178 calories
- Protein: 2g protein.
- Total Fat: 8g fat (5g saturated fat)
- Sodium: 83mg sodium
- Fiber: 1g fiber)
- Total Carbohydrate: 27g carbohydrate (20g sugars
- Cholesterol: 9mg cholesterol

140. Crispy Mexican Truffles

Serving: 2-1/2 dozen. | Prep: 30mins | Cook: 0mins | Ready in:

Ingredients

- 6 ounces cream cheese, softened
- 2 cups confectioners' sugar
- 8 ounces bittersweet chocolate, melted and cooled
- 2 teaspoons vanilla extract
- 1 cup crushed cornflakes
- 2 teaspoons ground cinnamon
- 1/2 teaspoon cayenne pepper

Direction

- Beat cream cheese till smooth in a big bowl. Beat vanilla, chocolate and confectioners' sugar in; cover. Refrigerate till easy to handle for 1 hour minimum.
- Mix cayenne, cinnamon and cornflakes in a small bowl. Form chocolate mixture to 1-inch balls then roll into cornflake mixture. Keep in an airtight container in the fridge.

Nutrition Information

- Calories: 98 calories
- Total Fat: 5g fat (3g saturated fat)
- Sodium: 33mg sodium
- Fiber: 1g fiber)
- Total Carbohydrate: 14g carbohydrate (10g sugars
- Cholesterol: 6mg cholesterol
- Protein: 1g protein.

141. Crunchy Chocolate Clusters

Serving: 3/4 pound (12 pieces) | Prep: 20mins | Cook: 5mins | Ready in:

Ingredients

- 3/4 cup coarsely crushed pretzels
- 1/4 cup raisins
- 2 tablespoons pine nuts, toasted
- 1-1/3 cups (8 ounces) semisweet chocolate chips
- 1/2 teaspoon instant coffee granules
- 1/4 teaspoon ground cinnamon
- 1/4 cup sour cream
- Coarse sea salt

Direction

- Add pine nuts, raisins and pretzels into a bowl. Melt chocolate chips in a microwave; mix till smooth. Stir in sour cream, cinnamon and coffee granules. Microwave in more 5- to 10-second intervals to reheat. Add them into the pretzel mixture; toss to combine.
- Onto a waxed paper-lined baking sheet, drop heaping tablespoonfuls of the mixture. Sprinkle salt on top.
- Chill in refrigerator for about 10 minutes until set. Keep refrigerated in an airtight container for storage.

Nutrition Information

- Calories: 139 calories
- Cholesterol: 1mg cholesterol
- Protein: 2g protein.
- Total Fat: 8g fat (4g saturated fat)
- Sodium: 86mg sodium
- Fiber: 1g fiber)
- Total Carbohydrate: 19g carbohydrate (12g sugars

142. Crunchy Chocolate Pudding Squares

Serving: 12-15 servings. | Prep: 30mins | Cook: 0mins | Ready in:

Ingredients

- 2 cups self-rising flour
- 1-1/2 cups finely chopped pecans
- 2/3 cup packed brown sugar
- 1 cup butter, melted
- 1 package (8 ounces) cream cheese, softened
- 1 cup confectioners' sugar
- 1 carton (8 ounces) frozen whipped topping, thawed, divided
- 3 cups cold milk
- 1 package (5.9 ounces) instant chocolate pudding mix
- Colored sprinkles, optional

Direction

- Combine the brown sugar, pecans and flour in a bowl. Mix butter into the mixture. Press into a 13-in. x 9-in. ungreased baking dish. Bake to a light brown, at 375° for 15-20 minutes. Let it cool down on a wire rack.
- Beat together cream cheese and confectioners' sugar in a bowl till smooth. Fold 1 cup whipped topping into the mixture. Spread atop the crust. In a different bowl, whisk

together pudding mix and milk for 2 minutes. Spoon this mixture onto the cream cheese layer. Chill in refrigerator until set, for 15 minutes. Spread the remaining whipped topping on top. Chill till set. Garnish with sprinkles if you wish. Slice into squares.

Nutrition Information

- Calories: 475 calories
- Sodium: 553mg sodium
- Fiber: 2g fiber)
- Total Carbohydrate: 47g carbohydrate (29g sugars
- Cholesterol: 56mg cholesterol
- Protein: 6g protein.
- Total Fat: 30g fat (15g saturated fat)

143. Crunchy Chocolate Sauce

Serving: about 1-1/2 cups. | Prep: 10mins | Cook: 0mins | Ready in:

Ingredients

- 1 cup chopped walnuts or pecans
- 1/2 cup butter, cubed
- 1 cup (6 ounces) semisweet chocolate chips
- Ice cream

Direction

- Sauté nuts in butter until they turn golden brown in a skillet. Put away from the heat; mix in chocolate chips until melted. Pour onto ice cream, serve while still warm (sauce will harden). Preserve the leftover in the fridge. This sauce can be microwaved to reheat.

Nutrition Information

- Calories: 180 calories
- Protein: 3g protein.
- Total Fat: 17g fat (7g saturated fat)
- Sodium: 78mg sodium
- Fiber: 1g fiber)
- Total Carbohydrate: 8g carbohydrate (6g sugars
- Cholesterol: 20mg cholesterol

144. Crunchy Peanut Bark

Serving: 10 dozen. | Prep: 15mins | Cook: 5mins | Ready in:

Ingredients

- 2 pounds white candy coating, coarsely chopped
- 1 cup peanut butter
- 3 cups crisp rice cereal
- 2 cups dry roasted peanuts
- 2 cups miniature marshmallows

Direction

- Microwave candy coating for 60 seconds at 70% power and mix. Keep heating in the microwave for a few more times, 10-20 seconds each time, mixing well until smooth. Stir in the rest of the ingredients. Scoop the mixture by heaping tablespoonfuls onto waxed paper. Let sit to set.

Nutrition Information

- Calories: 144 calories
- Total Fat: 9g fat (5g saturated fat)
- Sodium: 72mg sodium
- Fiber: 1g fiber)
- Total Carbohydrate: 15g carbohydrate (12g sugars
- Cholesterol: 0 cholesterol
- Protein: 2g protein.

145. Crunchy Peanut Butter Balls

Serving: 2-1/2 dozen. | Prep: 30mins | Cook: 0mins | Ready in:

Ingredients

- 1 cup peanut butter
- 1 jar (7 ounces) marshmallow creme
- 1-1/2 cups crisp rice cereal
- 1-1/2 cups (9 ounces) semisweet chocolate chips
- 4 teaspoons shortening

Direction

- Mix together marshmallow crème and peanut butter in a big bowl, then put in cereal and stir until well-coated.
- Melt shortening and chocolate chips in a microwave, mix until smooth. Roll cereal mixture into 1 inch balls. Dip into the chocolate and let excess drip off. Arrange on a pan lined with waxed paper, then chill until set.

Nutrition Information

- Calories: 123 calories
- Cholesterol: 0 cholesterol
- Protein: 3g protein.
- Total Fat: 7g fat (3g saturated fat)
- Sodium: 59mg sodium
- Fiber: 1g fiber)
- Total Carbohydrate: 14g carbohydrate (10g sugars

146. Custard Cups

Serving: 6 servings. | Prep: 15mins | Cook: 5mins | Ready in:

Ingredients

- 1-3/4 cups milk
- 1/4 cup sugar
- 3 eggs, beaten
- 1/4 teaspoon salt
- 1/2 teaspoon vanilla extract
- Ground cinnamon

Direction

- Heat the milk in a 1-quart microwavable dish without a cover on high setting until hot, about 3 minutes (don't boil). Beat together vanilla, salt, eggs and sugar using an electric mixer. Put into 6 ungreased 4-oz microwavable custard cups, then sprinkle cinnamon over top. Microwave without a cover on high setting until a knife inserted in the center exits clean, about 3 1/2 to 4 1/2 minutes. Allow to stand about 5 minutes before serving. Chill the leftovers.

Nutrition Information

- Calories: 114 calories
- Total Carbohydrate: 12g carbohydrate (12g sugars
- Cholesterol: 116mg cholesterol
- Protein: 5g protein.
- Total Fat: 5g fat (2g saturated fat)
- Sodium: 165mg sodium
- Fiber: 0 fiber)

147. Deep Fried Candy Bars On A Stick

Serving: 2 dozen. | Prep: 20mins | Cook: 5mins | Ready in:

Ingredients

- 1-1/2 cups all-purpose flour
- 4-1/2 teaspoons baking powder
- 1 tablespoon sugar
- 1 tablespoon brown sugar

- 1/8 teaspoon salt
- 1/8 teaspoon ground cinnamon
- 1 large egg
- 1/2 cup water
- 1/2 cup 2% milk
- 1/4 teaspoon vanilla extract
- 24 fun-size Snickers and/or Milky Way candy bars, frozen
- Oil for deep-fat frying
- Wooden skewers
- Confectioners' sugar, optional

Direction

- Combine the first 6 ingredients. Beat vanilla, milk, water and egg and in a separate bowl; pour into dry ingredients and whisk just until wet.
- Put oil in a deep frying-pan or electric pan and heat to reach 375 degrees. Cover a few candy bars at a time in batter and fry for 30 seconds on each side until golden brown. Transfer to paper towels and drain.
- Attach skewers to the bars. Sprinkle with confectioners' sugar (optional).

Nutrition Information

- Calories: 136 calories
- Sodium: 130mg sodium
- Fiber: 1g fiber)
- Total Carbohydrate: 16g carbohydrate (9g sugars
- Cholesterol: 11mg cholesterol
- Protein: 2g protein.
- Total Fat: 7g fat (2g saturated fat)

148. Deep Fried Cherry Pies

Serving: 4 servings. | Prep: 20mins | Cook: 10mins | Ready in:

Ingredients

- 1 cup all-purpose flour
- 1/4 teaspoon baking powder
- 1/4 teaspoon salt
- 2 tablespoons shortening
- 1/3 cup boiling water
- 1 cup cherry pie filling
- Oil for deep-fat frying
- 1/4 cup maple syrup
- 1/4 cup whipped topping

Direction

- Combine salt, baking powder, and flour in a small bowl. Cut shortening into flour mixture until mixture looks like coarse crumbs. Whisk in water just until moistened. Transfer dough to a work surface lightly dusted with flour, and knead for 8 to 10 times.
- Split dough into 4 parts; roll out each portion into a circle, about 8 inches in size. Add 1/4 cup of pie filling into the middle of each circle. Fold dough over the filling; use toothpicks to secure.
- Heat 1 inch of oil to 375° in a deep-fat fryer or an electric skillet. Fry pies in oil, folded side down, for 2 to 3 minutes or until light brown. Flip over; fry for 2 to 3 minutes more. Transfer to paper towels to drain. Pick out toothpicks. Serve pies with whipped topping and syrup.

Nutrition Information

- Calories: 309 calories
- Total Carbohydrate: 57g carbohydrate (29g sugars
- Cholesterol: 0 cholesterol
- Protein: 3g protein.
- Total Fat: 7g fat (2g saturated fat)
- Sodium: 187mg sodium
- Fiber: 1g fiber)

149. Double Chip Bars

Serving: 3 dozen. | Prep: 10mins | Cook: 25mins | Ready in:

Ingredients

- 1/2 cup butter, melted
- 1-1/2 cups graham cracker crumbs
- 1 can (14 ounces) sweetened condensed milk
- 2 cups (12 ounces) semisweet chocolate chips
- 1 cup peanut butter chips

Direction

- Put in a 9"x13" baking pan with butter. Sprinkle over butter evenly with cracker crumbs. Pour over crumbs evenly with milk, then sprinkle chips over top and press them down firmly.
- Bake at 350 degrees until turn golden brown, about 25 to 30 minutes. Allow to cool on a wire rack prior to cutting.

Nutrition Information

- Calories: 140 calories
- Protein: 2g protein.
- Total Fat: 8g fat (4g saturated fat)
- Sodium: 74mg sodium
- Fiber: 1g fiber)
- Total Carbohydrate: 17g carbohydrate (13g sugars
- Cholesterol: 11mg cholesterol

150. Double Chocolate Walnut Fudge

Serving: about 2-1/2 pounds. | Prep: 10mins | Cook: 20mins | Ready in:

Ingredients

- 1 teaspoon butter
- 1 package (12 ounces) semisweet chocolate chips
- 1 can (14 ounces) sweetened condensed milk, divided
- 1 cup chopped walnuts, divided
- 2 teaspoons vanilla extract, divided
- 1 package (11-1/2 ounces) milk chocolate chips

Direction

- Line foil on a 9-inch square pan. Coat the foil with butter.
- Combine 3/4 cup of milk and semisweet chocolate chips in a large heavy saucepan over low heat. Discard from the heat. Then stir in one teaspoon of vanilla and half a cup of walnuts. Spread into the prepared pan.
- Combine the remaining milk and milk chocolate chips in another saucepan. Discard from the heat. Then stir in the remaining walnuts and vanilla. Spread the mixture over the first layer. Cover and place in refrigerator until firm, about 120 mins. Lift fudge out of the pan with foil. Discard the foil; slice the fudge into 1-inch squares. Preserve in airtight container between layers of the waxed paper.

Nutrition Information

- Calories: 69 calories
- Total Fat: 4g fat (2g saturated fat)
- Sodium: 10mg sodium
- Fiber: 0 fiber)
- Total Carbohydrate: 8g carbohydrate (7g sugars
- Cholesterol: 3mg cholesterol
- Protein: 1g protein.

151. Double Chocolate Holiday Pie

Serving: 8 servings. | Prep: 25mins | Cook: 0mins | Ready in:

Ingredients

- 1/2 cup dark chocolate chips
- 1/4 cup sweetened condensed milk
- 1 Ready Crust, 2 Extra Servings graham cracker crust (9 ounces)
- 2 tablespoons plus 1/3 cup slivered almonds, divided
- 1 cup cold 2% milk
- 1 package (3.3 ounces) instant white chocolate pudding mix
- 1 envelope unflavored gelatin
- 2 cups heavy whipping cream, divided
- 2 tablespoons sugar
- 1/4 teaspoon almond extract
- 1 can (14 ounces) whole-berry cranberry sauce
- 1/4 teaspoon grated orange zest

Direction

- Put the milk and the chocolate chips in a small microwavable bowl. Place inside the microwave, without any cover. Set on high for half to 1 minute or just until the chocolate melts; mix until the consistency turns smooth. Spread the melted chocolate into the crust; scatter using 2 tablespoons of almonds.
- Prepare a big bowl, whisk in the pudding mix and milk and mix for roughly 2 minutes; put aside. Pour the gelatin on half a cup of cream in a small saucepan; let it sit for a minute. Place the pan over low heat and stir until the gelatin is entirely dissolved. Take if off from heat.
- Beat the rest of the cream in a large bowl until it starts to get thick. Add the extract and sugar; continue beating until soft peaks have formed. Beat in the gelatin mixture little by little. Fold into the pudding and pour into crust. Place in fridge for 4 hours or until set.
- Put the cranberry sauce in a food processor; place the cover and process till combined. Add the orange zest and stir to blend. Drizzle over and top it off with the rest of the almonds. Keep the leftovers in the fridge.

Nutrition Information

- Calories: 655 calories
- Protein: 7g protein.
- Total Fat: 40g fat (20g saturated fat)
- Sodium: 413mg sodium
- Fiber: 2g fiber)
- Total Carbohydrate: 72g carbohydrate (55g sugars
- Cholesterol: 87mg cholesterol

152. Double Decker Banana Cups

Serving: Makes 4 servings. | Prep: 5mins | Cook: | Ready in:

Ingredients

- 1-1/2 cups cold fat-free milk
- 1 pkg. (4-serving size) JELL-O Vanilla Flavor Sugar Free Fat Free Instant Pudding
- 1 cup thawed COOL WHIP LITE Whipped Topping
- 2 Tbsp. graham cracker crumbs
- 2 medium banana s, sliced

Direction

- 1. Add to a big bowl with milk. Put in dry pudding mix and use a wire whisk to beat until well-mixed, about 2 minutes. Stir in the whipped topping gently. Allow to stand about 5 minutes.
- 2. Layer in 4 separate dessert dishes with 1/2 each of the pudding mixture, graham crumbs and bananas, then repeat all layers.
- 3. Chill until serving, for a minimum of an hour. Keep the leftovers dessert in the fridge for storage.

Nutrition Information

- Calories: 170
- Sodium: 380 mg

- Total Fat: 3 g
- Saturated Fat: 2.5 g
- Cholesterol: 0 mg
- Protein: 4 g
- Fiber: 2 g
- Sugar: 17 g
- Total Carbohydrate: 32 g

153. Doughnut Parfaits

Serving: 4 servings. | Prep: 20mins | Cook: 0mins | Ready in:

Ingredients

- 2 cups cold milk
- 1 package (3.4 ounces) instant vanilla pudding mix
- 16 powdered sugar doughnut holes, halved
- 1 to 2 medium firm bananas, cut into 1/4-inch slices
- 2 cups whipped topping
- Chopped nuts and maraschino cherries

Direction

- Beat pudding mix and milk for 2 minutes in a large bowl. Allow it to stand for 2 minutes or until set to soft. In each of 4 parfait glasses, put four doughnut hole halves. Place half of the pudding, bananas, and whipped topping on top. Continue layers. Decorate with cherries and nuts.

Nutrition Information

- Calories: 528 calories
- Sodium: 706mg sodium
- Fiber: 2g fiber)
- Total Carbohydrate: 71g carbohydrate (42g sugars
- Cholesterol: 37mg cholesterol
- Protein: 7g protein.
- Total Fat: 23g fat (11g saturated fat)

154. Easy Black Forest Torte

Serving: 12-16 servings. | Prep: 20mins | Cook: 60mins | Ready in:

Ingredients

- 5 cups miniature marshmallows
- 1 package chocolate cake mix (regular size)
- 1 can (21 ounces) cherry pie filling
- 1 carton (8 ounces) frozen whipped topping, thawed

Direction

- Sprinkle marshmallow in 13x9-in. greased baking pan. Follow package directions to prep cake batter; put on marshmallows. Put pie filling on batter; bake for 1 hour at 350° or till inserted toothpick in middle exits clean. Cool; frost using whipped topping. Keep in the fridge.

Nutrition Information

- Calories:
- Protein:
- Total Fat:
- Sodium:
- Fiber:
- Total Carbohydrate:
- Cholesterol:

155. Easy Cocoa Mousse

Serving: 6 servings. | Prep: 15mins | Cook: 0mins | Ready in:

Ingredients

- 1 envelope unflavored gelatin
- 1/4 cup cold water

- 1-1/4 cups fat-free milk
- Artificial sweetener equivalent to 1/3 cup sugar
- 1/4 cup baking cocoa
- 1 teaspoon vanilla extract
- 1-3/4 cups reduced-fat whipped topping, divided

Direction

- Sprinkle gelatin on water in small saucepan; stand for 5 minutes. Cook on low heat till gelatin melts.
- Mix vanilla, cocoa, sweetener and milk in blender; add gelatin mixture slowly. Fold 1 1/2 cups whipped topping in; put in serving dishes. Cover; chill for 1 hour minimum. Use leftover topping to garnish.

Nutrition Information

- Calories: 81 calories
- Total Fat: 3g fat (0 saturated fat)
- Sodium: 29mg sodium
- Fiber: 0 fiber)
- Total Carbohydrate: 10g carbohydrate (0 sugars
- Cholesterol: 1mg cholesterol
- Protein: 3g protein. Diabetic Exchanges: 1 fat

156. Easy Elephant Ears

Serving: about 2-1/2 dozen. | Prep: 20mins | Cook: 15mins | Ready in:

Ingredients

- 1/2 cup sugar
- 2 teaspoons ground cinnamon
- 1 package (17.3 ounces) frozen puff pastry, thawed

Direction

- Set oven to 375°F for preheating. Combine sugar and cinnamon.
- On a work surface that's slightly floured, roll a pastry sheet into an 11x8-inch rectangle. Dust with a quart cup of cinnamon sugar. Roll up pastry sheet into a jelly-roll shape starting from the short sides towards the center. Using a plastic, wrap the dough and place in freezer for 10 minutes. Do the same procedure for the remaining dough.
- Remove plastic wrap and slice dough into half an inch size each; arrange slices on baking sheets lined with parchment paper. Bake until crisp and golden brown, about 12-15 minutes. Allow to cool on wire racks.

Nutrition Information

- Calories: 87 calories
- Fiber: 1g fiber)
- Total Carbohydrate: 12g carbohydrate (3g sugars
- Cholesterol: 0 cholesterol
- Protein: 1g protein.
- Total Fat: 4g fat (1g saturated fat)
- Sodium: 51mg sodium

157. Easy Grasshopper Ice Cream Pie

Serving: 8 servings. | Prep: 15mins | Cook: 0mins | Ready in:

Ingredients

- 4 cups mint chocolate chip ice cream, softened
- 1 chocolate crumb crust (8 inches)
- 5 Oreo cookies, chopped
- 1/3 cup chocolate-covered peppermint candies
- Chocolate hard-shell ice cream topping

Direction

- In crust, spread ice cream in. Sprinkle candies and cookies on. Drizzle ice cream topping on. Freeze till firm. 15 minutes before serving, remove from freezer.

Nutrition Information

- Calories: 374 calories
- Sodium: 182mg sodium
- Fiber: 1g fiber)
- Total Carbohydrate: 47g carbohydrate (35g sugars
- Cholesterol: 25mg cholesterol
- Protein: 4g protein.
- Total Fat: 19g fat (9g saturated fat)

158. Easy Peanut Butter Balls

Serving: about 6-1/2 dozen, 39 servings, 2 per serving. | Prep: 20mins | Cook: 0mins | Ready in:

Ingredients

- 1 cup light corn syrup
- 1/2 cup sugar
- 1 cup peanut butter
- 1 teaspoon vanilla extract
- 4 to 5 cups cornflakes

Direction

- Boil sugar and corn syrup in big saucepan; add peanut butter. Take off heat; mix cornflakes and vanilla in.
- By heaping teaspoonfuls, drop onto waxed paper; keep in airtight container.

Nutrition Information

- Calories: 83 calories
- Sodium: 62mg sodium
- Fiber: 0 fiber)
- Total Carbohydrate: 13g carbohydrate (8g sugars
- Cholesterol: 0 cholesterol
- Protein: 2g protein.
- Total Fat: 3g fat (1g saturated fat)

159. Easy Raspberry Sauce

Serving: 2 cups. | Prep: 10mins | Cook: 40mins | Ready in:

Ingredients

- 2 cups fresh or frozen raspberries
- 1-3/4 cups plus 1 tablespoon water, divided
- 1/3 cup sugar
- 2 tablespoons cornstarch

Direction

- Mix sugar, 1 3/4 cups of water, and raspberries in a saucepan. Boil. Turn down the heat; simmer without a cover for half an hour.
- Mash the raspberry mixture and drain into a 2-cup measuring cup through a fine sieve; then discard the seeds. If necessary, pour in water to measure 2 cups of puree. Place back into the saucepan.
- Mix the remaining water and cornstarch until smooth; add into the raspberry mixture and stir gradually. Boil on medium heat and stir continuously. Stir and cook for 1 more minute. Remove from the heat; let cool. Keep in the fridge.

Nutrition Information

- Calories: 27 calories
- Sodium: 0 sodium
- Fiber: 1g fiber)
- Total Carbohydrate: 7g carbohydrate (5g sugars
- Cholesterol: 0 cholesterol
- Protein: 0 protein. Diabetic Exchanges: 1/2 starch.
- Total Fat: 0 fat (0 saturated fat)

160. Easy Strawberry Sherbet

Serving: 1-1/2 quarts. | Prep: 10mins | Cook: 20mins | Ready in:

Ingredients

- 1 can (14 ounces) sweetened condensed milk
- 1 package (16 ounces) frozen unsweetened strawberries, thawed
- 2 cups strawberry soda

Direction

- Mix together strawberries and milk in a blender; blend while covered until the mixture is smooth. Pour into a big bowl and mix in soda.
- Transfer mixture to an ice cream freezer's cylinder; following the instructions from the manufacturer, freeze the mixture. Put ice cream into a freezer container; put into the freezer for 2 to 4 hours, then serve. The ice cream can be kept frozen for a maximum of 30 days.

Nutrition Information

- Calories: 162 calories
- Sodium: 48mg sodium
- Fiber: 1g fiber)
- Total Carbohydrate: 33g carbohydrate (32g sugars
- Cholesterol: 11mg cholesterol
- Protein: 3g protein.
- Total Fat: 3g fat (2g saturated fat)

161. Eggnog Pudding

Serving: 6 | Prep: 10mins | Cook: 2hours | Ready in:

Ingredients

- 1 (5.1 ounce) package instant vanilla pudding mix
- 4 dashes ground cinnamon
- 2 dashes ground nutmeg
- 2 dashes ground cloves
- 1 pinch ground ginger
- 3 cups cold milk

Direction

- In a bowl, mix together cloves, ginger, nutmeg, cinnamon and dry pudding mix until well-combined. Whisk in milk while stirring for 2 minutes, until there are no lumps anymore.
- Transfer the pudding into serving dishes and chill until set, about 2 hours.

Nutrition Information

- Calories: 154 calories;
- Sodium: 394
- Total Carbohydrate: 28.8
- Cholesterol: 10
- Protein: 4.1
- Total Fat: 2.8

162. Fancy Fuss Free Torte

Serving: 10 servings. | Prep: 15mins | Cook: 0mins | Ready in:

Ingredients

- 1 loaf (10-3/4 ounces) frozen pound cake, thawed
- 1 can (21 ounces) cherry pie filling or flavor of your choice
- 1 carton (8 ounces) frozen whipped topping, thawed
- 1/2 cup chopped pecans

Direction

- Slice the cake into 3 horizontal layers with a long-serrated knife. Put the bottom layer of cake on a plate. Apply half of the pie filling over it. Add layers by repeating the steps. Top with the rest of the cake layer with frosting on the sides and top of the cake. Garnish with pecans.

Nutrition Information

- Calories: 287 calories
- Total Fat: 13g fat (7g saturated fat)
- Sodium: 122mg sodium
- Fiber: 1g fiber)
- Total Carbohydrate: 38g carbohydrate (25g sugars
- Cholesterol: 44mg cholesterol
- Protein: 3g protein.

163. Fancy Sugar Cookie Bars

Serving: 2 dozen. | Prep: 10mins | Cook: 20mins | Ready in:

Ingredients

- 1 tube (16-1/2 ounces) refrigerated sugar cookie dough
- 1 cup semisweet chocolate chips
- 1/2 cup sweetened shredded coconut
- 1/4 cup chopped pecans

Direction

- Soften dough for 5 to 10 minutes at room temperature. Pat dough into an ungreased 13x9-inch baking pan. Bake in the oven at 350 degrees until golden browned, about 10 to 12 minutes.
- Scatter pecans, coconut and chocolate chips on top. Bake for 10 minutes longer. Place on a wire rack to cool.

Nutrition Information

- Calories: 137 calories
- Cholesterol: 6mg cholesterol
- Protein: 1g protein.
- Total Fat: 8g fat (3g saturated fat)
- Sodium: 88mg sodium
- Fiber: 1g fiber)
- Total Carbohydrate: 17g carbohydrate (9g sugars

164. Fast Light Lemon Mousse

Serving: 10 servings. | Prep: 20mins | Cook: 0mins | Ready in:

Ingredients

- 3/4 cup sugar
- 1/2 cup cornstarch
- 3 cups fat-free milk
- 2/3 cup lemon juice
- 1-1/2 teaspoons grated lemon zest
- 1/4 teaspoon vanilla extract
- 2 cups reduced-fat whipped topping
- 3 drops yellow food coloring, optional

Direction

- Mix cornstarch and sugar in big saucepan; mix milk in slowly till smooth. Boil, constantly mixing, on medium heat; mix and cook till bubbly and thickened or for 2 minutes. Take off heat; mix vanilla, zest and lemon juice in.
- Put saucepan in ice; mix for 5 minutes till mixture reaches room temperature. Fold food coloring (optional) and whipped topping in; put in dessert dishes using spoon. Refrigerate before serving for 1 hour minimum.

Nutrition Information

- Calories: 145 calories
- Fiber: 0 fiber)

- Total Carbohydrate: 29g carbohydrate (0 sugars
- Cholesterol: 1mg cholesterol
- Protein: 3g protein. Diabetic Exchanges: 1 starch
- Total Fat: 2g fat (0 saturated fat)
- Sodium: 39mg sodium

165. Festive Fruit Pie

Serving: 2 pies (6-8 servings each). | Prep: 10mins | Cook: 20mins | Ready in:

Ingredients

- 1 cup sugar
- 1/4 cup all-purpose flour
- 1 can (21 ounces) cherry pie filling
- 1 can (14 ounces) pineapple tidbits, drained
- 1 package (3 ounces) orange gelatin
- 3 to 4 medium firm bananas, sliced
- 1 cup chopped pecans
- 2 pastry shells, baked (9 inches)
- Whipped topping, optional

Direction

- Mix the flour and sugar in a big saucepan. Mix in the pineapple and pie filling. Boil over medium heat; cook and mix until thickened, or about 2 minutes. Discard from the heat; mix in the gelatin. Cool. Mix in the pecans and bananas.
- Transfer into the pie shells. Refrigerate for about 3 hours. If desired, decorate with whipped topping.

Nutrition Information

- Calories:
- Protein:
- Total Fat:
- Sodium:
- Fiber:
- Total Carbohydrate:
- Cholesterol:

166. Festive Mint Sundaes

Serving: 6 servings. | Prep: 10mins | Cook: 0mins | Ready in:

Ingredients

- 1 jar (8 ounces) green maraschino cherries, undrained
- Vanilla ice cream
- 18 mint Andes candies

Direction

- In a blender, add cherries, then place a cover and chop. Scoop into bowls with ice cream, then put cherries on top. In a small microwaveable bowl, arrange 6 mints and microwaved till just melted; mix till smooth.
- Remove to a small resealable plastic bag, then cut in the corner of a plastic or pastry bag with a small hole. Squeeze over sundaes with melted chocolate, then use leftover mints to decorate.

Nutrition Information

- Calories: 135 calories
- Sodium: 3mg sodium
- Fiber: 1g fiber)
- Total Carbohydrate: 33g carbohydrate (31g sugars
- Cholesterol: 0 cholesterol
- Protein: 1g protein.
- Total Fat: 3g fat (2g saturated fat)

167. Five Minute Blueberry Pie

Serving: 6-8 servings. | Prep: 15mins | Cook: 0mins | Ready in:

Ingredients

- 1/2 cup sugar
- 2 tablespoons cornstarch
- 3/4 cup water
- 4 cups fresh or frozen blueberries, thawed
- 1 graham cracker crust (9 inches)
- Whipped cream, optional

Direction

- In a large saucepan, mix cornstarch and sugar. Blend in water until smooth. Heat to a boil on medium heat; cook and stir for 2 minutes. Add in blueberries. Cook about 3 minutes, stirring occasionally. Spread into crust. Let chill. Garnish the top with whipped cream if wanted.

Nutrition Information

- Calories: 202 calories
- Fiber: 2g fiber)
- Total Carbohydrate: 39g carbohydrate (29g sugars
- Cholesterol: 0 cholesterol
- Protein: 1g protein.
- Total Fat: 6g fat (1g saturated fat)
- Sodium: 122mg sodium

168. Flaky Fruit Dessert

Serving: 6 servings. | Prep: 10mins | Cook: 15mins | Ready in:

Ingredients

- 1 can (21 ounces) fruit pie filling of your choice
- 1 teaspoon lemon juice
- 1/4 cup packed brown sugar
- 2 tablespoons butter, softened
- 1 teaspoon ground cinnamon
- 2 cups cornflakes

Direction

- In bowl, mix lemon juice and pie filling. Move into lightly greased 1-quart baking plate.
- In a separate bowl, mix the cinnamon, butter and brown sugar; put in the cornflakes. Spread on the filling. Bake at 350 degrees till thoroughly heated or for 15 to 20 minutes. Serve while warm.

Nutrition Information

- Calories: 217 calories
- Fiber: 1g fiber)
- Total Carbohydrate: 45g carbohydrate (33g sugars
- Cholesterol: 10mg cholesterol
- Protein: 1g protein.
- Total Fat: 4g fat (2g saturated fat)
- Sodium: 128mg sodium

169. Fluffy Lemon Pie

Serving: 8 servings. | Prep: 15mins | Cook: 0mins | Ready in:

Ingredients

- 1 package (1 ounce) sugar-free instant vanilla pudding mix
- 1 teaspoon Crystal Light lemonade drink mix
- 1 cup cold fat-free milk
- 1 carton (8 ounces) frozen reduced-fat whipped topping, thawed, divided
- 1 reduced-fat graham cracker crust (8 inches)

Direction

- Mix the soft drink mix and pudding mix. Stir the pudding mixture and milk in a small bowl for 2 minutes. Let it sit for 2 minutes, the pudding will become stiff.

- Fold in 1/2 of the whipped topping. Pour into the crust. Add the remaining whipped topping on top. Cover and refrigerate until set for 2-3 hrs.

Nutrition Information

- Calories: 189 calories
- Total Carbohydrate: 27g carbohydrate (12g sugars
- Cholesterol: 1mg cholesterol
- Protein: 2g protein. Diabetic Exchanges: 1-1/2 starch
- Total Fat: 6g fat (4g saturated fat)
- Sodium: 259mg sodium
- Fiber: 0 fiber)

170. Fourth Of July Jell O

Serving: 6-8 servings. | Prep: 15mins | Cook: 0mins | Ready in:

Ingredients

- 1 package (3 ounces) berry blue gelatin
- 2 cups boiling water, divided
- 1/2 cup cold water, divided
- 1 package (3 ounces) strawberry gelatin
- 1 can (15 ounces) pear halves, drained and cubed

Direction

- Melt berry gelatin in 1 cup of boiling water in a big bowl. Mix in 1/4 cup of cold water. Put in a 9x5-inch loaf pan, but do not grease it. Chill until firm. Do the same with the strawberry gelatin and the rest of the boiling and cold water.
- Once the gelatin is set, slice into cubes. In individual dishes or a big glass bowl, lightly mix pears with gelatin cubes right before serving.

Nutrition Information

- Calories: 117 calories
- Sodium: 51mg sodium
- Fiber: 1g fiber)
- Total Carbohydrate: 29g carbohydrate (27g sugars
- Cholesterol: 0 cholesterol
- Protein: 2g protein.
- Total Fat: 0 fat (0 saturated fat)

171. Freezer Raspberry Sauce

Serving: 4 pints. | Prep: 20mins | Cook: 0mins | Ready in:

Ingredients

- 10 cups fresh raspberries, divided
- 3 cups sugar
- 1 cup light corn syrup
- 1 package (3 ounces) liquid fruit pectin
- 2 tablespoons lemon juice

Direction

- Use boiling water to rinse 4 lids and 1-pint plastic containers; dry well. Crush 6 cups of raspberries thoroughly, one cup at a time, to get exactly 3 cups; put into a big bowl. Mix in corn syrup and sugar; stand for 10 minutes, occasionally mixing.
- Mix lemon juice and liquid pectin in a small bowl. Put into raspberry mixture; constantly mix to evenly distribute pectin for 3 minutes. Mix in the leftover whole raspberries.
- To within 1/2-in. of tops, fill all containers immediately. Wipe off the container's top edges; cover using lids immediately. Stand till partially set or for 24 hours at room temperature; freeze for a maximum of 1 year or refrigerate for a maximum of 3 weeks.
- Before using, thaw frozen sauce in the fridge.

Nutrition Information

- Calories: 58 calories
- Total Carbohydrate: 15g carbohydrate (12g sugars
- Cholesterol: 0 cholesterol
- Protein: 0 protein.
- Total Fat: 0 fat (0 saturated fat)
- Sodium: 6mg sodium
- Fiber: 1g fiber)

172. French Toasted Buns

Serving: 6 servings. | Prep: 15mins | Cook: 15mins | Ready in:

Ingredients

- 4 eggs
- 1/2 cup milk
- 1 teaspoon sugar
- 1/2 teaspoon vanilla extract
- 1/4 teaspoon salt
- 1/4 teaspoon ground cinnamon
- 6 day-old hamburger buns, split
- 1 cup maple syrup
- 1/3 cup chopped dried fruit

Direction

- Mix well the first 6 ingredients together in a shallow bowl. Dip into egg mixture with both sides of each bun, then cook on a greased hot griddle until both sides turn golden brown. At the same time, mix together dried fruit and syrup in a saucepan. Cook on medium heat until heated through. Serve together with French Toasted buns.

Nutrition Information

- Calories:
- Protein:
- Total Fat:
- Sodium:
- Fiber:
- Total Carbohydrate:
- Cholesterol:

173. Fresh Glazed Raspberry Pie

Serving: 6-8 servings. | Prep: 25mins | Cook: 0mins | Ready in:

Ingredients

- 4 cups fresh raspberries, divided
- 1/3 cup water
- 3/4 cup sugar
- 7-1/2 teaspoons cornstarch
- Dash salt
- 1 pastry shell (9 inches), baked
- Whipped cream, optional

Direction

- Crush 1 cup of berries in a small saucepan. Put in water, then simmer for 3 minutes. Drain, keeping the juice; discard seeds and pulp. Put enough water into juice to have 1 cup of liquid. Combine the salt, cornstarch and sugar in a large saucepan. Gradually stir in raspberry liquid. Heat to a boil; cook while stirring for 2 minutes until thickened. Take away from the heat; let cool slightly.
- Put the rest of the raspberries in pastry shell, then pour glaze over top. Put in the refrigerator for 2 to 3 hours or until set. If preferred, serve along with whipped cream.

Nutrition Information

- Calories: 232 calories
- Total Fat: 7g fat (3g saturated fat)
- Sodium: 119mg sodium
- Fiber: 4g fiber)
- Total Carbohydrate: 41g carbohydrate (22g sugars

- Cholesterol: 5mg cholesterol
- Protein: 2g protein.

174. Fried Banana Sundaes

Serving: 6 servings. | Prep: 15mins | Cook: 0mins | Ready in:

Ingredients

- 3 medium ripe bananas, peeled and halved lengthwise
- 2 tablespoons butter
- 2 teaspoons honey
- Vanilla ice cream
- Ground nutmeg

Direction

- Sauté bananas with butter in a big frying pan until turning pale golden brown, flip once. Put on serving dishes; drizzle honey over. Put one scoop of ice cream on top; sprinkle nutmeg over.

Nutrition Information

- Calories:
- Protein:
- Total Fat:
- Sodium:
- Fiber:
- Total Carbohydrate:
- Cholesterol:

175. Fried Egg Candy

Serving: about 3-1/2 dozen. | Prep: 30mins | Cook: 0mins | Ready in:

Ingredients

- 1 package (15 ounces) pretzel sticks
- 1 package (12 ounces) vanilla or white chips
- 48 yellow M&M's

Direction

- Arrange groups of 2 pretzel sticks on waxed paper, keep a small gap between each group. Put vanilla chips into a microwave safe bowl, heat the bowl at 70% power till the chips are melted; stir till the mixture becomes smooth. Use the vanilla chip liquid to make tablespoonful drops on each pair of pretzel sticks. To make "yolks", lay 1 or 2 M&M in the center of each "egg".

Nutrition Information

- Calories: 176 calories
- Protein: 3g protein.
- Total Fat: 6g fat (3g saturated fat)
- Sodium: 327mg sodium
- Fiber: 1g fiber)
- Total Carbohydrate: 27g carbohydrate (2g sugars
- Cholesterol: 4mg cholesterol

176. Fried Ice Cream

Serving: 8 | Prep: 15mins | Cook: 2mins | Ready in:

Ingredients

- 1 quart vanilla ice cream
- 3 cups crushed cornflakes cereal
- 1 teaspoon ground cinnamon
- 3 egg whites
- 2 quarts oil for frying

Direction

- Scoop ice cream into eight 1/2-cup sized balls and arrange on baking sheet to freeze for an hour, until firm.

- Mix together cinnamon and cornflakes in a shallow dish. Beat egg whites in another dish until foamy. Roll ice cream balls into egg whites, and then into cornflakes to cover ice cream fully. Repeat coating if needed. Freeze balls again for another 3 hours, until firm.
- Heat oil in a deep fryer or big, heavy saucepan to 190°C or 375°F.
- With a slotted spoon or basket, fry 1-2 ice cream balls at a time until golden, about 10-15 seconds. Transfer to paper towels to drain ice cream balls quickly. Serve instantly.

Nutrition Information

- Calories: 372 calories;
- Cholesterol: 29
- Protein: 4.4
- Total Fat: 29.3
- Sodium: 150
- Total Carbohydrate: 25

177. Frosty Freezer Pie

Serving: 8-10 servings. | Prep: 10mins | Cook: 0mins | Ready in:

Ingredients

- 1 package (8 ounces) cream cheese, softened
- 1 jar (7 ounces) marshmallow creme
- 2 cups raspberry, orange or lime sherbet, softened
- 2 to 3 cups whipped topping
- 1 graham cracker crust (9 inches)

Direction

- Beat marshmallow crème and cream cheese in a big bowl until smooth, then stir in sherbet. Fold in whipped topping.
- Transfer into crust, then freeze until firm. Take out of the freezer about 10 minutes prior to serving. You can freeze for a maximum of 3 months.

Nutrition Information

- Calories: 310 calories
- Protein: 3g protein.
- Total Fat: 15g fat (9g saturated fat)
- Sodium: 194mg sodium
- Fiber: 0 fiber)
- Total Carbohydrate: 40g carbohydrate (30g sugars
- Cholesterol: 27mg cholesterol

178. Frosty Pistachio Delight

Serving: 15 servings. | Prep: 15mins | Cook: 10mins | Ready in:

Ingredients

- 2-1/2 cups chocolate graham cracker crumbs
- 2/3 cup butter, melted
- 1 carton (1-1/2 quarts) vanilla ice cream, softened
- 2 packages (3.4 ounces each) instant pistachio pudding mix
- 1 cup plus 2 tablespoons pistachios, chopped, divided
- 3 drops green food coloring, optional
- 1 carton (8 ounces) frozen whipped topping, thawed
- 1 jar (11-3/4 ounces) hot fudge ice cream topping, warmed

Direction

- Mix together the butter and cracker crumbs in a small bowl, then press it on a 13x9-inch baking dish that's greased. Let it bake for 7 to 9 minutes at 350 degrees or until it becomes set. Let it cool on a wire rack.
- Mix together the food coloring (if preferred), 1 cup pistachios, pudding mixes and ice cream in a big bowl, then fold in the whipped topping. Spread on top of the crust. Put cover and let it freeze for a minimum of 4 hours.

- Take it out of the freezer 10 minutes prior to serving. Drizzle fudge topping on top and sprinkle it with the leftover pistachios.

Nutrition Information

- Calories: 476 calories
- Protein: 6g protein.
- Total Fat: 25g fat (13g saturated fat)
- Sodium: 444mg sodium
- Fiber: 2g fiber)
- Total Carbohydrate: 57g carbohydrate (35g sugars
- Cholesterol: 49mg cholesterol

179. Frozen Banana Split Pie

Serving: 8 servings | Prep: 25mins | Cook: | Ready in:

Ingredients

- 1 pt. frozen chocolate low-fat yogurt , softened
- 1 pt. frozen strawberry low-fat yogurt , softened
- 1 ready-to-use chocolate flavor crumb crust (6 oz.)
- 1 small banana , thinly sliced
- 1 cup sliced strawberries
- 2 Tbsp. chocolate fudge ice cream topping
- 2 Tbsp. strawberry ice cream topping
- 1/2 cup thawed COOL WHIP LITE Whipped Topping

Direction

- Alternately, put strawberry yogurt and chocolate scoops into curst.
- Freeze till firm for 3 hours.
- Before serving, put cool whip, ice cream toppings and banana slices on top.

Nutrition Information

- Calories: 260
- Total Fat: 9 g
- Saturated Fat: 4 g
- Sugar: 32 g
- Total Carbohydrate: 44 g
- Protein: 5 g
- Sodium: 170 mg
- Fiber: 4 g
- Cholesterol: 20 mg

180. Frozen Banana Treats

Serving: 8 servings. | Prep: 15mins | Cook: 0mins | Ready in:

Ingredients

- 1-1/2 cups granola without raisins, crushed
- 1 cup (6 ounces) semisweet chocolate chips
- 1/3 cup creamy peanut butter
- 8 Popsicle sticks
- 4 large firm bananas, halved widthwise

Direction

- Sprinkle on a big piece of waxed paper with granola then put aside. Melt chocolate chips in a microwave and stir until smooth. Stir in peanut butter until combined.
- Insert into each banana half with a Popsicle stick. Spread chocolate mixture over and roll in granola. Wrap in the foil and freeze about 24 hours.

Nutrition Information

- Calories: 307 calories
- Total Fat: 15g fat (5g saturated fat)
- Sodium: 60mg sodium
- Fiber: 7g fiber)
- Total Carbohydrate: 44g carbohydrate (23g sugars
- Cholesterol: 0 cholesterol
- Protein: 8g protein.

181. Frozen Lime Cake

Serving: 9 servings. | Prep: 15mins | Cook: 0mins | Ready in:

Ingredients

- 1-1/2 cups ground almonds
- 3/4 cup crushed gingersnap cookies (about 15 cookies)
- 1/3 cup butter, melted
- 2 pints pineapple-coconut or vanilla ice cream, softened
- 2 pints lime sherbet, softened
- Whipped topping, optional

Direction

- Mix butter, cookies and almonds in a small bowl. Push onto the bottom of a 9-in. square dish. Put in the freezer for 15 minutes.
- Put ice cream evenly on top of crust. Cover and put in the freezer for at least half an hour. Garnish with sherbet. Cover and put in the freezer for 4 hours or overnight.
- Take out from the freezer for 10 minutes prior to serving. Top servings with whipped topping (optional).

Nutrition Information

- Calories: 499 calories
- Sodium: 203mg sodium
- Fiber: 4g fiber)
- Total Carbohydrate: 54g carbohydrate (40g sugars
- Cholesterol: 98mg cholesterol
- Protein: 8g protein.
- Total Fat: 29g fat (13g saturated fat)

182. Frozen Orange Cream Pie

Serving: Makes 8 servings. | Prep: 20mins | Cook: | Ready in:

Ingredients

- 9 graham crackers , finely crushed (about 1-1/4 cups crumbs)
- 1/4 cup sugar
- 1/3 cup butter or margarine , melted
- 1 qt. (4 cups) frozen vanilla yogurt , softened
- 1 can (6 oz.) frozen orange juice concentrate , thawed
- 1 cup thawed COOL WHIP Whipped Topping
- 2 seedless orange slices , cut up

Direction

- Mix butter, sugar and graham crumbs. Up sides and bottom of 9-in. pie plate, firmly press in. Put aside.
- In a big bowl, beat orange juice and yogurt with an electric mixer at medium speed till blended well. Spread onto the crust.
- Freeze till firm for 4 hours. Put oranges and whipped topping on top prior to serving. Freeze leftovers.

Nutrition Information

- Calories: 370
- Cholesterol: 35 mg
- Protein: 5 g
- Total Fat: 16 g
- Saturated Fat: 9 g
- Fiber: 1 g
- Sugar: 37 g
- Sodium: 210 mg
- Total Carbohydrate: 53 g

183. Frozen Raspberry Cheesecake

Serving: 12 servings. | Prep: 20mins | Cook: 0mins | Ready in:

Ingredients

- 1-1/2 cups Oreo cookie crumbs
- 1/4 cup butter, melted
- 1 package (8 ounces) cream cheese, softened
- 3/4 cup confectioners' sugar
- 1 package (10 ounces) frozen sweetened raspberries, thawed
- 3/4 cup cranberry-raspberry juice, divided
- 1 teaspoon lemon juice
- 2 cups heavy whipping cream, whipped

Direction

- Mix butter and cookie crumbs and press down onto the bottom of a 9 inches springform pan that's ungreased. Beat confectioner's sugar and cream cheese in a big bowl until smooth. Beat in 1/2 cup cranberry-raspberry juice, raspberries and lemon juice until combined. Fold in whipped cream. Pour onto crust.
- Spoon leftover juice over the cheesecake; use knife to cut through batter and to swirl. Place cover and freeze overnight. Pull out of the freezer 15 minutes prior to serving.

Nutrition Information

- Calories: 319 calories
- Total Fat: 22g fat (12g saturated fat)
- Sodium: 186mg sodium
- Fiber: 2g fiber)
- Total Carbohydrate: 30g carbohydrate (21g sugars
- Cholesterol: 58mg cholesterol
- Protein: 3g protein.

184. Frozen Strawberry Delight

Serving: 10 servings. | Prep: 20mins | Cook: 0mins | Ready in:

Ingredients

- 1 can (14 ounces) sweetened condensed milk
- 1/4 cup lemon juice
- 4 cups sliced fresh strawberries, divided
- 1 carton (8 ounces) frozen whipped topping, thawed and divided
- 8 Oreo cookies, crushed

Direction

- Line foil on 8x4-in. loaf pan. Let edges hang on sides; put aside.
- Mix lemon juice and milk in a big bowl; fold in 2 cups whipped topping and 2 cups strawberries. Put 1/2 mixture in prepped pan; sprinkle cookie crumbs. Put leftover strawberry mixture over; cover. Freeze for 6 hours - overnight.
- Serve: Lift dessert from pan using foil. Invert onto serving plate; throw foil. Spread leftover whipped topping on sides and top of dessert; garnish using leftover strawberries. Cut to slices.

Nutrition Information

- Calories: 256 calories
- Sodium: 99mg sodium
- Fiber: 2g fiber)
- Total Carbohydrate: 39g carbohydrate (31g sugars
- Cholesterol: 13mg cholesterol
- Protein: 4g protein.
- Total Fat: 9g fat (6g saturated fat)

185. Fruity Rhubarb Sauce

Serving: 5 cups. | Prep: 30mins | Cook: 0mins | Ready in:

Ingredients

- 4 cups chopped fresh or frozen rhubarb
- 1 cup raisins
- 2/3 cup sugar
- 1/2 cup water
- 1 can (8 ounces) unsweetened crushed pineapple, undrained
- 1 cup sliced fresh strawberries
- Vanilla ice cream

Direction

- Mix water, sugar, raisins and rhubarb together in a large saucepan. Boil. Lower the heat; uncover and simmer for 20 to 22 minutes until rhubarb is softened. Put away from the heat. Fold strawberries and pineapple into the mixture. Serve while still warm or cooled on ice cream.

Nutrition Information

- Calories: 113 calories
- Sodium: 4mg sodium
- Fiber: 2g fiber)
- Total Carbohydrate: 29g carbohydrate (25g sugars
- Cholesterol: 0 cholesterol
- Protein: 1g protein.
- Total Fat: 0 fat (0 saturated fat)

186. Fruity Sherbet

Serving: about 5 pints (16-20 servings). | Prep: 5mins | Cook: 0mins | Ready in:

Ingredients

- 4 pints pineapple or lemon sherbet, softened
- 2 medium firm bananas, quartered lengthwise and thinly sliced
- 1 package (10 ounces) frozen sweetened raspberries, thawed
- 1 cup blueberries

Direction

- Mix all ingredients in a large bowl. Freeze, covered, for a maximum of 1 month.

Nutrition Information

- Calories: 111 calories
- Total Carbohydrate: 26g carbohydrate (20g sugars
- Cholesterol: 4mg cholesterol
- Protein: 1g protein.
- Total Fat: 1g fat (1g saturated fat)
- Sodium: 28mg sodium
- Fiber: 1g fiber)

187. Fruity Tapioca

Serving: 10 servings. | Prep: 15mins | Cook: 0mins | Ready in:

Ingredients

- 4 cups water
- 1 cup sugar
- 1/3 cup quick-cooking tapioca
- 1 can (6 ounces) frozen orange juice concentrate, thawed
- 1 can (29 ounces) sliced peaches, drained and diced
- 1 can (11 ounces) mandarin oranges, drained

Direction

- Mix together tapioca, sugar and water in a big saucepan, allowing to stand about 5 minutes. Bring the mixture to a full rolling boil. Take away from the heat and stir in orange juice concentrate. Allow to cool about 20 minutes.

- Stir in oranges and peaches, then remove to a serving bowl. Cover and chill until ready to serve.

Nutrition Information

- Calories:
- Sodium:
- Fiber:
- Total Carbohydrate:
- Cholesterol:
- Protein:
- Total Fat:

188. Fudge Berry Pie

Serving: 6-8 servings. | Prep: 15mins | Cook: 0mins | Ready in:

Ingredients

- 2 packages (10 ounces each) frozen sweetened raspberries or sliced strawberries, thawed and drained
- 1/4 cup corn syrup
- 1 carton (12 ounces) frozen whipped topping, thawed, divided
- 1 chocolate crumb crust (9 inches)
- 1 cup (6 ounces) semisweet chocolate chips

Direction

- Add berries into a blender; process with a cover until pureed. Pour the puree into a large bowl. Then stir in the corn syrup. Fold in 2 cups of the whipped topping. Put into the crust. Freeze with a cover for 2 hours until firm.
- Combine chocolate chips and 1 cup of whipped topping in a large saucepan; cook while stirring over low heat until it gets smooth. Spread over the filling. Freeze with a cover for 4 hours until firm.
- Take out from the freezer 30 minutes before serving. Put the rest of the whipped topping on top.

Nutrition Information

- Calories: 387 calories
- Total Fat: 18g fat (12g saturated fat)
- Sodium: 117mg sodium
- Fiber: 3g fiber)
- Total Carbohydrate: 54g carbohydrate (36g sugars
- Cholesterol: 0 cholesterol
- Protein: 2g protein.

189. Fudgy Chocolate Cookies

Serving: about 9 cookies. | Prep: 15mins | Cook: 15mins | Ready in:

Ingredients

- 8 ounces semisweet chocolate, chopped and divided
- 2 tablespoons butter, softened
- 1/3 cup packed brown sugar
- 1 egg
- 1/2 teaspoon vanilla extract
- 1/4 cup all-purpose flour
- 1/4 teaspoon baking powder
- 1 cup chopped pecans

Direction

- In the microwave, melt four 4 ounces chocolate; let cool down to the room temperature. Chop the leftover chocolate coarsely; put aside.
- In a small-sized bowl, cream the brown sugar and butter. Whip in the vanilla and egg. Put in the cooled chocolate; whip till blended. Mix the baking powder and flour; slowly put into the creamed mixture. Whisk in the chopped chocolate and pecans.

- Drop by quarter cupfuls onto the ungreased baking sheet. Bake at 350 degrees till firm and the tops become cracked or for 10 to 12 minutes. Allow it to rest for 2 minutes prior to gently taking out onto the wire racks to cool down totally.

Nutrition Information

- Calories: 181 calories
- Sodium: 47mg sodium
- Fiber: 2g fiber)
- Total Carbohydrate: 14g carbohydrate (10g sugars
- Cholesterol: 30mg cholesterol
- Protein: 3g protein.
- Total Fat: 14g fat (3g saturated fat)

190. Gelatin Parfaits

Serving: 6 servings. | Prep: 15mins | Cook: 0mins | Ready in:

Ingredients

- 1 package (3 ounces) lemon gelatin
- 1 package (3 ounces) orange gelatin
- 3 cups cubed pound cake (1-inch cubes)
- 2-1/4 cups whipped topping
- 2 tablespoons sugar
- 1/8 teaspoon ground cinnamon
- 6 maraschino cherries with stems

Direction

- Prepare the gelatins individually based on the package directions. Transfer onto individual 9x5-inch pans that are not greased. Store in the refrigerator until set. Slice into 1-inch cubes. Layer 1/4 cup cake cubes, 1/3cup cubed orange gelatin, 3 tablespoons whipped topping, 1/3 cup cubed lemon gelatin, 1/4 cup cake cubes, and 3 tablespoons whipped topping in each of six 1-1/2-cup parfait glasses or dessert dishes. Mix cinnamon and sugar; dust over whipped topping. Put a cherry on top.

Nutrition Information

- Calories: 299 calories
- Protein: 4g protein.
- Total Fat: 9g fat (7g saturated fat)
- Sodium: 156mg sodium
- Fiber: 0 fiber)
- Total Carbohydrate: 50g carbohydrate (42g sugars
- Cholesterol: 36mg cholesterol

191. German Chocolate Cookies

Serving: about 3-1/2 dozen. | Prep: 5mins | Cook: 10mins | Ready in:

Ingredients

- 1 package German chocolate cake mix (regular size)
- 1/2 cup butter, melted
- 1/2 cup quick-cooking oats
- 2 eggs
- 1 cup (6 ounces) semisweet chocolate chips
- 1/2 cup raisins

Direction

- Mix eggs, oats, butter and cake mix together until blended thoroughly in a large bowl. Mix in raisins and chocolate chips.
- Drop heaping tablespoonfuls of batter onto ungreased baking sheets, keeping a 2-inch distance away from each other. Bake at 350 degrees until edges are firm or for 9 to 11 minutes. Allow to cool for 5 minutes, then move to wire racks to cool thoroughly.

Nutrition Information

- Calories: 205 calories
- Sodium: 206mg sodium
- Fiber: 1g fiber)
- Total Carbohydrate: 29g carbohydrate (17g sugars
- Cholesterol: 32mg cholesterol
- Protein: 3g protein.
- Total Fat: 10g fat (5g saturated fat)

192. Gingerbread Men

Serving: 30 | Prep: 25mins | Cook: 12mins | Ready in:

Ingredients

- 1 (3.5 ounce) package cook and serve butterscotch pudding mix
- 1/2 cup butter
- 1/2 cup packed brown sugar
- 1 egg
- 1 1/2 cups all-purpose flour
- 1/2 teaspoon baking soda
- 1 1/2 teaspoons ground ginger
- 1 teaspoon ground cinnamon

Direction

- Add butter, brown sugar, and dry butterscotch pudding mix into a medium-sized bowl and cream together until texture is smooth. Add egg and stir together. Mix baking soda, cinnamon, ginger, and flour, and add into pudding mixture while stirring. Keep dough covered and chilled for around an hour until firm.
- Set oven temperature to 350 degrees F (175 degrees C) and leave aside to preheat. Prepare baking sheets with grease. Apply a coat of flour on a board, roll and flatten dough until thickness is about 1/8 inch, and use a cookie cutter to cut out man shapes. Arrange cookies with 2 inches distance on the baking sheets.
- Bake until cookies have golden edges, or for 10-12 minutes. Leave aside to cool on wire racks.

Nutrition Information

- Calories: 79 calories;
- Sodium: 63
- Total Carbohydrate: 11.5
- Cholesterol: 14
- Protein: 1
- Total Fat: 3.3

193. Gingersnap Pears

Serving: 8 servings. | Prep: 15mins | Cook: 15mins | Ready in:

Ingredients

- 4 cans (15-1/4 ounces each) sliced pears, drained
- 1 tablespoon all-purpose flour
- 1-1/2 cups finely crushed gingersnaps (about 32 cookies)
- 1/3 cup finely chopped walnuts
- 1/4 cup butter, melted
- Vanilla ice cream or whipped topping

Direction

- In a big bowl, add the pears, then sprinkle over with flour and gently toss to mix. Split between 8 ungreased 8-oz. custard cups. Mix together butter, walnuts and gingersnaps, then sprinkle over the pears.
- On a baking sheet, position custard cups. Bake for 15 to 20 minutes at 350°, until heated through, then serve warm together with whipped topping or ice cream.

Nutrition Information

- Calories: 236 calories
- Total Fat: 11g fat (4g saturated fat)
- Sodium: 245mg sodium
- Fiber: 1g fiber)

- Total Carbohydrate: 31g carbohydrate (18g sugars
- Cholesterol: 15mg cholesterol
- Protein: 3g protein.

194. Glazed Spiced Apples

Serving: 10 servings. | Prep: 5mins | Cook: 20mins | Ready in:

Ingredients

- 1/2 cup packed brown sugar
- 3 tablespoons cornstarch
- 1 can (12 ounces) diet cream soda
- 1/4 cup honey
- 1/4 teaspoon apple pie spice
- 1/4 teaspoon ground cinnamon
- 1/8 teaspoon ground nutmeg
- 8 large apples, peeled and sliced

Direction

- Mix together cornstarch and brown sugar in a microwavable bowl. Stir in nutmeg, cinnamon, apple pie spice, honey and soda until smooth. Microwave without a cover on high setting until thickened while stirring every minute, about 3 to 4 minutes
- Put into a 3-quart microwavable dish with apples then drizzle over apples with the sauce. Cover and cook on high setting for 5 1/2 minutes and stir. Cook without a cover until the apples are softened, about 5 1/2 to 8 more minutes, then stir and allow to stand for 5 minutes and serve warm.

Nutrition Information

- Calories: 187 calories
- Cholesterol: 0 cholesterol
- Protein: 1g protein.
- Total Fat: 1g fat (1g saturated fat)
- Sodium: 11mg sodium
- Fiber: 5g fiber)
- Total Carbohydrate: 47g carbohydrate (0 sugars

195. Gourmet Caramel Apples

Serving: 5 | Prep: 5mins | Cook: 45mins | Ready in:

Ingredients

- 5 large Granny Smith apples
- wooden craft sticks
- 1 (14 ounce) package individually wrapped caramels, unwrapped
- 2 tablespoons water
- 7 ounces chocolate candy bar, broken into pieces
- 2 tablespoons shortening, divided
- 1 cup colored candy coating melts

Direction

- Pour water in a large pot and bring to a boil. Briefly dip apples with a slotted spoon into the boiling water to remove any wax they may have. Wipe to dry, then set aside. Once cool, insert sticks into reach of the apple cores.
- Put waxed paper in a baking sheet and spray with cooking spray. Meanwhile, in a microwave-safe bowl, put unwrapped caramels and 2 tablespoons water. Cook in the microwave for 2 minutes on high power, then stir; continue to cook until the caramel melts completely, while stirring after every minute.
- Using the stick, dip the apples into the melted caramel and coat. Place on waxed paper until set; chill in the refrigerator for about 15 minutes to completely set.
- In a microwave-safe bowl, heat chocolate and 1 tablespoon shortening and mix together until the mixture becomes melted and smooth. Dip chilled apples into the chocolate mixture. Place on waxed paper to set.
- In another microwave-safe bowl, combine candy melts with the rest of the shortening;

heat in the microwave until the mixture is smooth, stirring every 30 seconds. Using a wooden stick or fork, flick colored designs with the melted candies onto the apples for an attractive, colorful finish. Chill the apples in the refrigerator overnight or until completely set.

Nutrition Information

- Calories: 831 calories;
- Total Fat: 34.8
- Sodium: 249
- Total Carbohydrate: 131.6
- Cholesterol: 22
- Protein: 8.1

196. Grape Ice

Serving: 6 servings. | Prep: 15mins | Cook: 0mins | Ready in:

Ingredients

- 3-1/2 cups water
- 3/4 cup sugar
- 1 can (12 ounces) frozen grape juice concentrate, thawed
- 1 tablespoon lemon juice

Direction

- Combine sugar and water in microwave-safe bowl. Microwave, covered, for 30 to 90 seconds on high; stir until the sugar dissolves. Stir in lemon juice and grape juice concentrate. Transfer to 1-1/2-quart freezer container. Freeze, covered, stirring several times, for at least half a day. It may be frozen up to 3 months. Before serving, using large spoon, break apart.

Nutrition Information

- Calories: 199 calories
- Sodium: 4mg sodium
- Fiber: 0 fiber)
- Total Carbohydrate: 50g carbohydrate (24g sugars
- Cholesterol: 0 cholesterol
- Protein: 0 protein.
- Total Fat: 0 fat (0 saturated fat)

197. Grilled Cake And Fruit

Serving: 4 servings. | Prep: 25mins | Cook: 5mins | Ready in:

Ingredients

- 4 slices angel food cake (1 inch thick)
- 1 ounce bittersweet chocolate
- 1 medium firm banana, cut into fourths
- 8 pineapple chunks
- 1 tablespoon lemon juice
- 1/4 cup sugar
- 1/4 teaspoon ground cinnamon
- 2 medium kiwifruit, peeled and diced
- 8 fresh strawberries, sliced

Direction

- On a cake slice, start cutting from the long side and stop within 1/2 inches of the opposite side to make a pocket. In every opening, add a piece of chocolate then put it to one side. Toss lemon juice, pineapple and banana together in a small bowl before draining it. Mix cinnamon and sugar together in a big resealable plastic bag before inserting the pineapple and banana, tossing to coat. Prepare skewers soaked wooden skewers or 4-inch metal skewers. Thread the fruits onto each one. Use cooking oil to dampen a paper towel. With long-handled tongs, use the towel to coat the grill rack lightly. Prep the grill for indirect heat. On a drip pan over indirect moderate heat, insert the fruit and grill until it is thoroughly heated. Cook for 4 to 6 minutes, flipping it over regularly during the process. Spend 30 to 60 seconds grilling each side of the cake until the chocolate melts. Get the fruit out of the skewers. Mix the grilled fruit with strawberries and kiwi and put together with the cake slices. Serve.

Nutrition Information

- Calories:
- Protein:
- Total Fat:
- Sodium:
- Fiber:
- Total Carbohydrate:
- Cholesterol:

198. Grilled Peaches 'n' Berries

Serving: 3 servings. | Prep: 10mins | Cook: 20mins | Ready in:

Ingredients

- 3 medium ripe peaches, halved and pitted
- 1 cup fresh blueberries
- 2 tablespoons brown sugar
- 2 tablespoons butter
- 1 tablespoon lemon juice

Direction

- Prepare a three 12-in square heavy-duty foil with double thickness and then put two halves of peaches, seam side up, on each. Add the butter, lemon juice, brown sugar, and blueberries on top. Tightly seal the mixture by folding a foil around.
- Place on grill rack; cover and cook until tender, 18 to 20 minutes over medium-low heat. Carefully open the foil to release steam.

Nutrition Information

- Calories: 172 calories
- Total Carbohydrate: 27g carbohydrate (23g sugars
- Cholesterol: 20mg cholesterol
- Protein: 1g protein.
- Total Fat: 8g fat (5g saturated fat)
- Sodium: 81mg sodium
- Fiber: 3g fiber)

199. Grilled Pear Sundaes

Serving: 6 servings. | Prep: 10mins | Cook: 5mins | Ready in:

Ingredients

- 4 medium ripe pears
- 1 tablespoon sugar
- 1/4 teaspoon ground cinnamon
- Dash pepper
- 2 cups reduced-fat no-sugar-added vanilla ice cream
- 3 teaspoons honey

Direction

- After peeling the pears, cut them up into halves. Cutting it along the long side, slice the halved pears up into six wedges and throw the core away. Combine pepper, cinnamon and sugar then scatter it over the fruits. Use cooking oil to dampen a paper towel then use long-handled tongs to coat the grill rack lightly by rubbing the towel on it. At moderate, indirect heat, grill the pears with a cover on for 2 to 3 minutes per side. They are ready when they become tender. Before serving, put the pears with a drizzle of honey and eat with ice cream.

Nutrition Information

- Calories: 150 calories

- Protein: 2g protein. Diabetic Exchanges: 1 starch
- Total Fat: 3g fat (2g saturated fat)
- Sodium: 39mg sodium
- Fiber: 3g fiber)
- Total Carbohydrate: 30g carbohydrate (20g sugars
- Cholesterol: 7mg cholesterol

200. Halloween Pretzel Treats

Serving: about 2 dozen. | Prep: 30mins | Cook: 5mins | Ready in:

Ingredients

- 8 ounces white baking chocolate, chopped
- 1 package (10 ounces) pretzel rods
- 1 cup orange candy coating disks
- Yellow, orange and brown jimmies

Direction

- Melt baking chocolate in a microwave, then stir until smooth. Dip into chocolate with halfway of each pretzel, letting excess drip off. Arrange on waxed paper and allow to stand until set.
- Melt candy coating disks in a microwave then stir until smooth. Drip into coating with pretzel tips, letting excess drip off, then use jimmies to sprinkle over. Allow to stand until set. Transfer into an airtight container to store.

Nutrition Information

- Calories: 143 calories
- Protein: 2g protein. Diabetic Exchanges: 1 starch
- Total Fat: 6g fat (4g saturated fat)
- Sodium: 174mg sodium
- Fiber: 0 fiber)
- Total Carbohydrate: 20g carbohydrate (11g sugars
- Cholesterol: 2mg cholesterol

201. Heavenly Hash Bars

Serving: 2-1/2 dozen. | Prep: 25mins | Cook: 0mins | Ready in:

Ingredients

- 1 package (16 ounces) miniature marshmallows
- 1 can (11-1/2 ounces) mixed nuts
- 2 cups (12 ounces) semisweet chocolate chips
- 2 cups butterscotch chips
- 1 cup peanut butter

Direction

- In a 9"x13" pan coated with grease, sprinkle nuts and marshmallows over. Melt peanut butter and chips in a small saucepan on low heat while stirring continuously until smooth. Drizzle over marshmallows and nuts then allow to stand about 8 to 10 minutes. Stir gently to coat marshmallows, then refrigerate until set. Cut into bars.

Nutrition Information

- Calories: 303 calories
- Sodium: 133mg sodium
- Fiber: 2g fiber)
- Total Carbohydrate: 34g carbohydrate (26g sugars
- Cholesterol: 1mg cholesterol
- Protein: 5g protein.
- Total Fat: 18g fat (8g saturated fat)

202. Homemade Chocolate Pudding

Serving: 6-8 servings. | Prep: 5mins | Cook: 5mins | Ready in:

Ingredients

- 1 cup sugar
- 1/2 cup baking cocoa
- 1/4 cup cornstarch
- 1/2 teaspoon salt
- 4 cups milk
- 2 tablespoons butter
- 2 teaspoons vanilla extract
- M&M's, optional

Direction

- Mix together salt, cornstarch, cocoa and sugar in a heavy saucepan, then put in milk gradually. Bring the mixture to a boil on medium heat, then boil and stir about 2 minutes. Take away from the heat, stir in vanilla and butter. Scoop into separate serving dishes, then refrigerate until ready to serve. Sprinkle M&M's over top if you want.

Nutrition Information

- Calories: 196 calories
- Fiber: 0 fiber)
- Total Carbohydrate: 38g carbohydrate (0 sugars
- Cholesterol: 2mg cholesterol
- Protein: 5g protein. Diabetic Exchanges: 2 starch
- Total Fat: 4g fat (0 saturated fat)
- Sodium: 244mg sodium

203. Hot Fudge Sundaes

Serving: 2 cups, 16 servings, 2 tablespoons per serving. | Prep: 5mins | Cook: 10mins | Ready in:

Ingredients

- 3/4 cup sugar
- 6 tablespoons baking cocoa
- 1 can (5 ounces) evaporated milk
- 1/3 cup butter, cubed
- 3/4 cup miniature marshmallows
- 1 teaspoon vanilla extract
- Vanilla ice cream
- Nuts and maraschino cherries, optional

Direction

- Mix together the sugar and cocoa in a large saucepan; stir milk into the mix. Add in the butter. Heat till boiling on medium heat; cook and stir till the sugar dissolves. Add in the marshmallows; cook till they melt. Take off from heat and stir vanilla into the mix. Serve alongside ice cream. Add nuts and cherries on top if you wish.

Nutrition Information

- Calories: 95 calories
- Cholesterol: 13mg cholesterol
- Protein: 1g protein.
- Total Fat: 5g fat (3g saturated fat)
- Sodium: 48mg sodium
- Fiber: 0 fiber)
- Total Carbohydrate: 13g carbohydrate (11g sugars

204. Ice Cream Birthday Cake

Serving: 12 servings. | Prep: 20mins | Cook: 30mins | Ready in:

Ingredients

- 4 cups birthday cake-flavored ice cream or flavor of your choice, softened if necessary
- 1 funfetti cake mix (regular size)
- 1 carton (8 ounces) frozen whipped topping, thawed

- Sprinkles

Direction

- Line a 9-in. round pan using plastic wrap. Put ice cream into pan and spread. Put in the freezer for 2 hours or until set.
- Prepare and bake cake mix following package directions with two 9-in. round baking trays. Let cool in pans for 10 minutes before taking out to wire racks to cool completely.
- Remove tops of cakes with a serrated knife if domed. Put one cake layer on a serving platter. Flip ice cream onto cake layer; discard plastic wrap. Put leftover cake layer over. Put whipped topping over top and sides of cake. Top with sprinkles (optional). Put in the freezer for 2 hours more or until set.

Nutrition Information

- Calories: 374 calories
- Sodium: 315mg sodium
- Fiber: 1g fiber)
- Total Carbohydrate: 45g carbohydrate (27g sugars
- Cholesterol: 66mg cholesterol
- Protein: 5g protein.
- Total Fat: 19g fat (8g saturated fat)

205. Ice Cream Pie

Serving: 8 | Prep: 10mins | Cook: | Ready in:

Ingredients

- 3 tablespoons butter
- 3 tablespoons corn syrup
- 2 tablespoons brown sugar
- 2 1/2 cups crispy rice cereal (such as Rice Krispies®)
- 1/4 cup peanut butter, slightly melted
- 1 (12 ounce) jar chocolate fudge sauce, divided
- 1 teaspoon corn syrup, or to taste
- 2 quarts vanilla ice cream

Direction

- In a saucepan, mix brown sugar, 3 tbsp. corn syrup and butter; boil. Take off heat. Mix rice cereal in. Transfer then press mixture in a 9-in. pie plate. Freeze for 15-20 minutes till firm.
- In a bowl, mix 1 tsp. corn syrup, 1/4 cup fudge sauce and peanut butter. Onto crust, spread 1/2 peanut butter mixture on. Freeze for 10-15 minutes till set.
- Into fudge sauce jar, put leftover 1/2 peanut butter mixture. Mix well. Refrigerate the peanut butter fudge sauce for 10-15 minutes till firm.
- In crust, spoon then pack ice cream in. Freeze for 10-15 minutes till firm.
- In a microwave-safe bowl, put peanut butter chocolate sauce. Heat for 30 seconds to 1 minutes in microwave till warm. Serve it with the pie.

Nutrition Information

- Calories: 567 calories;
- Total Fat: 26.8
- Sodium: 392
- Total Carbohydrate: 76.6
- Cholesterol: 70
- Protein: 9.2

206. Jazzy Gelatin

Serving: 12 servings. | Prep: 10mins | Cook: 0mins | Ready in:

Ingredients

- 1 package (6 ounces) orange gelatin
- 2 cups boiling water
- 1 cup ice cubes
- 1 can (15 ounces) mandarin oranges, drained
- 1 can (8 ounces) unsweetened crushed pineapple, undrained

- 1 can (6 ounces) frozen orange juice concentrate, thawed
- Green grapes and fresh mint, optional

Direction

- Use boiling water to dissolve gelatin in a large bowl. Combine it with orange juice concentrate, pineapple, oranges and ice cubes. Coat with cooking-spray a 6-cup ring mold and pour in the mixture. Put it into the refrigerator until firm or overnight.
- Take it out of the mold and transfer to a plate before serving. Add grapes into the center and use mint to decorate if you want.

Nutrition Information

- Calories: 107 calories
- Fiber: 1g fiber)
- Total Carbohydrate: 26g carbohydrate (25g sugars
- Cholesterol: 0 cholesterol
- Protein: 2g protein.
- Total Fat: 0 fat (0 saturated fat)
- Sodium: 35mg sodium

207. Jelly Bean Bark

Serving: 2 pounds. | Prep: 10mins | Cook: 5mins | Ready in:

Ingredients

- 1 tablespoon butter
- 1-1/4 pounds white candy coating, coarsely chopped
- 2 cups small jelly beans

Direction

- Using foil, line a 15x10x1-in. pan; grease foil with butter. Melt candy coating in a microwave; mix until smooth. Lather into lined and greased pan. Put jellybeans over, push down to adhere. Let sit until firm.
- Slice or crack bark into pieces. Put in an airtight container to store.

Nutrition Information

- Calories: 154 calories
- Total Carbohydrate: 27g carbohydrate (23g sugars
- Cholesterol: 1mg cholesterol
- Protein: 0 protein.
- Total Fat: 5g fat (5g saturated fat)
- Sodium: 10mg sodium
- Fiber: 0 fiber)

208. Kahlua Fudge

Serving: about 2-1/2 pounds. | Prep: 20mins | Cook: 5mins | Ready in:

Ingredients

- 1 teaspoon plus 2 tablespoons butter, divided
- 24 ounces Baker's white baking chocolate, coarsely chopped
- 1 cup sweetened condensed milk
- 1/2 cup chopped pecans, toasted
- 1/3 cup Kahlua (coffee liqueur)

Direction

- Use foil to line a pan of 9 inches square; use 1 teaspoon butter to grease the foil. Put white chocolate in a big heavy saucepan over low heat; cook while stirring to melt. Pour in remaining butter and milk; whisk until combined. Take away from the heat; mix in Kahlua and pecans.
- Transfer to the prepped pan. Cover and keep chilled in the refrigerator until firm, about 2 hours. Discard foil and slice fudge into square pieces of an inch. Keep refrigerated in between wax paper layers in a tightly sealed container to store.

Nutrition Information

- Calories: 65 calories
- Total Carbohydrate: 8g carbohydrate (8g sugars
- Cholesterol: 2mg cholesterol
- Protein: 1g protein.
- Total Fat: 4g fat (2g saturated fat)
- Sodium: 14mg sodium
- Fiber: 0 fiber)

209. Kahlua Truffles

Serving: 1-1/2 dozen. | Prep: 10mins | Cook: 10mins | Ready in:

Ingredients

- 1 cup (6 ounces) semisweet chocolate chips
- 1/4 cup butter, cubed
- 1 egg yolk, lightly beaten
- 3 tablespoons Kahlua (coffee liqueur)
- 2 tablespoons cream cheese, softened
- 2/3 cup salted roasted almonds or pistachios, chopped

Direction

- Melt butter and chocolate chips in the top of a metal bowl over simmering water or a double boiler; stir well until smooth.
- Whisk a small amount of the hot mixture into the egg yolk in a small bowl; bring all back to the double boiler and whisk constantly. Over low heat, cook until the mixture reaches 160° while constantly whisking.
- Remove from the heat; stir in cream cheese and Kahlua until combined. Allow to cool to room temperature, occasionally stirring. Cover and chill until it's easy to shape, for 60 minutes.
- In a small bowl, put in almonds. Form the mixture into 1-in. balls; then roll in almonds. Cover and chill until firm, for about 2 hours. Keep in an airtight container in the fridge.

Nutrition Information

- Calories: 116 calories
- Total Carbohydrate: 9g carbohydrate (7g sugars
- Cholesterol: 19mg cholesterol
- Protein: 2g protein.
- Total Fat: 9g fat (4g saturated fat)
- Sodium: 53mg sodium
- Fiber: 1g fiber)

210. Kitchen Sink Cookies

Serving: 60 | Prep: 15mins | Cook: 12mins | Ready in:

Ingredients

- 1 cup butter, softened
- 2 cups packed brown sugar
- 2 eggs
- 2 teaspoons vanilla extract
- 2 1/3 cups all-purpose flour
- 1 teaspoon baking soda
- 1 teaspoon salt
- 2 cups rolled oats
- 1 cup semisweet chocolate chips
- 1 cup vanilla baking chips
- 1/2 cup butterscotch chips
- 1 cup chopped pecans

Direction

- Set oven to 190°C (375°F) and start preheating.
- Beat brown sugar and butter in a big bowl until smooth. Beat in eggs, one at a time; mix in vanilla. Mix together salt, baking soda and flour; whisk into the beaten mixture. Stir in chopped pecans, butterscotch chips, vanilla chips, chocolate chips and oats. Scoop dough by tablespoonfuls and place onto unprepared

cookie sheets, laying at least 2 inches from each other.

- Bake at 190°C (375°F) for 8-10 minutes. Cool for 5 minutes on baking sheet, then transfer to a wire rack to cool entirely.

Nutrition Information

- Calories: 142 calories;
- Total Fat: 7.1
- Sodium: 97
- Total Carbohydrate: 18.2
- Cholesterol: 14
- Protein: 1.7

211. Kool Aid Sherbet

Serving: about 3 cups. | Prep: 10mins | Cook: 0mins | Ready in:

Ingredients

- 1 cup sugar
- 1 envelope unsweetened orange Kool-Aid mix or flavor of your choice
- 3 cups 2% milk

Direction

- Mix together milk, Kool-Aid mix and sugar in a big bowl until sugar has dissolved. Transfer the mixture into a shallow freezer container, then put on a cover and freeze the mixture until thickened a bit, about an hour.
- Remove the mixture into a big bowl and beat until smooth. Turn mixture back to freezer container then cover and freeze until firm. Take out of the freezer about 20 minutes prior to serving.

Nutrition Information

- Calories: 204 calories
- Protein: 4g protein.
- Total Fat: 4g fat (3g saturated fat)
- Sodium: 96mg sodium
- Fiber: 0 fiber)
- Total Carbohydrate: 39g carbohydrate (38g sugars
- Cholesterol: 17mg cholesterol

212. Layered Toffee Cake

Serving: 12-14 servings. | Prep: 20mins | Cook: 0mins | Ready in:

Ingredients

- 2 cups heavy whipping cream
- 1/2 cup caramel or butterscotch ice cream topping
- 1/2 teaspoon vanilla extract
- 1 prepared angel food cake (8 to 10 ounces)
- 9 Heath candy bar (1.4 ounces each), chopped

Direction

- Beat cream in a bowl thoroughly until it thickens. Slowly mix in vanilla and ice cream topping and continue to beat until soft peaks appear. Slice the cake horizontally to make 3 layers. On a serving plate, put the bottom layer; evenly spread 1 cup of cream mixture over the surface then sprinkle with half cup of candy bar. Repeat this procedure. Put on the top layer, cover the top surface and the sides with the rest of the cream mixture, sprinkle the remaining candy bar on top. Chill in the refrigerator before serving.

Nutrition Information

- Calories:
- Sodium:
- Fiber:
- Total Carbohydrate:
- Cholesterol:
- Protein:

- Total Fat:

213. Lazy Day Grasshopper Pie

Serving: 6-8 servings. | Prep: 10mins | Cook: 0mins | Ready in:

Ingredients

- 1 jar (7 ounces) marshmallow creme
- 1/4 cup milk
- 6 to 8 drops peppermint extract
- 6 to 8 drops green food coloring
- 1 cup heavy whipping cream, whipped
- 1 chocolate crumb crust (9 inches)
- Shaved chocolate and additional whipped cream, optional

Direction

- Blend food coloring, extract, milk and marshmallow crème in a bowl until forming a smooth mixture. Fold whipped cream into the mixture. Scoop into the pie shell. Freeze while covered until the pie firms up, or overnight.
- Take out of the freezer about 20 minutes prior to serving. Top with whipped cream (optional) and shaved chocolate (optional).

Nutrition Information

- Calories: 242 calories
- Sodium: 132mg sodium
- Fiber: 1g fiber)
- Total Carbohydrate: 36g carbohydrate (24g sugars
- Cholesterol: 22mg cholesterol
- Protein: 2g protein.
- Total Fat: 10g fat (5g saturated fat)

214. Lemon Angel Cake

Serving: 10-12 servings. | Prep: 30mins | Cook: 0mins | Ready in:

Ingredients

- 1 cup heavy whipping cream
- 1 tablespoon confectioners' sugar
- 1 can (15-3/4 ounces) lemon pie filling
- 1 prepared angel food cake (8 to 10 ounces)

Direction

- Place the cream in a small bowl and whisk it until thick. Mix in the confectioners' sugar and whisk it until stiff peaks are formed. Put the pie filling in a separate bowl and add in the whipped cream then fold.
- Slice the cake to make two horizontal layers. Put the first layer on a serving plate and coat the top with a cup of lemon mixture. Place the second layer on top. Spread the remaining lemon mixture over top and sides of the cake. Allow it to chill for 15 minutes or until it's time to serve. Keep any leftovers in the refrigerator.

Nutrition Information

- Calories:
- Cholesterol:
- Protein:
- Total Fat:
- Sodium:
- Fiber:
- Total Carbohydrate:

215. Lemon Basil Cookies

Serving: 3-1/2 dozen. | Prep: 10mins | Cook: 10mins | Ready in:

Ingredients

- 1 package (8 ounces) cream cheese, softened
- 1/4 cup butter, softened
- 1 egg yolk
- 1 teaspoon lemon juice
- 1 package lemon cake mix (regular size)
- 1/4 cup sweetened shredded coconut
- 1/4 cup chopped pecans
- 1 tablespoon dried basil
- 1/2 teaspoon grated lemon peel

Direction

- Cream butter and cream cheese in a big bowl until the mixture is fluffy. Whisk in lemon juice and egg yolk, then put in cake mix gradually and blend well. Stir in lemon peel, basil, pecans and coconut.
- Drop the mixture onto baking sheets coated with grease by teaspoonfuls with 2 inches apart, then bake at 350 degrees until turn golden brown, or for 10 to 14 minutes. Allow to cool for 2 minutes prior to transferring to wire racks.

Nutrition Information

- Calories: 87 calories
- Sodium: 107mg sodium
- Fiber: 0 fiber)
- Total Carbohydrate: 11g carbohydrate (6g sugars
- Cholesterol: 14mg cholesterol
- Protein: 1g protein.
- Total Fat: 5g fat (2g saturated fat)

216. Lemon Fluff Dessert

Serving: 12 servings. | Prep: 25mins | Cook: 0mins | Ready in:

Ingredients

- 1 can (12 ounces) evaporated milk
- 1 package (3 ounces) lemon gelatin
- 1 cup sugar
- 1-1/3 cups boiling water
- 1/4 cup lemon juice
- 1-3/4 cups graham cracker crumbs
- 5 tablespoons butter, melted

Direction

- Add milk to a small metal bowl and place the mixer beaters in the bowl. Cover and put into a refrigerator for a minimum of 2 hours.
- At the same time, add sugar, gelatin and boiling water to a big bowl and stir until dissolved. Whisk in lemon juice. Then cover and put into a refrigerator for approximately one and a half hours until syrupy.
- Mix the butter and crumbs in a small bowl then put aside 2 tbsp. for decoration. Press the remaining crumbs onto the bottom of a 13x9-inch dish. Beat the cold milk until soft peaks form. Beat the gelatin mixture until tiny bubbles form. Add milk to gelatin mixture and fold. Add the mixture to the prepared dish. Drizzle reserved crumbs over the mixture. Then cover and put into a refrigerator until set. Slice into squares.

Nutrition Information

- Calories: 221 calories
- Sodium: 151mg sodium
- Fiber: 0 fiber)
- Total Carbohydrate: 35g carbohydrate (29g sugars
- Cholesterol: 22mg cholesterol
- Protein: 3g protein. Diabetic Exchanges: 2 starch
- Total Fat: 8g fat (5g saturated fat)

217. Lemon Pineapple Dessert

Serving: 12-14 servings. | Prep: 10mins | Cook: 0mins | Ready in:

Ingredients

- 1 can (20 ounces) crushed pineapple, drained
- 1 can (15-3/4 ounces) lemon pie filling
- 1 can (14 ounces) sweetened condensed milk
- 1 carton (8 ounces) frozen whipped topping, thawed
- Lemon slices, optional

Direction

- Mix together condensed milk, pie filling and pineapple in a bowl, then fold in whipped topping. Scoop into bowls and use lemon to decorate if you want.

Nutrition Information

- Calories: 271 calories
- Fiber: 0 fiber)
- Total Carbohydrate: 48g carbohydrate (43g sugars
- Cholesterol: 52mg cholesterol
- Protein: 4g protein.
- Total Fat: 7g fat (5g saturated fat)
- Sodium: 62mg sodium

218. Lemon Plum Sorbet

Serving: 6 servings. | Prep: 20mins | Cook: 5mins | Ready in:

Ingredients

- 8 medium plums
- 2 cups sugar
- 1 cup water
- 1/3 cup lemon juice
- 2 teaspoons grated lemon peel

Direction

- Pour 8 cups of water in a big saucepan and boil. Toss in the plums and boil, covered, for another 30 to 45 seconds. Remove the plums and immediately immerse them in ice water. Pat dry to remove the water. Once plums are cool enough, peel off the skins. Slice in half and remove the seeds.
- Combine 1 cup of water and sugar in a small saucepan and boil. Stir constantly while cooking to dissolve the sugar. Mix in lemon juice and zest then put aside to cool.
- In a food processor, put the plums in then add the sugar syrup. Put the cover back and process until creamy, about 2 to 3 minutes. Pour puree in an 8-inch square dish and freeze until edges starts to set, about 1 hour. Stir the mixture then return in the freezer for 2 more hours or until it's set.
- When about to serve, transfer sorbet into a food processor. Put the cover on and process until mixture turns a creamy consistency, about 2 to 3 minutes.

Nutrition Information

- Calories: 310 calories
- Protein: 1g protein.
- Total Fat: 1g fat (0 saturated fat)
- Sodium: 0 sodium
- Fiber: 1g fiber)
- Total Carbohydrate: 79g carbohydrate (76g sugars
- Cholesterol: 0 cholesterol

219. Lemon Lime Mousse

Serving: 6 servings. | Prep: 20mins | Cook: 10mins | Ready in:

Ingredients

- 1/2 cup sugar
- 2 tablespoons cornstarch
- Pinch salt
- 3 large egg yolks
- 2/3 cup 2% milk
- 1/4 cup lemon juice

- 1 tablespoon lime juice
- 1-1/2 teaspoons grated lemon zest
- 1/2 teaspoon grated lime zest
- 1 cup heavy whipping cream
- Lime slices, optional

Direction

- Mix salt, cornstarch and sugar in small saucepan; whisk milk and egg yolks in till smooth. Whisk citrus juices in till blender; boil on medium heat, constantly mixing. Mix and cook for 2 more minutes; mix citrus zests in.
- Put mixture in bowl; use plastic wrap to cover surface then refrigerate till cold.
- Serve: Beat cream till soft peaks form in small bowl; fold into citrus mixture. Put in serving dishes; top with lime slices if desired.

Nutrition Information

- Calories: 257 calories
- Total Fat: 18g fat (10g saturated fat)
- Sodium: 57mg sodium
- Fiber: 0 fiber)
- Total Carbohydrate: 23g carbohydrate (20g sugars
- Cholesterol: 149mg cholesterol
- Protein: 3g protein.

220. Lime Cheesecake Pie

Serving: 8 servings. | Prep: 5mins | Cook: 0mins | Ready in:

Ingredients

- 1 package (8 ounces) cream cheese, softened
- 1 can (14 ounces) sweetened condensed milk
- 1/3 cup lime juice
- 1-1/2 teaspoons vanilla extract
- 1 graham cracker crust (9 inches)
- 1 carton (8 ounces) frozen whipped topping, thawed
- Lime slices and fresh mint, optional

Direction

- Whisk the cream cheese in a big bowl until smooth. Add vanilla, lime juice, and milk; whisk until smooth. Pour the mixture into the crust. Chill for 2 hours. Spread the topping over, chill for another 60 minutes. Use mint and lime to garnish if you want.

Nutrition Information

- Calories: 446 calories
- Protein: 7g protein.
- Total Fat: 24g fat (15g saturated fat)
- Sodium: 268mg sodium
- Fiber: 0 fiber)
- Total Carbohydrate: 49g carbohydrate (41g sugars
- Cholesterol: 48mg cholesterol

221. Lime Sherbet Molded Salad

Serving: 16 servings. | Prep: 20mins | Cook: 0mins | Ready in:

Ingredients

- 2 packages (3 ounces each) lime gelatin
- 2 cups boiling water
- 2 pints lime sherbet, softened
- 1 carton (8 ounces) whipped topping, thawed

Direction

- In a big bowl with boiling water, dissolve gelatin. Mix in sherbet till well blended. Keep chilled till it becomes syrupy.
- Scoop whipped topping to a big bowl. Slowly whip in the gelatin mixture on low speed till well blended. Add to a 12-cup mold coated using cooking spray. Keep chilled in the refrigerator till set or for 6 to 8 hours.

Nutrition Information

- Calories: 110 calories
- Total Fat: 3g fat (3g saturated fat)
- Sodium: 29mg sodium
- Fiber: 0 fiber)
- Total Carbohydrate: 19g carbohydrate (15g sugars
- Cholesterol: 2mg cholesterol
- Protein: 1g protein.

222. Low Fat Fudge Pops

Serving: 12 servings. | Prep: 15mins | Cook: 0mins | Ready in:

Ingredients

- 1 can (14 ounces) fat-free sweetened condensed milk
- 1/2 cup sugar
- 1/2 cup baking cocoa
- 2-1/2 cups fat-free milk
- Sugar substitute equivalent to 1/2 cup sugar
- 1 teaspoon vanilla extract
- 12 disposable plastic cups (3 ounces)
- 12 Popsicle sticks

Direction

- Mix cocoa, sugar, and condensed milk together in a heavy pot and stir until smooth. Boil the mixture on medium-low heat then cook and stir for a minute. Stir in skim milk gradually; continue stirring until the sugar and cocoa dissolve. Take off heat then mix in vanilla and sweetener.
- Transfer into cups; use heavy-duty foil to cover each cup. Put sticks through the foil and let it hold the sticks up. Put the cups in a 13x9-in pan. Place in the freezer for 5hrs until firm. Discard the foil and the cups then serve.

Nutrition Information

- Calories: 158 calories
- Total Carbohydrate: 34g carbohydrate (31g sugars
- Cholesterol: 5mg cholesterol
- Protein: 5g protein. Diabetic Exchanges: 2 starch.
- Total Fat: 0 fat (0 saturated fat)
- Sodium: 55mg sodium
- Fiber: 1g fiber)

223. Macadamia Chip Cookies

Serving: 5-1/2 dozen. | Prep: 15mins | Cook: 15mins | Ready in:

Ingredients

- 1 cup butter, softened
- 3/4 cup packed brown sugar
- 1/4 cup sugar
- 2 eggs
- 1 teaspoon vanilla extract
- 2-1/4 cups all-purpose flour
- 1 package (3.4 ounces) instant vanilla pudding mix
- 1 teaspoon baking soda
- 1/4 teaspoon salt
- 1 package (10 to 12 ounces) white baking chips
- 2 jars (3-1/4 ounces each) macadamia nuts, chopped
- 1/2 cup finely crushed peanut brittle

Direction

- Beat butter with sugars in a big bowl until light and fluffy. Add one egg at a time, whisking well before adding another. Mix in vanilla. Mix the salt, baking soda, dry pudding mix and flour together and add them to the creamed mixture, little by little and combine together. Mix in peanut brittle, nuts and chips.
- Grease baking trays. Take rounded tablespoonfuls of the batter and put each 2

inches apart from another on the prepared baking trays. Set oven at 375°F and start baking until they turn golden brown, about 10 to 12 minutes. Take the cookies to a wire rack and let cool.

Nutrition Information

- Calories:
- Cholesterol:
- Protein:
- Total Fat:
- Sodium:
- Fiber:
- Total Carbohydrate:

224. Make Ahead Tiramisu

Serving: 12 servings | Prep: 20mins | Cook: | Ready in:

Ingredients

- 2 Tbsp. MAXWELL HOUSE Instant Coffee
- 1/4 cup boiling water
- 32 reduced-fat vanilla wafers
- 1 tub (8 oz.) PHILADELPHIA 1/3 Less Fat than Cream Cheese
- 1/4 cup powdered sugar
- 1 tub (8 oz.) COOL WHIP FREE Whipped Topping, thawed
- 1 cup fresh raspberries
- 1 tsp. unsweetened cocoa powder

Direction

- Dissolve coffee granules in boiling water by stirring. Use 16 wafers to cover the bottom of an 8-inch square dish. Shower with 1 tbsp. coffee.
- In a medium bowl, gradually add 2 tbsp. of the leftover coffee to the reduced-fat cream cheese, use a whisk to beat until combined. Add sugar and mix well. Next, stir in COOL WHIP, scoop 1/2 over wafers in a dish. Then cover with the leftover wafers. Drizzle with the leftover coffee and place the leftover cream cheese mixture on top.
- Chill overnight. Just before serving, put raspberries on top and dust with cocoa powder.

Nutrition Information

- Calories: 130
- Saturated Fat: 3 g
- Sodium: 130 mg
- Fiber: 1 g
- Sugar: 10 g
- Cholesterol: 15 mg
- Protein: 2 g
- Total Fat: 5 g
- Total Carbohydrate: 20 g

225. Malted Milk Pie

Serving: 2 pies (6-8 servings each). | Prep: 10mins | Cook: 0mins | Ready in:

Ingredients

- 1 package (7 ounces) malted milk balls, chopped
- 1 pint vanilla ice cream, softened
- 1 carton (8 ounces) frozen whipped topping, thawed
- 2 chocolate crumb crusts (9 inches)
- Additional whipped topping, optional

Direction

- Put a quarter cup of malted milk balls aside to use for topping. In a big bowl, put ice cream, then fold the rest of malted milk balls and whipped topping in. Scoop into the crust. Place in freezer with cover.
- Jazz up using the reserved malted milk balls and extra whipped topping if wished. Take out of the from freezer 20 minutes prior to serving.

Nutrition Information

- Calories: 271 calories
- Fiber: 1g fiber)
- Total Carbohydrate: 34g carbohydrate (20g sugars
- Cholesterol: 11mg cholesterol
- Protein: 3g protein.
- Total Fat: 14g fat (7g saturated fat)
- Sodium: 152mg sodium

226. Maple Apple Topping

Serving: 8 servings. | Prep: 10mins | Cook: 20mins | Ready in:

Ingredients

- 1/2 cup butter, cubed
- 3 large tart apples, peeled and sliced
- 1-1/2 cups maple syrup
- 1 teaspoon ground cinnamon
- 1/2 cup chopped nuts

Direction

- Add butter in a large skillet and melt. Add cinnamon, syrup, and apples. Cook over medium-low heat and stir until the apples have softened. Add nuts and stir. Top on pancakes or waffles to serve.

Nutrition Information

- Calories: 338 calories
- Protein: 2g protein.
- Total Fat: 16g fat (7g saturated fat)
- Sodium: 121mg sodium
- Fiber: 1g fiber)
- Total Carbohydrate: 50g carbohydrate (45g sugars
- Cholesterol: 31mg cholesterol

227. Maple Mocha Pops

Serving: 1 dozen. | Prep: 15mins | Cook: 0mins | Ready in:

Ingredients

- 2 cups heavy whipping cream
- 1/2 cup half-and-half cream
- 1/4 cup maple syrup
- 1/4 cup chocolate syrup
- 1 tablespoon instant coffee granules
- 12 freezer pop molds or 12 paper cups (3 ounces each) and wooden pop sticks

Direction

- Whisk coffee granules, chocolate syrup, maple syrup, half-and-half and whipping cream till coffee melts in a big bowl.
- Fill cups/molds with 1/4 cup of cream mixture. Put holders on top of molds. Top with foil for cups (if used) and insert sticks through foil then freeze till firm.

Nutrition Information

- Calories: 185 calories
- Cholesterol: 59mg cholesterol
- Protein: 1g protein.
- Total Fat: 16g fat (10g saturated fat)
- Sodium: 25mg sodium
- Fiber: 0 fiber)
- Total Carbohydrate: 10g carbohydrate (8g sugars

228. Marbled Orange Fudge

Serving: about 2-1/2 pounds. | Prep: 30mins | Cook: 0mins | Ready in:

Ingredients

- 1-1/2 teaspoons plus 3/4 cup butter, divided
- 3 cups sugar
- 3/4 cup heavy whipping cream
- 1 package white baking chips (10 to 12 ounces)
- 1 jar (7 ounces) marshmallow creme
- 3 teaspoons orange extract
- 12 drops yellow food coloring
- 5 drops red food coloring
- green shoestring licorice, optional

Direction

- Use 1-1/2 teaspoons butter to grease a 13x9-inch baking pan and put aside.
- Mix together remaining butter, cream and sugar in a big heavy saucepan. Over low heat, cook while stirring to dissolve sugar. Boil the mixture and cook while stirring for 4 minutes. Take away from the heat; mix in marshmallow crème and chips until the mixture is smooth.
- Reserve a cup of mixture. Put food coloring and orange extract into the remaining mixture; whisk until combined. Transfer to greased pan. Scoop saved marshmallow mixture by tablespoonfuls and place on top; swirl by cutting through with a knife. Chill while covered till set. Slice into triangular pieces and use licorice to decorate (optional).

Nutrition Information

- Calories: 109 calories
- Sodium: 12mg sodium
- Fiber: 0 fiber)
- Total Carbohydrate: 20g carbohydrate (15g sugars
- Cholesterol: 7mg cholesterol
- Protein: 0 protein.
- Total Fat: 3g fat (2g saturated fat)

229. Marshmallow Witches

Serving: 1 dozen. | Prep: 30mins | Cook: 0mins | Ready in:

Ingredients

- 1/2 cup vanilla frosting, divided
- 36 miniature semisweet chocolate chips
- 12 large marshmallows
- 1 drop each green, red and yellow food coloring, optional
- 1/4 cup sweetened shredded coconut
- 12 chocolate wafers
- 12 miniature peanut butter cups
- 12 milk chocolate kisses

Direction

- Put dab of frosting on bottom of 3 chocolate chips for face of each witch; press 1 for nose and 2 for eyes onto each marshmallow.
- Hair: In small resealable plastic bag, mix 1 drop of water and green food coloring. Add coconut; shake well. Spread a little bit of frosting on sides of marshmallows; press the coconut hair to frosting. In heavy-duty, small resealable plastic bag, put 3 tablespoons frosting; use yellow and red food coloring to tint orange. Put aside.
- Hats: In middle of chocolate wafers, spread some leftover frosting; press peanut butter cups into frosting, upside down. Spread frosting on bottoms of chocolate kisses lightly; put onto peanut butter cups. Cut small hole in corner of plastic/pastry bag; insert small star tip. Use frosting to fill bag; pipe stars around base of every peanut butter cup. Use dab of frosting to secure hat to each witch.

Nutrition Information

- Calories: 121 calories
- Sodium: 69mg sodium
- Fiber: 1g fiber)
- Total Carbohydrate: 18g carbohydrate (11g sugars
- Cholesterol: 2mg cholesterol
- Protein: 2g protein.
- Total Fat: 5g fat (3g saturated fat)

230. Master Cookie Mix

Serving: 144 | Prep: | Cook: | Ready in:

Ingredients

- 9 cups all-purpose flour
- 4 teaspoons baking soda
- 2 teaspoons salt
- 3 cups packed brown sugar
- 3 cups white sugar
- 4 cups shortening
- 8 cups semisweet chocolate chips
- 4 cups butterscotch chips

Direction

- Stir white sugar, brown sugar, salt, baking soda and flour together in the largest bowl. Put in shortening; stir until mealy. Mix in butterscotch chips and chocolate chips lightly until evenly distributed. Add four cups master mix to each 1-qt jar.
- Stick these directions onto the jar: Start preheating the oven to 375°F (190°C). Beat one teaspoon vanilla and 2 eggs in a medium bowl until blended well. Put entire contents of jar into bowl, mix until combined. Drop onto the cookie sheet by teaspoonfuls. Bake for 10-12 mins in prepared oven. It makes about two dozen.

Nutrition Information

- Calories: 184 calories;
- Sodium: 75
- Total Carbohydrate: 23.5
- Cholesterol: 0
- Protein: 1.2
- Total Fat: 9.9

231. Microwave Marshmallow Fudge

Serving: about 2 pounds. | Prep: 10mins | Cook: 5mins | Ready in:

Ingredients

- 1 teaspoon butter
- 1 can (16 ounces) chocolate frosting
- 2 cups (12 ounces) semisweet chocolate chips
- 1/2 cup chopped walnuts
- 1/2 cup miniature marshmallows

Direction

- Use foil to line a 9-inch square pan and use butter to coat the foil, then put aside. Melt chocolate chips and frosting together in a microwave, then stir until the mixture is smooth. Mix in walnuts and allow to cool about 10 minutes. Stir in marshmallows then remove to prepped pan. Cover and chill until firm.
- Lift fudge out of pan with foil. Get rid of the foil and slice fudge into squares with 1-inch size. Keep in an airtight container in the fridge for storage.

Nutrition Information

- Calories: 51 calories
- Fiber: 0 fiber)
- Total Carbohydrate: 6g carbohydrate (5g sugars
- Cholesterol: 0 cholesterol
- Protein: 0 protein.
- Total Fat: 3g fat (1g saturated fat)
- Sodium: 17mg sodium

232. Microwave Truffles

Serving: 2 dozen. | Prep: 15mins | Cook: 20mins | Ready in:

Ingredients

- 1/3 cup finely chopped pecans, toasted, divided
- 8 ounces semisweet chocolate
- 1/4 cup butter
- 1/4 cup heavy whipping cream
- 1/4 teaspoon almond extract

Direction

- Put 24 small foil candy cups on a baking sheet or in miniature muffin cups. Put half a teaspoon of the pecans into each. Put the remaining pecans and cups aside.
- Combine butter and chocolate in a 2-quart microwave-safe bowl. Microwave for 1 minute at 50% power, until melted. Mix in extract and cream. Using an electric mixer, beat until they are thickened slightly, occasionally scraping sides of the bowl. Transfer to prepared cups immediately. Sprinkle with the remaining pecans. Place in the refrigerator until set.

Nutrition Information

- Calories: 86 calories
- Protein: 1g protein.
- Total Fat: 9g fat (4g saturated fat)
- Sodium: 40mg sodium
- Fiber: 0 fiber)
- Total Carbohydrate: 2g carbohydrate (1g sugars
- Cholesterol: 17mg cholesterol

233. Mini Coffee Cakes

Serving: about 1 dozen. | Prep: 10mins | Cook: 20mins | Ready in:

Ingredients

- 1/3 cup butter, softened
- 1/4 cup sugar
- 1 egg
- 1-1/2 cups all-purpose flour
- 1 package (3.4 ounces) instant vanilla pudding mix
- 1 tablespoon baking powder
- 1/4 teaspoon salt
- 1-1/4 cups 2% milk
- 1/2 cup chopped walnuts
- TOPPING:
- 1/2 cup chopped walnuts
- 1/3 cup packed brown sugar
- 2 tablespoons butter, melted
- 1/4 teaspoon ground cinnamon

Direction

- Cream sugar and butter in a big bowl till fluffy and light. Whisk in the egg. Mix salt, baking powder, pudding mix and flour; gently put into creamed mixture alternating with the milk, whipping thoroughly after each addition. Mix in the walnuts.
- Fill muffin cups lined with paper 2/3 full. Mix ingredients for topping; scatter on top of batter. Bake for 20 to 25 minutes at 375° till a toothpick pricked in the middle gets out clean. Let cool for 10 minutes; transfer from the pan to the wire rack.

Nutrition Information

- Calories: 273 calories
- Protein: 6g protein.
- Total Fat: 14g fat (5g saturated fat)
- Sodium: 354mg sodium
- Fiber: 1g fiber)
- Total Carbohydrate: 32g carbohydrate (17g sugars
- Cholesterol: 40mg cholesterol

234. Mini Rum Cakes

Serving: 6 servings. | Prep: 10mins | Cook: 0mins | Ready in:

Ingredients

- 2 cups cold 2% milk
- 1 package (3.4 ounces) instant vanilla pudding mix
- 1 teaspoon rum extract
- 6 individual round sponge cakes
- 1-1/2 cups whipped topping
- Fresh or frozen raspberries

Direction

- Beat the pudding mix and milk in a small bowl for 2 minutes; add the extract and stir. Allow to stand until soft-set, for 2 minutes.
- On the dessert plates, arrange sponge cakes; add the pudding on top. Add the raspberries and whipped topping to decorate.

Nutrition Information

- Calories: 238 calories
- Sodium: 320mg sodium
- Fiber: 0 fiber)
- Total Carbohydrate: 37g carbohydrate (27g sugars
- Cholesterol: 34mg cholesterol
- Protein: 4g protein.
- Total Fat: 7g fat (5g saturated fat)

235. Minister's Delight

Serving: 12 servings. | Prep: 5mins | Cook: 02hours00mins | Ready in:

Ingredients

- 1 can (21 ounces) cherry or apple pie filling
- 1 package yellow cake mix (regular size)
- 1/2 cup butter, melted
- 1/3 cup chopped walnuts, optional

Direction

- Put the pie filling in a slow cooker, 1-1/2-quart in size. Mix butter and cake mix, mixture will become crumbly); scatter on top of filling. Scatter walnuts over if wished. Cook with cover for 2 to 3 hours on low. Put in bowls to serve.

Nutrition Information

- Calories: 304 calories
- Total Fat: 12g fat (6g saturated fat)
- Sodium: 357mg sodium
- Fiber: 1g fiber)
- Total Carbohydrate: 48g carbohydrate (31g sugars
- Cholesterol: 20mg cholesterol
- Protein: 2g protein.

236. Mint Candy Cookies

Serving: about 3-1/2 dozen. | Prep: 20mins | Cook: 10mins | Ready in:

Ingredients

- 1 package (17-1/2 ounces) sugar cookie mix
- 40 to 45 mint Andes candies
- 6 ounces pink candy coating disks
- Heart-shaped decorating sprinkles, optional

Direction

- Make the cookie dough according to the directions in the package. Cover and let chill until it becomes easy to handle or for 15 to 20 minutes.
- Pat a scant tablespoonful of dough in a thin layer, encircling each mint candy. Put on baking sheets without grease, leaving 2-inch space apart. Bake until set or for 7 to 9 minutes at 375 degrees. Let to cool for 1 minutes then allow to cool completely by transferring wire racks from pans.
- Melt candy coating in a microwave-safe bowl then mix until it becomes smooth. Drizzle on

top of cookies. If desired, put decorating sprinkles on top.

Nutrition Information

- Calories:
- Sodium:
- Fiber:
- Total Carbohydrate:
- Cholesterol:
- Protein:
- Total Fat:

237. Mint Chocolate Pie

Serving: 6-8 servings. | Prep: 15mins | Cook: 0mins | Ready in:

Ingredients

- 2 cups heavy whipping cream
- 2 tablespoons confectioners' sugar
- 2 cups cold 2% milk
- 1-1/2 teaspoons peppermint extract
- 5 to 6 drops green food coloring, optional
- 2 packages (3.4 ounces each) instant vanilla pudding mix
- 1 cup miniature semisweet chocolate chips
- 1 pastry shell (9 inches), baked

Direction

- Whip cream and sugar in a small bowl until soft peaks appear. Mix the food coloring, extract and milk in a big bowl if desired. Put in pudding mixes and whip for 2 minutes or until thickened. Fold in chocolate chips and cream mixture.
- Add to pastry crust. Chill for 3 hours or until firm.

Nutrition Information

- Calories: 523 calories
- Fiber: 1g fiber)
- Total Carbohydrate: 44g carbohydrate (29g sugars
- Cholesterol: 95mg cholesterol
- Protein: 5g protein.
- Total Fat: 38g fat (22g saturated fat)
- Sodium: 325mg sodium

238. Mocha Dessert Fondue

Serving: 2-1/2 cups. | Prep: 5mins | Cook: 10mins | Ready in:

Ingredients

- 8 ounces semisweet chocolate, chopped
- 1 can (14 ounces) sweetened condensed milk
- 1/3 cup strong brewed coffee
- Assorted fresh fruit

Direction

- On low heat, melt the chocolate in a heavy saucepan while stirring continuously Add in the coffee and stir thoroughly. Keep warm. Best serve with fruit.

Nutrition Information

- Calories: 241 calories
- Protein: 5g protein.
- Total Fat: 11g fat (6g saturated fat)
- Sodium: 50mg sodium
- Fiber: 2g fiber)
- Total Carbohydrate: 35g carbohydrate (33g sugars
- Cholesterol: 13mg cholesterol

239. Moist Walnut Brownies

Serving: 2 dozen. | Prep: 10mins | Cook: 35mins | Ready in:

Ingredients

- 4 cups Brownie Mix
- 4 eggs
- 2 teaspoons vanilla extract
- 1-1/3 cups chopped walnuts
- 1 cup (6 ounces) semisweet chocolate chips

Direction

- Whisk together vanilla, eggs and brownie mix in a bowl. Fold in chocolate chips and walnuts. Grease a 13x9-inch baking pan and spread the mixture into the prepared pan. Bake in 350-degree oven until a toothpick is clean when coming out from the center, about 35 minutes. Place on a wire rack to cool.

Nutrition Information

- Calories:
- Fiber:
- Total Carbohydrate:
- Cholesterol:
- Protein:
- Total Fat:
- Sodium:

240. Mom's Buttermilk Cookies

Serving: about 3 dozen. | Prep: 20mins | Cook: 10mins | Ready in:

Ingredients

- 1/2 cup butter, softened
- 1 cup granulated sugar
- 1 large egg
- 1 teaspoon vanilla extract
- 2-1/2 cups all-purpose flour
- 1/2 teaspoon baking soda
- 1/2 teaspoon salt
- 1/2 cup buttermilk
- FROSTING:
- 3 tablespoons butter, softened
- 3-1/2 cups confectioners' sugar
- 1/4 cup whole milk
- 1 teaspoon vanilla extract
- 1/2 cup finely chopped walnuts, optional

Direction

- Preheat an oven to 375°. Cream granulated sugar and butter till fluffy and light; beat in vanilla and egg. Whisk salt, baking soda and flour in another bowl; alternately with buttermilk, add to creamed mixture, beating well after each.
- By rounded tablespoonfuls, drop onto greased baking sheets, 2-in. apart. Bake for 10-12 minutes till edges brown lightly. Transfer to wire racks; cool.
- Frosting: Beat vanilla, milk, confectioners' sugar and butter till smooth; spread on cookies. Sprinkle chopped walnuts, if desired.

Nutrition Information

- Calories: 135 calories
- Cholesterol: 15mg cholesterol
- Protein: 1g protein.
- Total Fat: 4g fat (2g saturated fat)
- Sodium: 88mg sodium
- Fiber: 0 fiber)
- Total Carbohydrate: 24g carbohydrate (17g sugars

241. Moonbeam Munchies

Serving: 6 dozen whole moons. | Prep: 15mins | Cook: 10mins | Ready in:

Ingredients

- 2 cups sugar
- 1 cup shortening
- 1 egg

- 2 teaspoons lemon extract
- 5-1/4 cups all-purpose flour
- 1 teaspoon baking soda
- 1/2 teaspoon salt
- 1 cup buttermilk
- 1/2 cup water
- 5 drops yellow food coloring

Direction

- Cream shortening and sugar together in a big bowl. Put in extract and egg. Mix salt, baking soda and flour together, then put into the creamed mixture together with sour milk, alternately, mixing well. Chill about 2 hours or overnight.
- Roll dough to the thickness of 1/4 inch on a surface coated lightly with flour. Use a round cookie cutter to cut the dough. You can halve some circles and shape them into half-moon shapes, if wanted. Arrange on baking sheets coated with grease.
- Bake at 350 degrees until edges start to brown, about 8 to 10 minutes. Transfer to wire racks to cool.
- Mix together food coloring and water, brush over the cooled cookies with this mixture. Allow to dry thoroughly, then keep in airtight containers for storage.

Nutrition Information

- Calories: 166 calories
- Sodium: 73mg sodium
- Fiber: 0 fiber)
- Total Carbohydrate: 25g carbohydrate (11g sugars
- Cholesterol: 7mg cholesterol
- Protein: 2g protein.
- Total Fat: 6g fat (2g saturated fat)

242. No Bake Cheesecake

Serving: | Prep: | Cook: | Ready in:

Ingredients

- 20 sheets Graham crackers
- 2 tablespoons packed brown sugar
- 3/4 stick unsalted butter, melted
- 450 grams cream cheese, at room temperature
- 1 can sweetened condensed milk
- 2 tablespoons freshly squeezed lemon juice
- 1 tablespoon vanilla extract

Direction

- Preparation:
- Create the crust: In a food processor fitted with the blade attachment, put the salt, sugar and graham crackers and pulse into an equal crumb, about 10 pulses. Add in the butter and blend to combine. The mixture should come together in your hand when squeezed.
- Push down the crust into the pan; place the crust mixture into a 9-inch springform pan. Push down the crumbs equally over the bottom and 1 inch up the sides of pan, using a heavy-bottomed cup as necessary to press the mixture into the pan.
- Crust chilling: place in the refrigerator for 10 minutes. In the meantime, make the filling.
- Create the filling: In a large bowl, put the cream cheese and use an electric mixer to beat on medium speed until turn smooth. Put in the vanilla, lemon juice and sweetened condensed milk and keep on beating for about 2 minutes until fully smooth.
- Chill the filling: place the filling into the crust and use an offset spatula to smooth the top. Put in the refrigerator for at least 4 hours, but ideally overnight. Take from the pan and serve: prior serving, take the sides of the springform pan. Slice the cheesecake using a long, thin knife dipped in hot water then dried.

243. No Bake Strawberry Dessert

Serving: 20 servings. | Prep: 20mins | Cook: 0mins | Ready in:

Ingredients

- 1 loaf (10-1/2 ounces) angel food cake, cut into 1-inch cubes
- 2 packages (.3 ounce each) sugar-free strawberry gelatin
- 2 cups boiling water
- 1 package (20 ounces) frozen unsweetened whole strawberries, thawed
- 2 cups cold 1% milk
- 1 package (1 ounce) sugar-free instant vanilla pudding mix
- 1 carton (8 ounces) frozen reduced-fat whipped topping, thawed
- Chopped fresh strawberries, optional

Direction

- In a 13"x9" dish, put one single layer of cake cubes. Dissolve gelatin in boiling water in a bowl, then stir in strawberries. Pour the mixture over cake and press cake down gently. Chill for an hour, until set.
- Whisk together pudding mix and milk in a big bowl about 2 minutes. Allow to stand until soft-set, about 2 minutes.
- Scoop over gelatin layer then spread with whipped topping. Chill until serving. Use chopped fresh strawberries to decorate if you want.

Nutrition Information

- Calories: 92 calories
- Protein: 2g protein. Diabetic Exchanges: 1 starch.
- Total Fat: 2g fat (1g saturated fat)
- Sodium: 172mg sodium
- Fiber: 1g fiber)
- Total Carbohydrate: 16g carbohydrate (0 sugars
- Cholesterol: 2mg cholesterol

244. No Cook Pumpkin Mousse

Serving: 6 servings. | Prep: 10mins | Cook: 0mins | Ready in:

Ingredients

- 1 carton (4 ounces) whipped cream cheese with cinnamon and brown sugar
- 1 cup pumpkin pie filling
- 1/2 cup whipped topping
- 6 individual graham cracker tart shells
- Additional whipped topping and ground cinnamon

Direction

- Mix the pumpkin and cream cheese in a small bowl till incorporated. Fold in the whipped topping. Stuff the tart shells. Jazz up each using more whipped topping and scatter cinnamon on top. Keep in refrigerator.

Nutrition Information

- Calories: 243 calories
- Sodium: 277mg sodium
- Fiber: 2g fiber)
- Total Carbohydrate: 28g carbohydrate (17g sugars
- Cholesterol: 23mg cholesterol
- Protein: 3g protein.
- Total Fat: 13g fat (6g saturated fat)

245. No Fuss Truffles

Serving: about 4-1/2 dozen. | Prep: 50mins | Cook: 0mins | Ready in:

Ingredients

- 2 packages (10 to 12 ounces each) milk chocolate or butterscotch chips
- 1 carton (8 ounces) frozen whipped topping, thawed
- 1-1/4 cups ground toasted almonds, graham cracker crumbs or finely chopped salted peanuts

Direction

- Melt chips in microwave-safe bowl; mix till smooth. Cool for 30 minutes, mixing several times, to room temperature.
- Fold whipped topping in; drop on waxed paper-lined baking sheets by rounded teaspoonfuls. Freeze till firm or for 1 1/2 hours.
- Form to balls; roll in peanuts/crumbs/almonds. Refrigerate/freeze in airtight container. Remove from freezer about 30 minutes prior to serving if frozen.

Nutrition Information

- Calories: 103 calories
- Protein: 2g protein.
- Total Fat: 7g fat (4g saturated fat)
- Sodium: 9mg sodium
- Fiber: 1g fiber)
- Total Carbohydrate: 9g carbohydrate (7g sugars
- Cholesterol: 2mg cholesterol

246. Nuts About You Cookie Sticks

Serving: about 2-1/2 dozen. | Prep: 5mins | Cook: 5mins | Ready in:

Ingredients

- 1 cup semisweet chocolate chips
- 1 tablespoon shortening
- 2 tablespoons creamy peanut butter
- 1 can (13-1/2 ounces) Pirouette cookies
- 1/2 cup chopped nuts

Direction

- Melt the peanut butter, shortening and chocolate chips in a microwave. Mix until it becomes smooth. Dunk 1 end of each cookie in the chocolate mixture and let the excess drip off. Sprinkle using nuts and put it on waxed paper. Let rest until set.

Nutrition Information

- Calories: 111 calories
- Protein: 1g protein.
- Total Fat: 7g fat (3g saturated fat)
- Sodium: 34mg sodium
- Fiber: 1g fiber)
- Total Carbohydrate: 13g carbohydrate (8g sugars
- Cholesterol: 5mg cholesterol

247. Nutter Butter Truffles

Serving: 4 dozen. | Prep: 60mins | Cook: 0mins | Ready in:

Ingredients

- 1 package (1 pound) Nutter Butter sandwich cookies
- 1 package (8 ounces) cream cheese, softened
- 8 ounces milk chocolate candy coating, melted
- 8 ounces white candy coating, melted
- 3 ounces bittersweet chocolate, melted

Direction

- In food processor, process cookies till finely crushed, covered. Add cream cheese; process till blended then roll to 1-in. balls.
- Dip 1/2 of the balls into milk chocolate; let excess drip off. Put onto waxed paper; repeat

with leftover white coating and balls. Drizzle bittersweet chocolate on truffles. Let stand till set. Keep in airtight container in the fridge.

Nutrition Information

- Calories: 120 calories
- Total Fat: 7g fat (4g saturated fat)
- Sodium: 49mg sodium
- Fiber: 0 fiber)
- Total Carbohydrate: 14g carbohydrate (10g sugars
- Cholesterol: 5mg cholesterol
- Protein: 1g protein.

248. Nutty Cookies & Cream Dessert

Serving: 15 servings. | Prep: 25mins | Cook: 0mins | Ready in:

Ingredients

- 1 package (15-1/2 ounces) Oreo cookies, crushed
- 1/2 cup butter, melted
- 1/2 gallon cookies and cream ice cream, softened
- 1-1/2 cups salted peanuts, coarsely chopped
- 2/3 cup hot fudge ice cream topping
- 2/3 cup caramel ice cream topping
- 1 carton (8 ounces) frozen whipped topping, thawed

Direction

- Mix together butter and cookie crumbs in a big bowl, then put aside 1 cup of mixture. Press into an ungreased 13"x9" dish with the rest of crumbs. Spread ice cream over, then layer with peanuts, ice cream toppings and whipped topping. Sprinkle 1 cup of reserved crumbs over top and freeze, covered, until firm.
- Take out of the freezer about 15 minutes before serving.

Nutrition Information

- Calories: 559 calories
- Protein: 8g protein.
- Total Fat: 31g fat (13g saturated fat)
- Sodium: 409mg sodium
- Fiber: 3g fiber)
- Total Carbohydrate: 66g carbohydrate (34g sugars
- Cholesterol: 43mg cholesterol

249. Nutty Ice Cream Delight

Serving: 12-15 servings. | Prep: 30mins | Cook: 0mins | Ready in:

Ingredients

- 3 cups cream-filled chocolate sandwich cookie crumbs
- 1/2 cup butter, melted
- 1/8 teaspoon ground cinnamon
- CHOCOLATE SAUCE:
- 2 cups confectioners' sugar
- 2 tablespoons malted milk powder
- 1 can (12 ounces) evaporated milk
- 1 cup (6 ounces) semisweet chocolate chips
- 1/2 cup butter, cubed
- 1/2 teaspoon vanilla extract
- 1/2 teaspoon orange extract, optional
- 2 cups salted peanuts
- 1/2 gallon peanut butter ice cream with peanut butter cup pieces or peanut butter swirl ice cream

Direction

- Mix together the cookie crumbs, butter and cinnamon in a large bowl. Pat them into a greased 13-in. x 9-in. dish. Freeze, covered, till firm.

- In the meantime, mix together the butter, malted milk powder, milk, chocolate chips and confectioners' sugar in a large saucepan. Heat until boiling; cook and stir for 7-8 minutes. Take off heat; stir vanilla and orange extract into the mix if you wish. Let it cool down thoroughly.
- Sprinkle peanuts atop the crust; spread with ice cream. Freeze. Add chocolate sauce on top. Freeze, covered, till firm, for about 3 hours. You can freeze it for up to 3 months.

Nutrition Information

- Calories:
- Total Carbohydrate:
- Cholesterol:
- Protein:
- Total Fat:
- Sodium:
- Fiber:

250. Oatmeal Chip Cookie Mix

Serving: 2-1/2 dozen. | Prep: 20mins | Cook: 10mins | Ready in:

Ingredients

- 1-1/4 cups quick-cooking oats
- 1 cup all-purpose flour
- 1/2 teaspoon baking powder
- 1/2 teaspoon baking soda
- 1/4 teaspoon salt
- 3/4 cup milk chocolate chips
- 1/3 cup white baking chips
- 1/2 cup slivered almonds
- 1/4 cup sweetened shredded coconut
- 1/2 cup packed brown sugar
- 1/2 cup granulated sugar
- ADDITIONAL INGREDIENTS:
- 1/2 cup butter, softened
- 1 large egg
- 1/2 teaspoon vanilla extract

Direction

- In a food processor, pulse oats until ground finely; put aside. Mix together salt, baking soda, baking powder and flour.
- In a glass jar of 1 quart, layer oats, flour mixture, chips, almonds, coconut, brown sugar and granulated sugar, packing thoroughly between each layer. Cover up and keep in a cool and dry place for up to 6 months. Yield: 1 batch (approximately 4 cups in total).
- For cookies: Preheat the oven to 375°. Cream the butter until fluffy and light. Beat in vanilla and egg. Put in cookie mixture; mix well (mixture will be dry). Add by rounded tablespoonfuls onto ungreased baking sheets, 2 inches apart. Bake in about 10-15 minutes, until lightly browned in color. Let cool for 2 minutes prior to transferring onto wire racks.

Nutrition Information

- Calories: 260 calories
- Cholesterol: 33mg cholesterol
- Protein: 4g protein.
- Total Fat: 13g fat (7g saturated fat)
- Sodium: 178mg sodium
- Fiber: 2g fiber)
- Total Carbohydrate: 33g carbohydrate (19g sugars

251. Oatmeal Shortbread

Serving: about 5 dozen. | Prep: 10mins | Cook: 30mins | Ready in:

Ingredients

- 1 cup butter, softened
- 3/4 cup sugar
- 1-1/2 cups all-purpose flour
- 1-1/2 cups quick-cooking oats

- 3/4 teaspoon salt

Direction

- Cream sugar and butter together in a bowl until fluffy and light. Slowly put in salt, oats and flour. Press to 13x9-inch baking pan that's greased. If preferred, use a fork to prick it. Bake at 325 degrees until browned lightly or 30 to 35 minutes. Allow to cool for 10 minutes, then slice.

Nutrition Information

- Calories: 111 calories
- Sodium: 121mg sodium
- Fiber: 1g fiber)
- Total Carbohydrate: 12g carbohydrate (5g sugars
- Cholesterol: 16mg cholesterol
- Protein: 1g protein.
- Total Fat: 6g fat (4g saturated fat)

252. Orange Cream Dessert

Serving: 12-15 servings. | Prep: 15mins | Cook: 0mins | Ready in:

Ingredients

- 2 cups cream-filled chocolate sandwich cookie crumbs
- 1/3 cup butter, melted
- 1 package (6 ounces) orange or lime gelatin
- 2 cups boiling water
- 1 quart vanilla ice cream, softened

Direction

- Mix cookie crumbs with butter in a big bowl; put aside a quarter cup for garnishing. Push leftover crumb mixture into a greased 13-in. x 9-in. pan. Dissolve gelatin in water in a separate bowl; cover and chill for 10 minutes.
- Mix in ice cream until smooth. Add on top of crust. Scatter with saved crumb mixture. Refrigerate until set.

Nutrition Information

- Calories: 244 calories
- Sodium: 196mg sodium
- Fiber: 1g fiber)
- Total Carbohydrate: 32g carbohydrate (23g sugars
- Cholesterol: 26mg cholesterol
- Protein: 3g protein.
- Total Fat: 12g fat (6g saturated fat)

253. Orange Soda Sherbet

Serving: 2 quarts. | Prep: 35mins | Cook: 0mins | Ready in:

Ingredients

- 3 cans (12 ounces each) orange soda
- 1 can (14 ounces) sweetened condensed milk
- 1 can (8 ounces) crushed pineapple, undrained

Direction

- Chill pineapple, milk and unopened cans of soda together until fully cold. Mix together pineapple, milk and soda in a big bowl until blended.
- Fill cylinder of ice cream for a maximum of 2/3 full. Following manufacturer's instructions to freeze. (Chill any leftover mixture until ready to freeze.) Remove sherbet to freezer containers and let headspace for expansion. Freeze until firm, about 2 to 4 hours.

Nutrition Information

- Calories:
- Cholesterol:
- Protein:

- Total Fat:
- Sodium:
- Fiber:
- Total Carbohydrate:

254. Orange Swirl Yogurt Pie

Serving: 6-8 servings. | Prep: 25mins | Cook: 0mins | Ready in:

Ingredients

- 1/4 cup sugar
- 4 teaspoons cornstarch
- 1 can (6 ounces) frozen orange juice concentrate, thawed
- 1/3 cup water
- 2 tablespoons butter
- 1 tablespoon grated orange zest
- 6 cups low-fat vanilla frozen yogurt, divided
- CRUST:
- 1-1/4 cups crushed gingersnaps (about 20 cookies)
- 1/3 cup butter, melted

Direction

- Mix cornstarch and sugar in a small saucepan. Mix water and orange juice concentrate in till smooth. Boil. Stir and cook till thickened for 1-2 minutes. Take off heat. Mix orange zest and butter in. Cool it down to room temperature, mixing a few times.
- Soften 4 frozen yogurt cups. Meanwhile, mix butter and gingersnaps in a small bowl. Up the sides and bottom of a 9-in. greased pie plate, press it on.
- Spoon the softened yogurt onto crust. Put 1/2 orange sauce on top. With a knife, cut through to swirl. Put leftover frozen yogurt scoops on filling. Drizzle with leftover orange sauce.
- Cover. Freeze for 8 hours minimum then cut. You can freeze this for up to 3 months.

Nutrition Information

- Calories: 409 calories
- Sodium: 281mg sodium
- Fiber: 1g fiber)
- Total Carbohydrate: 62g carbohydrate (46g sugars
- Cholesterol: 43mg cholesterol
- Protein: 6g protein.
- Total Fat: 17g fat (9g saturated fat)

255. Parfaits

Serving: 4 servings. | Prep: 10mins | Cook: 0mins | Ready in:

Ingredients

- 2 ounces cream cheese, softened
- 6 tablespoons peanut butter
- 3/4 cup whipped topping, divided
- 1/2 cup plus 2 tablespoons graham cracker crumbs
- 1 tablespoon sugar
- 4-1/2 teaspoons butter, melted
- 1-1/4 cups miniature semisweet chocolate chips

Direction

- Whisk peanut butter and cream cheese in a small bowl until smooth. Fold in 1/2 cup whipped topping into bowl; reserve mixture.
- Mix sugar and graham cracker crumbs in a small bowl. Put in butter, mixing until mixture is crumbly. Place and press 1 tbsp. of crumb mixture into four parfait glasses. Scoop 2 tbsp. peanut butter mixture on top of crumbs; drizzle with 2 tbsp. chocolate chips. Repeat layers. Put chocolate chips and the rest of the whipped topping on top.

Nutrition Information

- Calories: 594 calories

- Protein: 10g protein.
- Total Fat: 41g fat (20g saturated fat)
- Sodium: 283mg sodium
- Fiber: 5g fiber)
- Total Carbohydrate: 55g carbohydrate (40g sugars
- Cholesterol: 27mg cholesterol

256. Patriotic Trifle

Serving: 16 servings, about 2/3 cup each | Prep: 30mins | Cook: | Ready in:

Ingredients

- 1 pkg. (1 oz.) JELL-O Vanilla Flavor Sugar Free Fat Free Instant Pudding
- 1-1/2 cups cold fat-free milk
- 1 tub (8 oz.) COOL WHIP LITE Whipped Topping , thawed, divided
- 1 pkg. (13 oz.) angel food cake , cut into 1/2-inch cubes (about 6-1/2 cups)
- 2 cups fresh strawberries , sliced
- 1 cup blueberries

Direction

- Use whisk to beat milk and pudding mix for 2 minutes in medium bowl; mix 1 1/2 cups COOL WHIP in.
- Layer 1/2 each of berries and cake in big serving bowl; use pudding mixture to cover. Put layers of leftover cake, berries then COOL WHIP over.
- Refrigerate for 1 hour.

Nutrition Information

- Calories: 120
- Saturated Fat: 2 g
- Sugar: 18 g
- Total Carbohydrate: 23 g
- Cholesterol: 0 mg
- Total Fat: 2 g
- Sodium: 250 mg
- Fiber: 1 g
- Protein: 2 g

257. Peach Mallow Pie

Serving: 6-8 servings. | Prep: 15mins | Cook: 0mins | Ready in:

Ingredients

- 35 large marshmallows
- 1/2 cup milk
- 1-1/2 cups frozen sliced peaches, thawed or1 package (10 ounces) frozen sweetened raspberries, thawed, undrained
- 1/8 teaspoon almond extract
- 1 carton (8 ounces) frozen whipped topping, thawed
- 1 graham cracker crust (9 inches)

Direction

- In a big microwavable bowl, put the milk and marshmallows. Microwave on high, with no cover, for 30 to 90 seconds. Mix till smooth and put aside.
- Chop peaches finely then pulse in a food processor or use a fork to lightly mash till chopped finely. Put into mixture of marshmallow. Mix in extract. Fold in the whipped topping and transfer into crust. Chill about two hours.

Nutrition Information

- Calories:
- Total Fat:
- Sodium:
- Fiber:
- Total Carbohydrate:
- Cholesterol:
- Protein:

258. Peaches & Cream Dessert

Serving: 15 servings. | Prep: 20mins | Cook: 10mins | Ready in:

Ingredients

- 1 package (16 ounces) pecan shortbread cookies, crushed
- 1/2 cup butter, melted
- 1 cup sugar
- 1 package (3 ounces) peach gelatin
- 2 tablespoons cornstarch
- 1 can (12 ounces) lemon-lime soda
- 1 package (8 ounces) cream cheese, softened
- 1 cup confectioners' sugar
- 1 carton (8 ounces) frozen whipped topping, thawed
- 6 cups fresh or frozen sliced peeled peaches, thawed
- 1/3 cup unsweetened pineapple juice

Direction

- Mix the butter and cookies crumbs in a small bowl then press onto the bottom of an ungreased 13x9-inch dish.
- Mix the cornstarch, gelatin, and the sugar in a small saucepan and whisk in soda until smooth. Bring the mixture to a boil. Cook while stirring until the mixture is a bit thickened, 5-7 minutes. Let it cool to room temperature while stirring occasionally.
- At the same time, beat the confectioners' sugar and cream cheese in a big bowl until smooth. Put in whipped topping and continue beating until blended. Pour over the crust. Mix together the pineapple juice and peaches. Place over the cream cheese layer. Spread the gelatin mixture over the cake top. Cover and keep in a refrigerator overnight.

Nutrition Information

- Calories: 446 calories
- Total Fat: 21g fat (12g saturated fat)
- Sodium: 241mg sodium
- Fiber: 2g fiber)
- Total Carbohydrate: 60g carbohydrate (36g sugars
- Cholesterol: 39mg cholesterol
- Protein: 4g protein.

259. Peachy Cream Pie

Serving: 8 servings. | Prep: 25mins | Cook: 0mins | Ready in:

Ingredients

- 3/4 cup sugar
- 5 teaspoons cornstarch
- 1-1/2 cups cold water
- 1 package (3 ounces) peach, apricot or orange gelatin
- 1-1/2 cups frozen unsweetened peach slices, thawed
- 3 ounces cream cheese, softened
- 3 tablespoons confectioners' sugar
- 1 tablespoon whole milk
- 1-1/2 cups whipped topping
- 1 extra-servings-size graham cracker crust (9 ounces)

Direction

- Mix sugar with cornstarch in a big saucepan. Mix in water until smooth. Heat up to a boil; cook and mix for 1-2 minutes or until thickened. Take off from the heat; mix in gelatin until dissolved. Put in peaches. Chill about 20 minutes until thickened slightly,
- Whip the milk, confectioners' sugar and cream cheese in a big bowl until smooth. Fold in whipped topping. Scoop into pie crust. Scoop gelatin mixture on top of cream cheese layer. Chill about 3 hours until firm.

Nutrition Information

- Calories: 376 calories
- Fiber: 1g fiber)
- Total Carbohydrate: 60g carbohydrate (50g sugars
- Cholesterol: 12mg cholesterol
- Protein: 3g protein.
- Total Fat: 14g fat (6g saturated fat)
- Sodium: 239mg sodium

260. Peanut Butter Chocolate Bars

Serving: 1-1/2 to 2 dozen. | Prep: 30mins | Cook: 0mins | Ready in:

Ingredients

- 1 cup sugar
- 1 cup light corn syrup
- 1 cup peanut butter
- 6 cups crisp rice cereal
- 2 cups (12 ounces) semisweet chocolate chips, melted

Direction

- Cook peanut butter, corn syrup and sugar in big saucepan on medium low heat till sugar melts. Take of heat; add cereal. Mix till coated. Spread in 13x9-in. greased pan; lightly press. Spread melted chocolate on bars; chill.

Nutrition Information

- Calories: 227 calories
- Sodium: 132mg sodium
- Fiber: 1g fiber)
- Total Carbohydrate: 36g carbohydrate (25g sugars
- Cholesterol: 0 cholesterol
- Protein: 4g protein.
- Total Fat: 10g fat (4g saturated fat)

261. Peanut Butter Chocolate Pie

Serving: 8 servings. | Prep: 10mins | Cook: 0mins | Ready in:

Ingredients

- 1 package (6 ounces) peanut butter cups
- 1 cup cold 2% milk
- 1 package (3.9 ounces) instant chocolate pudding mix
- 1 carton (8 ounces) frozen whipped topping, thawed
- 1 chocolate crumb crust (8 inches)

Direction

- Slice four peanut butter cups into halves; chop up the rest of the cups roughly and put aside. Whisk together milk and pudding mix in a large bowl for 2 minutes (the mixture will get thick). Fold the whipped topping into this mixture.
- Fold the chopped peanut butter cups into the mixture. Spoon it into crust. Decorate the top with halved peanut butter cups. Chill in refrigerator for no less than 15 minutes before serving.

Nutrition Information

- Calories: 364 calories
- Sodium: 388mg sodium
- Fiber: 2g fiber)
- Total Carbohydrate: 46g carbohydrate (31g sugars
- Cholesterol: 5mg cholesterol
- Protein: 5g protein.
- Total Fat: 17g fat (9g saturated fat)

262. Peanut Butter Cookie Cups

Serving: 3 dozen. | Prep: 25mins | Cook: 15mins | Ready in:

Ingredients

- 1 package (17-1/2 ounces) peanut butter cookie mix
- 36 miniature peanut butter cups, unwrapped

Direction

- Preheat an oven to 350°. Follow package direction to prep cookie mix; roll dough to 1-in. balls. Put into greased mini muffin cups; evenly press dough up sides and bottom of every cup.
- Bake till set for 11-13 minutes; put peanut butter cup immediately in every cup and gently press down. Cool for 10 minutes; remove from pans carefully.

Nutrition Information

- Calories: 119 calories
- Sodium: 89mg sodium
- Fiber: 1g fiber)
- Total Carbohydrate: 13g carbohydrate (3g sugars
- Cholesterol: 6mg cholesterol
- Protein: 2g protein.
- Total Fat: 7g fat (2g saturated fat)

263. Peanut Butter Cookie Parfait

Serving: 1 serving. | Prep: 15mins | Cook: 0mins | Ready in:

Ingredients

- 3 peanut butter cookies, coarsely chopped
- 2/3 cup vanilla ice cream
- 3 tablespoons hot fudge ice cream topping, warmed

Direction

- Reserve one large cookie piece. Pour half of the chopped cookies in a parfait; put half of the ice cream and hot fudge topping on top. Continue. Decorate with reserved cookie piece.

Nutrition Information

- Calories: 573 calories
- Total Carbohydrate: 81g carbohydrate (47g sugars
- Cholesterol: 39mg cholesterol
- Protein: 9g protein.
- Total Fat: 24g fat (9g saturated fat)
- Sodium: 316mg sodium
- Fiber: 3g fiber)

264. Peanut Butter Cup Pie

Serving: 8 | Prep: 20mins | Cook: | Ready in:

Ingredients

- 1 (3 ounce) package non-instant vanilla pudding mix
- 2 cups milk
- 1 (16 ounce) jar peanut butter
- 1 (9 inch) pie crust, baked
- 1 (3.9 ounce) package instant chocolate pudding mix
- 2 cups milk
- 1 cup frozen whipped topping, thawed (optional)

Direction

- Mix 2 cups milk with vanilla pudding mix; prepare following directions on package. When pudding heats up, put in peanut butter. Mix continuously until peanut butter is melted and mixture is thick and smooth. Add mixture to pie shell.

- Following package directions, mix chocolate pudding mix and 2 cups milk. Let it set up 5 minutes, then put on top of peanut butter pudding layer. Refrigerate for a few hours before serving. Top with whipped topping (optional).

Nutrition Information

- Calories: 597 calories;
- Total Fat: 38.8
- Sodium: 689
- Total Carbohydrate: 48.6
- Cholesterol: 10
- Protein: 19.4

265. Peanut Butter Drops

Serving: 48 | Prep: | Cook: | Ready in:

Ingredients

- 2 cups white sugar
- 1/2 cup milk
- 3 tablespoons unsweetened cocoa powder
- 1/2 cup butter
- 1/2 cup peanut butter
- 3 cups quick cooking oats

Direction

- Use whisk to mix milk, cocoa and sugar in saucepan. Slice butter into mixture on low heat till all is melted and mixed.
- Put on rolling boil; boil for 2 1/2 minutes. To test: Put a spoonful of mixture into cup of cold water; if it makes a ball, it boiled for long enough, if not, it's not ready. This can take 3 minutes.
- Turn heat off; add peanut butter. Mix till combined. Use heavy spoon to mix oats in; mix all together. By spoonfuls, drop onto waxed paper.

Nutrition Information

- Calories: 86 calories;
- Total Fat: 3.7
- Sodium: 27
- Total Carbohydrate: 12.6
- Cholesterol: 5
- Protein: 1.5

266. Peanut Butter Graham Bars

Serving: 20 bars. | Prep: 15mins | Cook: 0mins | Ready in:

Ingredients

- 10 whole graham crackers, broken into quarters, divided
- 1 cup graham cracker crumbs (about 14 squares)
- 3/4 cup sugar
- 1/2 cup packed brown sugar
- 1/2 cup butter, cubed
- 1/3 cup milk
- 1/2 cup semisweet chocolate chips
- 1/4 cup creamy peanut butter

Direction

- Press half of the graham crackers to the bottom of an 11x7-in. greased dish; put aside. In a 2-qt. microwave-safe bowl, combine the milk, butter, sugars and crumbs. Microwave on high, uncovered, for 45 seconds; mix. Microwave for another 1-1/2 to 2 minutes on high. Pour half of the mixture over crackers in greased pan right away. Place the remaining graham crackers on top; layer the remaining sugar mixture on top.

- In a small microwave-safe bowl, heat peanut butter and chocolate chips on high, uncovered, until chips are melted, for 30-45 seconds. Mix until blended and smooth. Evenly spread onto bars. Refrigerate, covered, for 1-1/2 hours before slicing.

Nutrition Information

- Calories: 182 calories
- Fiber: 1g fiber)
- Total Carbohydrate: 26g carbohydrate (18g sugars
- Cholesterol: 13mg cholesterol
- Protein: 2g protein.
- Total Fat: 9g fat (4g saturated fat)
- Sodium: 139mg sodium

267. Peanut Butter Jumbos

Serving: 9 dozen. | Prep: 15mins | Cook: 15mins | Ready in:

Ingredients

- 1-1/2 cups peanut butter
- 1/2 cup butter, softened
- 1 cup sugar
- 1 cup packed brown sugar
- 3 large eggs
- 1 teaspoon vanilla extract
- 4-1/2 cups quick-cooking oats
- 2 teaspoons baking soda
- 1 cup miniature semisweet chocolate chips
- 1 cup M&M's miniature baking bits

Direction

- Preheat an oven to 350°. Cream sugars, butter and peanut butter till blended in big bowl; beat vanilla and egg in. Whisk baking soda and oats in another bowl; beat into creamed mixture slowly. Mix baking bits and chocolate chips in.
- By heaping tablespoonfuls, drop on ungreased baking sheets, 2-in. apart. Bake till edges are browned for 12-14 minutes. Transfer from pans onto wire racks; cool. Keep in airtight containers.

Nutrition Information

- Calories: 153 calories
- Sodium: 106mg sodium
- Fiber: 1g fiber)
- Total Carbohydrate: 18g carbohydrate (13g sugars
- Cholesterol: 18mg cholesterol
- Protein: 4g protein. Diabetic Exchanges: 1 fat
- Total Fat: 8g fat (3g saturated fat)

268. Peanut Butter Kiss Cookies

Serving: 9 | Prep: | Cook: | Ready in:

Ingredients

- 1 cup white sugar
- 1 cup peanut butter
- 1 egg
- 18 milk chocolate candy kisses, unwrapped

Direction

- Preheat the oven to 350°F. Combine egg, peanut butter and sugar.
- Form dough into 1-inch balls and put on ungreased cookie sheet (NOTE: if dough is too sticky, chill for 30 minutes until can be easily handled)
- Allow to bake for 10 minutes. Remove from oven. Force 1 chocolate kiss into the center of each warm cookie.

Nutrition Information

- Calories: 311 calories;

- Total Fat: 17.9
- Sodium: 147
- Total Carbohydrate: 33.5
- Cholesterol: 23
- Protein: 8.5

269. Peanut Butter Silk Pie

Serving: 8 servings. | Prep: 10mins | Cook: 0mins | Ready in:

Ingredients

- 3/4 cup peanut butter
- 4 ounces cream cheese, softened
- 1 cup confectioners' sugar
- 1 carton (8 ounces) frozen whipped topping, thawed
- 1 graham cracker crust (9 inches)
- Salted chopped peanuts

Direction

- Beat confectioners' sugar, cream cheese and peanut butter in large bowl until they become smooth. Then fold in the whipped topping. Transfer to prepared crust. Top with nuts. Let chill until enjoying.

Nutrition Information

- Calories: 434 calories
- Sodium: 276mg sodium
- Fiber: 2g fiber)
- Total Carbohydrate: 40g carbohydrate (29g sugars
- Cholesterol: 16mg cholesterol
- Protein: 8g protein.
- Total Fat: 27g fat (11g saturated fat)

270. Peanut Ice Cream Squares

Serving: 20 servings. | Prep: 20mins | Cook: 10mins | Ready in:

Ingredients

- 2 cups confectioners' sugar
- 1 can (12 ounces) evaporated milk
- 2/3 cup chocolate chips
- 1 cup butter, divided
- 1 teaspoon vanilla extract
- 3 cups chocolate wafer crumbs (about 48 wafers)
- 1/2 gallon vanilla ice cream
- 2 cups salted dry roasted peanuts, crushed

Direction

- Bring together 1/2 cup of butter, chocolate chips, milk and sugar in a big saucepan to a boil. Lower heat, simmer without a cover for about 8 minutes. Take away from the heat and stir in vanilla. Allow to fully cool.
- Melt leftover butter and toss together with wafer crumbs. Press the mixture onto the bottom of a 13"x9" pan. Slice ice cream into slices with 1 1/2 inches slices, then place over the crust. Sprinkle nuts on top and freeze for a half hour.
- Spread over nuts with the cooled sauce. Place a cover and freeze until firm, about an hour. You can freeze for a maximum of 2 months. Take out of the freezer about 15 minutes before serving.

Nutrition Information

- Calories: 441 calories
- Cholesterol: 54mg cholesterol
- Protein: 8g protein.
- Total Fat: 27g fat (13g saturated fat)
- Sodium: 368mg sodium
- Fiber: 2g fiber)
- Total Carbohydrate: 45g carbohydrate (26g sugars

271. Peanutty Fries

Serving: about 3-1/2 dozen. | Prep: 20mins | Cook: 0mins | Ready in:

Ingredients

- 1 package (10 ounces) peanut butter chips
- 1 cup sweetened condensed milk
- Paper muffin cup liners (2-1/2-inch diameter)
- Red icing, optional

Direction

- Melt peanut butter chips with milk in a microwave, then stir until smooth. Transfer into a 9-inch square pan lined with foil and coated with grease. Allow to cool totally at room temperature. Lift out of the pan and invert on a cutting board.
- Take off the foil and cut into strips with 3x1/4-inch size. Fold muffin cup liners in half and press out creases, then fold in half one more time. Fold point under and use it as fries' holder. Use icing for ketchup if you want.

Nutrition Information

- Calories: 239 calories
- Sodium: 110mg sodium
- Fiber: 2g fiber)
- Total Carbohydrate: 29g carbohydrate (25g sugars
- Cholesterol: 10mg cholesterol
- Protein: 8g protein.
- Total Fat: 11g fat (5g saturated fat)

272. Pecan Candy Clusters

Serving: 16 candies. | Prep: 30mins | Cook: 0mins | Ready in:

Ingredients

- 2 cups milk chocolate chips, divided
- 64 pecan halves (about 1-1/2 cups)
- 28 caramels
- 2 tablespoons heavy whipping cream

Direction

- Use waxed paper to line a baking tray; put aside. Microwave a cup chocolate chips to melt; mix until smooth. Put chocolate by tablespoonfuls onto lined baking tray. Put 4 pecans over each chocolate drop quickly.
- In a 1-quart microwaveable pan, put the caramels; pour in cream. Microwave on high, with no cover, for 2 minutes, mixing once. Scoop onto the center of each cluster.
- Melt the leftover chocolate chips; mix until smooth. Smear on top of caramel. Let sit until firm.

Nutrition Information

- Calories:
- Sodium:
- Fiber:
- Total Carbohydrate:
- Cholesterol:
- Protein:
- Total Fat:

273. Pecan Cereal Clusters

Serving: about 5 dozen. | Prep: 20mins | Cook: 0mins | Ready in:

Ingredients

- 3/4 cup peanut butter
- 1 cup (6 ounces) semisweet chocolate chips
- 3 cups Cheerios
- 2-1/4 cups milk chocolate M&M's
- 3/4 cup pecan halves

Direction

- Use waxed paper to line three 15x10x1-in. pans. In a large heavy saucepan, cook and stir the chocolate chips and peanut butter over low heat until chips melt.
- Take off from heat; mix in pecans, M&M's and Cheerios until coated evenly. On the prepared pans, drop rounded tablespoonfuls of the dough. Keep in refrigerator for 4 hours or until firm.

Nutrition Information

- Calories: 160 calories
- Cholesterol: 2mg cholesterol
- Protein: 3g protein.
- Total Fat: 10g fat (4g saturated fat)
- Sodium: 66mg sodium
- Fiber: 2g fiber)
- Total Carbohydrate: 17g carbohydrate (12g sugars

274. Pecan Chocolate Candies

Serving: 3 dozen. | Prep: 25mins | Cook: 5mins | Ready in:

Ingredients

- 1 can (5 ounces) evaporated milk
- 1/2 cup sugar
- 1 cup (6 ounces) semisweet chocolate chips
- 2 teaspoons vanilla extract
- 2-1/2 cups crushed vanilla wafers (about 75 wafers)
- 1-1/2 cups chopped pecans, divided

Direction

- Boil sugar and milk in big saucepan on medium heat; take off heat. Mix vanilla and chocolate chips in till smooth. Add 1/3 cup pecans and vanilla wafers; mix till combined well. Put in bowl; refrigerate till set for 30 minutes.
- Form to 3/4-in. balls. Coat by rolling in leftover pecans. Put onto waxed paper-lined baking sheets then refrigerate till set.

Nutrition Information

- Calories: 108 calories
- Protein: 1g protein. Diabetic Exchanges: 1 starch
- Total Fat: 6g fat (2g saturated fat)
- Sodium: 29mg sodium
- Fiber: 1g fiber)
- Total Carbohydrate: 13g carbohydrate (9g sugars
- Cholesterol: 2mg cholesterol

275. Pecan Chocolate Chip Brownies

Serving: 2 dozen. | Prep: 15mins | Cook: 45mins | Ready in:

Ingredients

- 2 tubes (16-1/2 ounces each) refrigerated chocolate chip cookie dough
- 3/4 cup sweetened shredded coconut, divided
- 1 package fudge brownie mix (8-inch square pan size)
- 1/2 cup semisweet chocolate chips
- 1/2 cup chopped pecans

Direction

- Pat cookie dough into a 13x9" baking pan coated with cooking spray. Scatter half a cup of coconut and press tightly into the dough.
- Follow the instructions on the package, make brownie batter; then distribute this batter over the coconut. Scatter the rest of coconut on top, then sprinkle with pecans and chocolate chips.

- Bake for 40-45 minutes at 350 degrees until a toothpick inserted in the middle comes out without any remaining crumbs. Don't overbake. Place on a wire rack to cool.

Nutrition Information

- Calories:
- Total Carbohydrate:
- Cholesterol:
- Protein:
- Total Fat:
- Sodium:
- Fiber:

276. Pecan Grahams

Serving: about 4-1/2 dozen. | Prep: 20mins | Cook: 10mins | Ready in:

Ingredients

- 1/2 cup shortening
- 1/2 cup sugar
- 1/2 cup packed brown sugar
- 1 egg
- 1 cup all-purpose flour
- 1/2 teaspoon baking powder
- 1/2 teaspoon baking soda
- 1/4 teaspoon salt
- 1 cup graham cracker crumbs
- 1 cup ground pecans
- 54 to 60 pecan halves

Direction

- Cream sugars and shortening together in a bowl, then put egg in and mix well. Mix together salt, baking soda, baking powder and flour, then put into the creamed mixture. Stir in ground pecans and cracker crumbs, then mix well.
- Drop the batter on ungreased baking sheets by rounded teaspoonfuls with 2 inches apart. Put in the center of each cookie a pecan half, then press it down slightly.
- Bake at 350 degrees until browned slightly, about 9 to 11 minutes. Allow to cool about 2 minutes prior to moving to wire racks.

Nutrition Information

- Calories: 134 calories
- Sodium: 75mg sodium
- Fiber: 1g fiber)
- Total Carbohydrate: 14g carbohydrate (8g sugars
- Cholesterol: 8mg cholesterol
- Protein: 2g protein.
- Total Fat: 8g fat (1g saturated fat)

277. Peppermint Candy Cane Cookies

Serving: 3 dozen. | Prep: 25mins | Cook: 10mins | Ready in:

Ingredients

- 1/2 tube refrigerated sugar cookie dough, softened
- 2 tablespoons all-purpose flour
- 1/2 teaspoon peppermint extract
- 1/2 teaspoon red food coloring

Direction

- Beat extract, flour and cookie dough till smooth in a big bowl. Halve dough; mix food coloring into 1 portion.
- Form 1 tsp. white dough to 6-in. rope. Form 1 tsp. red dough to 6-in. rope. Put ropes side by side; lightly press together, then twist.
- Put onto ungreased baking sheet; to make handle of cane, curve top of cookie. Repeat with leftover dough, putting cookies on baking sheets, 2-in. apart.

- Bake at 350° till set or for 8-10 minutes; cool for 2 minutes. Transfer to wire racks carefully.

Nutrition Information

- Calories: 33 calories
- Sodium: 30mg sodium
- Fiber: 0 fiber)
- Total Carbohydrate: 5g carbohydrate (2g sugars
- Cholesterol: 2mg cholesterol
- Protein: 0 protein.
- Total Fat: 1g fat (0 saturated fat)

278. Peppermint Topping

Serving: 2-1/4 cups. | Prep: 5mins | Cook: 20mins | Ready in:

Ingredients

- 1-1/2 cups crushed peppermint candies
- 1 cup heavy whipping cream
- 1 jar (7 ounces) marshmallow creme

Direction

- Mix together marshmallow crème, whipping cream and crushed candies in a heavy saucepan. Cook and stir the mixture on low heat until the mixture is smooth and candy is melted thoroughly. Keep in the fridge for storage.

Nutrition Information

- Calories: 112 calories
- Protein: 0 protein.
- Total Fat: 5g fat (3g saturated fat)
- Sodium: 17mg sodium
- Fiber: 0 fiber)
- Total Carbohydrate: 17g carbohydrate (12g sugars
- Cholesterol: 18mg cholesterol

279. Pineapple Cheesecake

Serving: 8 | Prep: 10mins | Cook: | Ready in:

Ingredients

- 1 (8 ounce) package cream cheese, softened
- 1/2 cup white sugar
- 2 (15 ounce) cans crushed pineapple, drained
- 1 3/4 cups frozen whipped topping, thawed
- 1 (9 inch) prepared graham cracker crust

Direction

- Add sugar and cream cheese into a big bowl and mix. Pour whipped topping and 1 can of pineapple into the cream cheese bowl mix and stir. Continue mixing until it is smooth.
- Distribute mixture into the crust and pour the other can of pineapple on top. Keep covered and allow to chill for 2 hours.

Nutrition Information

- Calories: 380 calories;
- Cholesterol: 31
- Protein: 3.7
- Total Fat: 18.9
- Sodium: 234
- Total Carbohydrate: 50.1

280. Pineapple Coconut Snowballs

Serving: about 2 dozen. | Prep: 20mins | Cook: 0mins | Ready in:

Ingredients

- 1 package (8 ounces) cream cheese, softened

- 1 can (8 ounces) crushed pineapple, well drained
- 2-1/2 cups sweetened shredded coconut

Direction

- Beat pineapple and cream cheese till combined in a small bowl; cover. Refrigerate it for 30 minutes.
- Roll to 1-inch balls then roll in coconut and refrigerate for 6 hours - overnight.

Nutrition Information

- Calories: 67 calories
- Protein: 2g protein. Diabetic Exchanges: 1 fat
- Total Fat: 5g fat (5g saturated fat)
- Sodium: 55mg sodium
- Fiber: 1g fiber)
- Total Carbohydrate: 4g carbohydrate (0 sugars
- Cholesterol: 1mg cholesterol

281. Pineapple Ice Cream

Serving: Makes about 1 1/4 quarts | Prep: | Cook: | Ready in:

Ingredients

- 1 1/2 cups drained canned crushed pineapple in juice (from a 20-fl-oz can), reserving 1/2 cup plus 1 tablespoon juice
- 3/4 cup plus 2 tablespoons sugar
- 2 teaspoons cornstarch
- 1 1/4 cups whole milk
- 2 large egg yolks
- 1/4 teaspoon vanilla
- 1 cup chilled heavy cream
- Accompaniment: lacy rice noodle crisps
- an instant-read thermometer; an ice cream maker

Direction

- Boil 1/2 cup sugar, 1/2 cup leftover pineapple juice and pineapple in 2-3-qt. heavy saucepan, mixing till sugar melts. Lower heat; simmer, occasionally mixing, for 5 minutes till pineapple is soft. Mix leftover tbsp. pineapple juice and cornstarch in small bowl till cornstarch melts; add to pineapple mixture. Simmer, frequently mixing, for 1 minute till thick.
- Put milk on just a boil in 1 1/2-2-.qt heavy saucepan. Whisk big pinch of salt, leftover 1/4 cup and 2 tbsp. sugar and yolks in bowl; in a stream, add hot milk, whisking. Put custard back in saucepan; cook on medium low heat, using wooden spoon to mix, for 2-3 minutes till thermometer in custard reads 170-175°F. Through very fine-mesh sieve, put custard immediately into bowl; mix vanilla and pineapple mixture in then cool down to room temperature, occasionally mixing. Mix cream in; chill custard for 4 hours till very cold, covered.
- In ice cream maker, freeze custard; put into airtight container. Put in freezer for minimum of 12 hours to harden.
- You can make ice cream 3 days ahead.

Nutrition Information

- Calories: 232
- Fiber: 0 g(2%)
- Total Carbohydrate: 30 g(10%)
- Cholesterol: 77 mg(26%)
- Protein: 2 g(5%)
- Total Fat: 12 g(18%)
- Saturated Fat: 7 g(35%)
- Sodium: 32 mg(1%)

282. Pineapple Orange Cheesecake

Serving: 6 servings. | Prep: 5mins | Cook: 10mins | Ready in:

Ingredients

- 2 cups cubed fresh pineapple
- 2 tablespoons brown sugar
- 2 tablespoons butter
- 1/3 cup orange marmalade
- 1 package (30 ounces) frozen New York-style cheesecake, thawed
- Whipped topping, optional

Direction

- Sauté brown sugar and pineapple in butter in a big skillet for 8 minutes. On top of cheesecake, spread orange marmalade and layer pineapple mixture over. Top with whipped topping (optional).

Nutrition Information

- Calories: 575 calories
- Fiber: 1g fiber)
- Total Carbohydrate: 59g carbohydrate (54g sugars
- Cholesterol: 88mg cholesterol
- Protein: 8g protein.
- Total Fat: 36g fat (16g saturated fat)
- Sodium: 344mg sodium

283. Pineapple Caramel Sponge Cakes

Serving: 4 servings. | Prep: 5mins | Cook: 5mins | Ready in:

Ingredients

- 1 can (8 ounces) unsweetened crushed pineapple, drained
- 1/2 cup caramel ice cream topping
- 4 individual round sponge cakes
- 1 pint vanilla ice cream, softened

Direction

- Mix caramel topping and pineapple in a pot. Cook for 2-3 minutes over medium heat. Stir often. Cook until heated through.
- Put sponge cakes onto dessert plates. Put a scoop of ice cream on top, with a quarter cup of pineapple sauce. Serve right away.

Nutrition Information

- Calories: 355 calories
- Cholesterol: 57mg cholesterol
- Protein: 5g protein.
- Total Fat: 9g fat (6g saturated fat)
- Sodium: 376mg sodium
- Fiber: 1g fiber)
- Total Carbohydrate: 66g carbohydrate (27g sugars

284. Pistachio Cookie Dessert

Serving: 12-15 servings. | Prep: 20mins | Cook: 0mins | Ready in:

Ingredients

- 1 package (15-1/2 ounces) Oreo cookies
- 1/2 cup plus 2 tablespoons butter, melted
- 1-1/2 cups cold 2% milk
- 2 packages (3.4 ounces each) instant pistachio pudding mix
- 1 quart vanilla ice cream, softened
- 1 carton (16 ounces) frozen whipped topping, thawed

Direction

- Add cookies to a blender, process with the cover on until fine crumbs form. Whisk in butter. Put aside 1 cup for topping. Press the remaining crumb mixture into an ungreased 13x9-inch dish.
- Beat the pudding mix with milk in a big bowl for 2 minutes on low speed. Put in ice cream gradually. Fold in whipped topping.

- Pour over the crust. Drizzle reserved crumb mixture on top and slightly press down. Freeze with a cover overnight or for 4 hrs. Take out of the freezer 20 min prior to slicing.

Nutrition Information

- Calories: 446 calories
- Sodium: 459mg sodium
- Fiber: 1g fiber)
- Total Carbohydrate: 48g carbohydrate (30g sugars
- Cholesterol: 39mg cholesterol
- Protein: 4g protein.
- Total Fat: 25g fat (14g saturated fat)

285. Pistachio Cranberry Bark

Serving: about 1 pound. | Prep: 20mins | Cook: 0mins | Ready in:

Ingredients

- 2 cups (12 ounces) semisweet chocolate chips
- 1 cup chopped pistachios, toasted, divided
- 3/4 cup dried cranberries, divided
- 5 ounces white candy coating, melted

Direction

- Microwave chocolate chips in a microwaveable bowl until melted; mix until smooth. Mix in 1/2 of the cranberries and 3/4 cup of pistachios; smear onto a waxed paper-lined baking tray. Sprinkle with melted candy coating. Slice through layers, using a knife to swirl.
- Scatter with the leftover pistachios and cranberries. Chill until set.
- Break or slice into pieces. Put in an airtight container in the fridge to store.

Nutrition Information

- Calories: 215 calories
- Fiber: 2g fiber)
- Total Carbohydrate: 28g carbohydrate (24g sugars
- Cholesterol: 0 cholesterol
- Protein: 3g protein.
- Total Fat: 12g fat (6g saturated fat)
- Sodium: 36mg sodium

286. Pound Cake With Strawberries

Serving: 8 servings. | Prep: 5mins | Cook: 0mins | Ready in:

Ingredients

- 1 cup (8 ounces) sour cream
- 1 teaspoon sugar
- 1 loaf (10-3/4 ounces) frozen pound cake, thawed and cut into cubes
- 1 package (10 ounces) frozen sweetened sliced strawberries, thawed

Direction

- In a small bowl, mix together sugar and sour cream. Arrange the cake cubes in dessert bowls, topping them with sweetened sour cream and strawberries.

Nutrition Information

- Calories: 236 calories
- Cholesterol: 73mg cholesterol
- Protein: 4g protein.
- Total Fat: 11g fat (7g saturated fat)
- Sodium: 154mg sodium
- Fiber: 1g fiber)
- Total Carbohydrate: 30g carbohydrate (20g sugars

287. Praline Peach Brownie Sundaes

Serving: 6 servings. | Prep: 10mins | Cook: 10mins | Ready in:

Ingredients

- 1/4 cup packed brown sugar
- 1/4 cup heavy whipping cream
- 2 tablespoons butter
- 1/4 teaspoon ground cinnamon
- 2 medium peaches, peeled and sliced or 1 cup frozen unsweetened peach slices, thawed and patted dry
- 1/2 cup chopped pecans
- 1 teaspoon vanilla extract
- 6 prepared brownies
- 3 cups vanilla ice cream
- Additional peach slices, optional

Direction

- Whisk together cinnamon, butter, cream and brown sugar in a large saucepan till smooth. Boil the mixture; cook while stirring till thickened, 6-7 minutes. Take away from the heat; mix in vanilla, pecans and peaches. Allow to cool for 10 minutes.
- In dessert dishes, place brownies; put the peach sauce and ice cream on top. Use more peach slices for garnish if you want.

Nutrition Information

- Calories: 566 calories
- Protein: 7g protein.
- Total Fat: 32g fat (12g saturated fat)
- Sodium: 289mg sodium
- Fiber: 3g fiber)
- Total Carbohydrate: 69g carbohydrate (52g sugars
- Cholesterol: 63mg cholesterol

288. Pretzel Cereal Crunch

Serving: about 9 cups. | Prep: 15mins | Cook: 5mins | Ready in:

Ingredients

- 1-1/4 cups Golden Grahams
- 1-1/4 cups Apple Cinnamon Cheerios
- 1-1/4 cups miniature pretzels
- 1 cup chopped pecans, toasted
- 1 package (10 to 12 ounces) white baking chips
- 2 tablespoons creamy peanut butter

Direction

- Mix together pecans, pretzels and cereals in a big bowl. Melt chips in a microwavable bowl, the stir the mixture until smooth. Stir in peanut butter. Drizzle whole mixture over cereal mixture and toss to coat well. Transfer the mixture into a baking sheet lined with waxed paper and spread evenly. Allow to fully cool and break mixture into pieces. Keep in an airtight container to store.

Nutrition Information

- Calories: 190 calories
- Sodium: 105mg sodium
- Fiber: 1g fiber)
- Total Carbohydrate: 19g carbohydrate (14g sugars
- Cholesterol: 3mg cholesterol
- Protein: 3g protein.
- Total Fat: 12g fat (4g saturated fat)

289. Pretzel Jell O Dessert

Serving: 12 servings. | Prep: 30mins | Cook: 0mins | Ready in:

Ingredients

- 2 cups crushed pretzels

- 3/4 cup butter, melted
- 2 tablespoons sugar
- FILLING:
- 1 package (8 ounces) cream cheese, softened
- 1 cup sugar
- 1 carton (8 ounces) frozen whipped topping, thawed
- TOPPING:
- 2 packages (3 ounces each) strawberry gelatin
- 2 cups boiling water
- 1/2 cup cold water
- Fresh strawberries and additional whipped topping, optional

Direction

- Set the oven at 350° to preheat. Mix sugar, melted butter, and crushed pretzels; press onto the bottom of an ungreased 13x9-in. baking dish. Then bake for around 10 minutes. Let cool completely.
- To make the filling: Beat sugar and cream cheese until smooth. Add whipped topping, stir and spread over the crust. Cover and chill in the fridge until cold.
- Dissolve gelatin in a small bowl of boiling water. Stir in cold water; chill until set partially. Carefully pour over the filling. Cover and chill for 4-6 hours, until firm.
- Slice into squares. Serve with additional whipped topping and strawberries if desired.

Nutrition Information

- Calories: 401 calories
- Sodium: 401mg sodium
- Fiber: 1g fiber)
- Total Carbohydrate: 48g carbohydrate (37g sugars
- Cholesterol: 50mg cholesterol
- Protein: 4g protein.
- Total Fat: 22g fat (14g saturated fat)

290. Pretzel Sparklers

Serving: about 2 dozen. | Prep: 30mins | Cook: 0mins | Ready in:

Ingredients

- 8 ounces white baking chocolate, chopped
- 1 package (10 ounces) pretzel rods
- Colored candy stars or sprinkles

Direction

- Microwave chocolate in a microwaveable bowl at 70% power for a minute and whisk. Heat for additional 10-20-second intervals while whisking until smooth.
- Plunge each pretzel rod halfway into chocolate; wait for excess to drip off. Sprinkle stars on top. Allow to dry on waxed paper.

Nutrition Information

- Calories: 105 calories
- Cholesterol: 1mg cholesterol
- Protein: 3g protein.
- Total Fat: 2g fat (1g saturated fat)
- Sodium: 311mg sodium
- Fiber: 1g fiber)
- Total Carbohydrate: 20g carbohydrate (2g sugars

291. Pretzel Topped Sugar Cookies

Serving: about 4-1/2 dozen. | Prep: 15mins | Cook: 15mins | Ready in:

Ingredients

- 2 tubes (18 ounces each) refrigerated sugar cookie dough
- 2-1/2 cups vanilla or white chips, divided
- 1 package (7-1/2 ounces) white fudge-covered pretzels

Direction

- Crush cookie dough into small pieces into a large mixing bowl; add 1 1/2 cups chips and mix well, drop mixture onto ungreased baking sheets by tablespoonfuls, separating mounds 2 inches apart.
- Bake cookies for 15 to 18 minutes at 325° until lightly browned. Instantly insert a pretzel into the center of each cookie. Transfer cookies to wire rack and allow to cool.
- Melt the rest of chips in a microwave oven; whisk until no lumps remain. Drizzle over cookies to garnish.

Nutrition Information

- Calories: 102 calories
- Cholesterol: 5mg cholesterol
- Protein: 1g protein.
- Total Fat: 5g fat (2g saturated fat)
- Sodium: 60mg sodium
- Fiber: 0 fiber)
- Total Carbohydrate: 13g carbohydrate (4g sugars

292. Puddin' Cones

Serving: 8 servings. | Prep: 15mins | Cook: 0mins | Ready in:

Ingredients

- 1-1/2 cups cold milk
- 1 package (3.4 ounces) instant vanilla pudding mix
- 3 envelopes whipped topping mix (Dream Whip)
- 8 cake ice cream cones (about 3 inches)
- Chopped nuts, jimmies and miniature colored-coated baking chips or topping of your choice

Direction

- Beat the pudding mix and milk in a big bowl for 2 minutes on low speed. Fold in whipped topping mix; cover and chill for a minimum of 1 hour. Scoop 1/4 cup of the mixture into each cone, then drizzle the toppings on top.

Nutrition Information

- Calories: 173 calories
- Fiber: 0 fiber)
- Total Carbohydrate: 28g carbohydrate (22g sugars
- Cholesterol: 6mg cholesterol
- Protein: 2g protein.
- Total Fat: 5g fat (4g saturated fat)
- Sodium: 198mg sodium

293. Pumpkin Chip Cream Pie

Serving: 8 servings. | Prep: 20mins | Cook: 0mins | Ready in:

Ingredients

- 3/4 cup cold 2% milk
- 1 package (3.4 ounces) instant vanilla pudding mix
- 2/3 cup miniature semisweet chocolate chips
- 1/2 cup canned pumpkin
- 3/4 teaspoon pumpkin pie spice
- 1 carton (8 ounces) frozen whipped topping, thawed, divided
- 1 graham cracker crust (9 inches)
- Slivered almonds and chocolate curls, optional

Direction

- Beat pudding mix and milk in a big bowl for 2 minutes, mixture will become thick. Mix in pie spice, pumpkin and chocolate chips. Fold in 2 cups of whipped topping. Scoop into crust. Chill for 4 hours till set.

- Scatter the rest of whipped topping over; jazz up with chocolate curls and almonds if wished.

Nutrition Information

- Calories: 315 calories
- Sodium: 305mg sodium
- Fiber: 2g fiber)
- Total Carbohydrate: 43g carbohydrate (32g sugars
- Cholesterol: 2mg cholesterol
- Protein: 3g protein.
- Total Fat: 15g fat (9g saturated fat)

294. Quick & Easy Chocolate Sauce

Serving: 2-1/4 cups. | Prep: 5mins | Cook: 10mins | Ready in:

Ingredients

- 12 ounces (2 cups) semisweet chocolate chips
- 1 cup heavy whipping cream
- 3/4 cup sugar

Direction

- Mix together all the ingredients in a small heavy saucepan. Put over medium heat to boil, whisking continuously. Boil mixture while stirring for 2 minutes.
- Keep refrigerated in a tightly sealed container to store. Lightly warm, then serve.

Nutrition Information

- Calories: 169 calories
- Total Carbohydrate: 21g carbohydrate (19g sugars
- Cholesterol: 18mg cholesterol
- Protein: 1g protein.
- Total Fat: 11g fat (6g saturated fat)
- Sodium: 7mg sodium
- Fiber: 1g fiber)

295. Quick Apple Crisp

Serving: 8 servings. | Prep: 30mins | Cook: 0mins | Ready in:

Ingredients

- 1 cup graham cracker crumbs (about 16 squares)
- 1/2 cup all-purpose flour
- 1/2 cup packed brown sugar
- 1 teaspoon ground cinnamon
- 1/2 teaspoon ground nutmeg
- 1/2 cup butter, melted
- 8 medium tart apples, peeled and sliced
- Whipped topping or ice cream

Direction

- Mix the butter, nutmeg, brown sugar, cinnamon, flour and cracker crumbs in a big bowl. Put apples in a greased microwaveable 2-1/2 quarts dish. Put crumb mixture on top.
- Microwave on high for 8-9 minutes, with no cover, or until apples are tender. Serve while warm with ice cream or whipped topping.

Nutrition Information

- Calories: 289 calories
- Total Fat: 13g fat (7g saturated fat)
- Sodium: 150mg sodium
- Fiber: 3g fiber)
- Total Carbohydrate: 44g carbohydrate (30g sugars
- Cholesterol: 30mg cholesterol
- Protein: 2g protein.

296. Quick Chocolate Chip Cheesecake

Serving: 8 servings. | Prep: 20mins | Cook: 0mins | Ready in:

Ingredients

- 3/4 cup all-purpose flour
- 3/4 cup graham cracker crumbs
- 6 tablespoons sugar
- 3 tablespoons baking cocoa
- 1/2 cup butter, melted
- FILLING:
- 1 package (8 ounces) cream cheese, softened
- 2 tablespoons sugar
- 2 tablespoons 2% milk
- 1 large egg, beaten
- 1/2 cup plus 2 tablespoons miniature semisweet chocolate chips, divided

Direction

- Prepare a large bowl and combine all your dry ingredients together - the cracker crumbs, flour, sugar, and cocoa; add butter and mix it in. Measure 3/4 cup of the mixture to be used for the topping later, set it aside. Grease a 9-in. microwave-safe pie plate and press onto it the remaining mixture. Without covering the pie plate, microwave on high temperature setting for 1-2 minutes or until the crust has set.
- For the cheesecake filling, combine cream cheese, sugar and milk together and beat until smooth. Add an egg and beat on low speed just until combined. Once egg has been incorporated, add 1/2 cup of chocolate chips. Spread cheese mixture evenly over the prepared pie crust. Sprinkle remaining chocolate chips and the crumb mixture that was reserved earlier.
- Still uncovered, microwave the cheesecake on high temperature for 3-4 minutes or an inserted thermometer in the center reads 160 degrees, the cheesecake is ready. Cool for 1 hour on a wire rack then refrigerate until chilled. For best result, take cheesecake out of the refrigerator and kept at room temperature for 10 minutes before cutting.

Nutrition Information

- Calories: 405 calories
- Protein: 6g protein.
- Total Fat: 27g fat (16g saturated fat)
- Sodium: 225mg sodium
- Fiber: 2g fiber)
- Total Carbohydrate: 38g carbohydrate (23g sugars
- Cholesterol: 88mg cholesterol

297. Quick Chocolate Chip Cookie Mix

Serving: about 6 dozen per batch. | Prep: 10mins | Cook: 10mins | Ready in:

Ingredients

- 4-1/2 cups all-purpose flour
- 1-1/2 cups sugar
- 1-1/2 cups packed brown sugar
- 2 teaspoons baking soda
- 1-1/2 teaspoons salt
- 2 cups shortening
- 2 cups chopped pecans
- 2 packages (12 ounces each) semisweet chocolate chips
- ADDITIONAL INGREDIENTS:
- 2 eggs
- 2 teaspoons vanilla extract

Direction

- Mix together the first 5 ingredients in a big bowl. Cut shortening into mixture until coarse and crumbly. Mix in chocolate chips and pecans. Keep in a tightly sealed container in a cool, dry place for up to 6 months. This recipe makes 2 batches of 14 cups in total.

- To make cookies: Beat vanilla and eggs in a mixing bowl. Mix in 7 cups cookie mix until fully incorporated (put in 1 to 2 tablespoons water if the dough is dry). Scoop by teaspoonfuls and place 2 in. apart onto greased baking sheets. Bake in 375-degree oven until the color turns golden brown, about 7 to 9 minutes. Allow to cool for 1 to 2 minutes then transfer to wire racks.

Nutrition Information

- Calories: 80 calories
- Protein: 1g protein.
- Total Fat: 5g fat (1g saturated fat)
- Sodium: 45mg sodium
- Fiber: 0 fiber)
- Total Carbohydrate: 9g carbohydrate (6g sugars
- Cholesterol: 6mg cholesterol

298. Quick Cookie Mix

Serving: 8 cups. | Prep: 10mins | Cook: 0mins | Ready in:

Ingredients

- 1-1/2 cups butter, softened
- 3 teaspoons salt
- 2 teaspoons baking powder
- 6 cups all-purpose flour

Direction

- Beat together baking powder, salt and butter in a big bowl until mixed. Put in flour slowly and blend just until crumbly. Keep in an airtight container in the fridge for a maximum of one month.
- Quick Cookie Mix may be used to prepare the following recipes: Apricot Thumbprints, Butter Almond Cookies, Peanut Butter Blossoms and Toffee Triangles.

Nutrition Information

- Calories: 40 calories
- Total Carbohydrate: 4g carbohydrate (0 sugars
- Cholesterol: 6mg cholesterol
- Protein: 1g protein.
- Total Fat: 2g fat (1g saturated fat)
- Sodium: 77mg sodium
- Fiber: 0 fiber)

299. Quick Cream Topped Grapes

Serving: 6 servings. | Prep: 10mins | Cook: 0mins | Ready in:

Ingredients

- 1 pound seedless grapes
- 1 cup sour cream
- 1/4 cup packed dark brown sugar

Direction

- Divide grapes into six cups for serving. Mix together brown sugar and sour cream until it smoothens. Put into refrigerator until it is ready for serving. Top over grapes.

Nutrition Information

- Calories: 168 calories
- Fiber: 1g fiber)
- Total Carbohydrate: 24g carbohydrate (23g sugars
- Cholesterol: 27mg cholesterol
- Protein: 2g protein.
- Total Fat: 7g fat (5g saturated fat)
- Sodium: 25mg sodium

300. Quick Frozen Fruit Fluff

Serving: 12-16 servings. | Prep: 10mins | Cook: 0mins | Ready in:

Ingredients

- 3 medium firm bananas, sliced
- 1 can (29 ounces) peach halves, drained and diced
- 1 can (21 ounces) cherry pie filling
- 1 can (14 ounces) sweetened condensed milk
- 1 carton (8 ounces) frozen whipped topping, thawed

Direction

- Mix together milk, pie filling, peaches and bananas in a big bowl, blending well. Fold in whipped toppings, then transfer the mixture into a 9"x13" dish. Place a cover and freeze about 8 hours to overnight. You can freeze it for a maximum of one month.

Nutrition Information

- Calories: 220 calories
- Sodium: 42mg sodium
- Fiber: 1g fiber)
- Total Carbohydrate: 42g carbohydrate (38g sugars
- Cholesterol: 8mg cholesterol
- Protein: 3g protein.
- Total Fat: 5g fat (4g saturated fat)

301. Quick Peanut Butter Squares

Serving: 16 squares. | Prep: 15mins | Cook: 0mins | Ready in:

Ingredients

- 3/4 cup peanut butter
- 1/2 cup packed brown sugar
- 1/2 cup corn syrup
- 1 tablespoon butter
- 1 teaspoon vanilla extract
- 2 cups cornflakes
- 1 cup crisp rice cereal
- 1-1/2 cups semisweet chocolate chips

Direction

- Mix butter, corn syrup, brown sugar and peanut butter in a microwavable bowl. Microwave on high setting without a cover until butter is melted, about 45 seconds. Stir in vanilla until blended. Put in cereal and blend well. Spread into a greased 8 inches square pan.
- Melt the chocolate chips in a microwavable bowl and stir until smooth. Spread over cereal mixture then chill until chocolate is set. Break into pieces.

Nutrition Information

- Calories: 221 calories
- Protein: 4g protein.
- Total Fat: 11g fat (4g saturated fat)
- Sodium: 108mg sodium
- Fiber: 2g fiber)
- Total Carbohydrate: 31g carbohydrate (19g sugars
- Cholesterol: 0 cholesterol

302. Raspberry Coconut Cream Pie

Serving: 8 servings. | Prep: 25mins | Cook: 0mins | Ready in:

Ingredients

- 1/3 cup white baking chips, melted
- One 9-inch graham cracker crust (about 6 ounces)
- 2 cups cold whole milk

- 2 packages (3.4 ounces each) instant vanilla pudding mix
- 1/2 cup sweetened shredded coconut
- 1 carton (8 ounces) frozen whipped topping, thawed, divided
- 1 cup fresh raspberries
- Additional coconut, toasted

Direction

- Spread over the bottom of the crust with the melted baking chips. Beat the pudding mixes and milk for 2 minutes (so that the mixture will become thick). Add 1/2 cup of coconut and stir; fold in 2 cups of the whipped topping.
- Spread into the crust with 1/2 of the mixture. Dust with raspberries. Spread over the raspberries with the rest of the pudding mixture. Place the rest of the whipped topping on top. Dust with the toasted coconut. Chill in the fridge for 3 hours until set.

Nutrition Information

- Calories: 388 calories
- Sodium: 322mg sodium
- Fiber: 2g fiber)
- Total Carbohydrate: 54g carbohydrate (46g sugars
- Cholesterol: 8mg cholesterol
- Protein: 4g protein.
- Total Fat: 17g fat (10g saturated fat)

303. Raspberry Cream

Serving: 2 servings. | Prep: 10mins | Cook: 0mins | Ready in:

Ingredients

- 1 package (3 ounces) raspberry gelatin
- 1/2 cup boiling water
- 1 package (10 ounces) frozen sweetened raspberries
- 1 cup vanilla ice cream, softened
- Whipped cream

Direction

- Dissolve the gelatin in a bowl with boiling water, then stir in ice cream and raspberries until mixed. Scoop into 2 dessert dishes then cover and chill for a minimum of an hour. Use whipped cream to decorate.

Nutrition Information

- Calories: 433 calories
- Fiber: 6g fiber)
- Total Carbohydrate: 89g carbohydrate (79g sugars
- Cholesterol: 29mg cholesterol
- Protein: 7g protein.
- Total Fat: 7g fat (4g saturated fat)
- Sodium: 151mg sodium

304. Raspberry Icebox Dessert

Serving: 12-15 servings. | Prep: 20mins | Cook: 0mins | Ready in:

Ingredients

- 2 packages (3 ounces each) raspberry gelatin
- 2 cups boiling water
- 3 cups fresh or frozen raspberries
- 2 cups graham cracker crumbs (about 32 squares)
- 1/4 cup packed brown sugar
- 1/2 cup butter, melted
- 1-1/2 cups cold milk
- 1 package (3.4 ounces) instant vanilla pudding mix
- 1 package (8 ounces) cream cheese, softened

Direction

- Mix water and gelatin in a large bowl; mix till the gelatin is dissolved. Stir in raspberries. Place in the refrigerator till syrupy, 1 hour.
- Combine butter, brown sugar and cracker crumbs together in a small bowl. Press into a 13x9-in. dish coated with grease.
- Whisk pudding mix and milk in a large bowl for 2 minutes. Allow to sit till soft-set, 2 minutes.
- Beat cream cheese in another bowl, till smooth. Slowly put in pudding. Spread over the crust. Transfer the gelatin mixture on top. Keep chilled till set. Place any leftovers in the refrigerator.

Nutrition Information

- Calories: 239 calories
- Sodium: 291mg sodium
- Fiber: 2g fiber)
- Total Carbohydrate: 27g carbohydrate (18g sugars
- Cholesterol: 36mg cholesterol
- Protein: 4g protein.
- Total Fat: 13g fat (8g saturated fat)

305. Raspberry Oatmeal Bars

Serving: 24 | Prep: 15mins | Cook: 23mins | Ready in:

Ingredients

- 1 (18.25 ounce) package yellow cake mix
- 2 1/2 cups quick cooking oats
- 3/4 cup margarine, melted
- 1 cup raspberry jam
- 1 tablespoon water

Direction

- Set oven to 375°F (190°C) to preheat. Grease a 9x13 inch pan.
- Stir together melted margarine, cake mix, and oats in a big bowl until it forms a nice lumpy dough and there are no dry ingredients left. Push half of the oat's mixture evenly into the bottom of the greased pan. Stir jam and water in another bowl, smear evenly onto the crust. Scatter the leftover oat mixture on the top evenly.
- Bake in the heated oven until the top is lightly brown, or for 18 to 23 minutes. Let rest to cool before slicing into bars.

Nutrition Information

- Calories: 210 calories;
- Total Fat: 8.7
- Sodium: 208
- Total Carbohydrate: 31.8
- Cholesterol: < 1
- Protein: 2.1

306. Raspberry Rice Pudding

Serving: 4 servings. | Prep: 15mins | Cook: 0mins | Ready in:

Ingredients

- 1-1/2 cups heavy whipping cream
- 1/4 cup sugar
- 3/4 teaspoon vanilla extract
- 1-1/2 cups cold cooked rice
- 1/3 cup seedless raspberry jam
- 4 drops red food coloring, optional
- 1 cup fresh raspberries

Direction

- Beat together vanilla, sugar and cream in a bowl until soft peaks form. Stir in jam, food coloring, if wanted, and rice, then scoop the mixture into serving dishes. Use raspberries to decorate.

Nutrition Information

- Calories: 517 calories
- Total Fat: 33g fat (21g saturated fat)
- Sodium: 35mg sodium
- Fiber: 2g fiber)
- Total Carbohydrate: 53g carbohydrate (32g sugars
- Cholesterol: 122mg cholesterol
- Protein: 4g protein.

307. Raspberry Sorbet

Serving: 8 | Prep: | Cook: 15mins | Ready in:

Ingredients

- ¾ cups water
- 1¾ cups sugar
- 3 tablespoons lemon juice
- 1½ tablespoons crème de cassis
- 3 pints red raspberries

Direction

- In a medium saucepan, mix together sugar and water and heat until water starts to boil. Stir constantly until sugar is dissolved. Leave it boiling for 2 minutes then take pan off heat. Add in crème de cassis and lemon juice. Pour mixture to a medium bowl and let it completely cool.
- Put raspberries in a food processor and process until pureed. Pour into the sugar syrup bowl through a fine-meshed sieve to strain. Refrigerate sorbet mixture to chill then transfer to an ice cream maker and process according to manufacturing instructions. An alternate way is to pour mixture in an ice cube tray or shallow metal cake pan and freeze until firm. Crush into pieces and put in a food processor to process. Move sorbet into a freezer container for at least an hour or until frozen through.

Nutrition Information

- Calories: 232 calories;
- Fiber: 6
- Cholesterol: 0
- Total Fat: 1
- Saturated Fat: 0
- Total Carbohydrate: 57
- Sugar: 50
- Protein: 1
- Sodium: 3

308. Raspberry Sundaes

Serving: 1-1/2 cups sauce. | Prep: 20mins | Cook: 0mins | Ready in:

Ingredients

- 2 packages (10 ounces each) frozen sweetened raspberries, thawed
- 2 tablespoons cornstarch
- 1/2 teaspoon almond extract
- Vanilla ice cream

Direction

- Drain raspberries, keeping the juice; put berries aside. Combine 2 tablespoons of juice and cornstarch until smooth in a bowl. Bring the reserved juice and raspberries to a boil in a saucepan; stir in the cornstarch mixture. Cook for 1 to 2 minutes, or until the sauce thickened. Take away from the heat; stir in the almond extract. Allow to cool. Put over ice cream to serve.

Nutrition Information

- Calories: 30 calories
- Protein: 0 protein.
- Total Fat: 0 fat (0 saturated fat)
- Sodium: 0 sodium
- Fiber: 1g fiber)
- Total Carbohydrate: 7g carbohydrate (5g sugars

- Cholesterol: 0 cholesterol

309. Refreshing Strawberry Pie

Serving: 6-8 servings. | Prep: 30mins | Cook: 0mins | Ready in:

Ingredients

- 1 unbaked pastry shell (9 inches)
- 3/4 cup sugar
- 2 tablespoons cornstarch
- 1 cup water
- 1 package (3 ounces) strawberry gelatin
- 4 cups sliced fresh strawberries
- Fresh mint, optional

Direction

- Using a double thickness of heavy-duty foil, line an unpricked pastry shell. Bake for 8 minutes at 450°. Take the foil away; bake for 5 more minutes. Place on a wire rack to cool.
- Mix water, cornstarch and sugar in a small saucepan till smooth. Boil the mixture; cook while stirring till thickened, or for 2 minutes. Take away from the heat; mix in gelatin till dissolved. Place in the refrigerator till slightly cooled, or for 15-20 minutes.
- Meanwhile, spread strawberries into the crust. Transfer over the berries with the gelatin mixture. Keep in the refrigerator till set. Use mint for garnish if you want.

Nutrition Information

- Calories: 264 calories
- Sodium: 125mg sodium
- Fiber: 2g fiber)
- Total Carbohydrate: 49g carbohydrate (32g sugars
- Cholesterol: 5mg cholesterol
- Protein: 2g protein.
- Total Fat: 7g fat (3g saturated fat)

310. Refrigerator Lime Cheesecake

Serving: 12 servings. | Prep: 25mins | Cook: 5mins | Ready in:

Ingredients

- 32 soft ladyfingers, split
- 1 envelope unflavored gelatin
- 1/4 cup lime juice, chilled
- 2 packages (8 ounces each) cream cheese, softened
- 1 cup sugar
- 6 ounces white baking chocolate, melted and cooled
- 2 teaspoons grated lime zest
- 1 cup heavy whipping cream, whipped
- Fresh strawberry and lime slices, optional

Direction

- Organize 20 split ladyfingers around the edges then 12 split ladyfingers on the bottom of an 8-inch ungreased springform pan; put aside. Dust the gelatin on the cold lime juice in a small saucepan; allow to stand for a minute. Heat over low heat, mixing until gelatin is entirely dissolved; cool.
- In the meantime, beat the sugar and cream cheese until smooth. Beat in the gelatin mixture, lime zest and melted chocolate gradually. Fold in the whipped cream. Pour into the prepared pan. Cover then refrigerate for 3 hours, until set. Discard the pan sides. Serve with lime slices and strawberry if desired.

Nutrition Information

- Calories: 408 calories
- Protein: 6g protein.
- Total Fat: 25g fat (16g saturated fat)

- Sodium: 267mg sodium
- Fiber: 0 fiber)
- Total Carbohydrate: 42g carbohydrate (35g sugars
- Cholesterol: 100mg cholesterol

311. Rhubarb Ice Cream

Serving: about 2 quarts. | Prep: 15mins | Cook: 10mins | Ready in:

Ingredients

- 4 cups sliced rhubarb
- 2 cups sugar
- 2 cups water
- 3 cups miniature marshmallows
- 3 tablespoons lemon juice
- 5 to 7 drops red food coloring, optional
- 2 cups heavy whipping cream, whipped

Direction

- Boil water, sugar and rhubarb in a big saucepan. Lower heat; cover. Simmer till rhubarb is soft or for 10-12 minutes.
- Mix in food coloring (optional), lemon juice and marshmallows; cook and mix till marshmallows melt. Cover; refrigerate it for 1 hour.
- Fold in the whipped cream. Put into freezer container; cover. Freeze for a maximum of 2 months. 20 minutes before serving, remove from freezer.

Nutrition Information

- Calories: 236 calories
- Protein: 1g protein.
- Total Fat: 11g fat (7g saturated fat)
- Sodium: 17mg sodium
- Fiber: 1g fiber)
- Total Carbohydrate: 35g carbohydrate (31g sugars
- Cholesterol: 41mg cholesterol

312. Rhubarb Sundaes

Serving: 1 cup. | Prep: 5mins | Cook: 10mins | Ready in:

Ingredients

- 2 cups chopped fresh or frozen rhubarb
- 1/3 cup sugar
- 1/4 cup water
- 1/4 teaspoon ground cinnamon
- 1/2 teaspoon honey
- Vanilla ice cream
- Chopped walnuts, optional

Direction

- Bring cinnamon, water, sugar and rhubarb in a small saucepan to a boil. Lower heat and simmer without a cover until rhubarb is soft and the sauce obtains desired consistency, about 8 to 10 minutes. Take away from the heat and stir in honey. Serve over ice cream while still warm. Use walnuts to sprinkle over if you want.

Nutrition Information

- Calories: 80 calories
- Total Carbohydrate: 20g carbohydrate (18g sugars
- Cholesterol: 0 cholesterol
- Protein: 1g protein.
- Total Fat: 0 fat (0 saturated fat)
- Sodium: 3mg sodium
- Fiber: 1g fiber)

313. Rocky Road Freezer Pie

Serving: 16 servings. | Prep: 15mins | Cook: 0mins | Ready in:

Ingredients

- 1-1/2 cups half-and-half cream
- 1 package (3.9 ounces) instant chocolate pudding mix
- 1 carton (8 ounces) frozen whipped topping, thawed
- 1/3 cup semisweet chocolate chips
- 1/3 cup miniature marshmallows
- 1/3 cup chopped pecans
- 1 graham cracker crust (9 inches)
- Miniature marshmallows, chopped pecans and chocolate sauce, optional

Direction

- Beat pudding mix and cream in a big bowl for 2 minutes. Fold whipped topping into the mixture. Mix in pecans, marshmallows and chocolate chips. Pour into the pie shell. Put in the freezer for 6 hours until firm. Take out of the freezer for 10 minutes then serve.

Nutrition Information

- Calories: 184 calories
- Total Fat: 10g fat (5g saturated fat)
- Sodium: 175mg sodium
- Fiber: 1g fiber)
- Total Carbohydrate: 20g carbohydrate (15g sugars
- Cholesterol: 11mg cholesterol
- Protein: 2g protein.

314. Rocky Road Fudge Pops

Serving: 12 servings. | Prep: 10mins | Cook: 10mins | Ready in:

Ingredients

- 2-1/2 cups 2% milk
- 1 package (3.4 ounces) cook-and-serve chocolate pudding mix
- 1/2 cup chopped peanuts
- 1/2 cup miniature semisweet chocolate chips
- 12 disposable plastic cups (3 ounces each)
- 1/2 cup marshmallow creme
- 12 wooden pop sticks

Direction

- Whisk pudding mix and milk in a big microwave-safe bowl. Microwave on high, uncovered, until slightly thick and bubbly, or for 4-6 minutes, mixing every 2 minutes. Cool, mixing a few times, for 20 minutes.
- Meanwhile, mix chocolate chips and peanuts; distribute to plastic cups. Mix marshmallow crème into pudding then spoon into cups. Put wooden pop sticks in; freeze.

Nutrition Information

- Calories: 140 calories
- Sodium: 64mg sodium
- Fiber: 1g fiber)
- Total Carbohydrate: 18g carbohydrate (14g sugars
- Cholesterol: 7mg cholesterol
- Protein: 4g protein.
- Total Fat: 7g fat (3g saturated fat)

315. Rocky Toffee Fudge

Serving: 2-1/2 pounds. | Prep: 5mins | Cook: 5mins | Ready in:

Ingredients

- 1 teaspoon butter
- 1 can (14 ounces) sweetened condensed milk
- 2 cups (12 ounces) dark chocolate chips
- 1 cup (6 ounces) semisweet chocolate chips
- 1 cup miniature marshmallows
- 1/2 cup milk chocolate English toffee bits
- 1/3 cup Kahlua (coffee liqueur)

Direction

- Use foil to line a 9-inch square baking pan. Use butter to grease the foil; put aside.
- Mix the chips and milk in a big microwave-safe bowl. Microwave, uncovered, on high setting for 60 seconds; whisk. Cook till the chips melt or for 30 to 60 seconds more, whisking every 30 seconds. Whisk in Kahlua, toffee bits and marshmallows.
- Move into the prepped pan. Keep covered and refrigerated till firm or for 2 hours. Lift the fudge from pan using the foil. Lightly peel off the foil; chop the fudge into 1-inch square pieces. Keep stored in an airtight container.

Nutrition Information

- Calories:
- Sodium:
- Fiber:
- Total Carbohydrate:
- Cholesterol:
- Protein:
- Total Fat:

316. S'more Parfaits

Serving: 4 servings. | Prep: 10mins | Cook: 0mins | Ready in:

Ingredients

- 2 cups cold milk
- 1 package (3.9 ounces) instant chocolate fudge or chocolate pudding mix
- 2 cups coarsely crushed graham crackers (about 24 squares)
- 1 cup miniature marshmallows
- 4 tablespoons miniature semisweet chocolate chips

Direction

- Beat pudding mix and milk in a bowl for 2 minutes. Allow it to stand for 2 minutes or until soft-set.
- Into four parfait glasses, put 3 tablespoons each of the pudding mixture. Then layer each with 1/4 cup cracker crumbs, then 3 tablespoons pudding, 1/4 cup marshmallows and 1 tablespoon chocolate chips. Put the remaining pudding and crumbs on top. Keep for 1 hour in the refrigerator prior to serving.

Nutrition Information

- Calories: 218 calories
- Protein: 6g protein. Diabetic Exchanges: 2-1/2 starch
- Total Fat: 5g fat (2g saturated fat)
- Sodium: 361mg sodium
- Fiber: 2g fiber)
- Total Carbohydrate: 40g carbohydrate (0 sugars
- Cholesterol: 3mg cholesterol

317. Seven Layer Cake

Serving: 10-12 servings. | Prep: 25mins | Cook: 0mins | Ready in:

Ingredients

- 4 cups graham cracker crumbs (about 32 squares)
- 1/2 cup sugar
- 1/2 cup butter, melted
- 1 pint vanilla ice cream, softened
- 1 pint chocolate ice cream, softened
- 1 pint strawberry ice cream, softened

Direction

- Use heavy-duty aluminum foil to line the bottom and sides of a 9"x5" loaf pan. Mix together butter, sugar and graham cracker crumbs, then press into the pan with 1/4 of the mixture. Freeze about 15 minutes.
- Spread over crumbs with vanilla ice cream, then use another 1/4 of crumbs to sprinkle

over and press down gently. Freeze until firm, about 45 to 60 minutes.

- Use chocolate ice cream to spread over, then sprinkle with another 1/4 of the crumbs and press down gently. Freeze until firm. Use strawberry ice cream to spread over and put leftover crumbs on top. At last, the pan will become very full. Place a cover and freeze for several hours to overnight. You can freeze for a maximum of 2 months.
- Take out of the freezer about 10 minutes before serving. Lift cake from pan using the foil, then get rid of foil. Use a serrated knife to slice cake.

Nutrition Information

- Calories: 352 calories
- Sodium: 294mg sodium
- Fiber: 1g fiber)
- Total Carbohydrate: 47g carbohydrate (23g sugars
- Cholesterol: 44mg cholesterol
- Protein: 4g protein.
- Total Fat: 17g fat (9g saturated fat)

318. Shortcake Squares

Serving: 9 servings. | Prep: 10mins | Cook: 20mins | Ready in:

Ingredients

- 2 cups all-purpose flour
- 1 tablespoon baking powder
- 1 tablespoon sugar
- 1/2 teaspoon salt
- 1/3 cup shortening
- 1 egg
- 1/2 cup milk
- 2 tablespoons butter, softened
- Sweetened raspberries or fruit of your choice
- Whipped cream

Direction

- Mix salt, sugar, baking powder and flour in a bowl; cut shortening in till mixture is similar to coarse crumbs. Beat milk and egg in a bowl till well incorporated; put to dry ingredients. Mix using a fork till moistened. Pat into a square 9-inch greased baking pan. Allow to bake for 18 to 20 minutes at 375° till golden brown. Let cool on a wire rack. Slice into squares. Halve every square horizontally and butter cut sides. Put whipped cream and berries on top.

Nutrition Information

- Calories: 211 calories
- Protein: 4g protein.
- Total Fat: 11g fat (4g saturated fat)
- Sodium: 304mg sodium
- Fiber: 1g fiber)
- Total Carbohydrate: 23g carbohydrate (3g sugars
- Cholesterol: 32mg cholesterol

319. Shortcut Shortcake

Serving: 12-15 servings. | Prep: 20mins | Cook: 0mins | Ready in:

Ingredients

- 2 cups cold milk
- 1 package (5.1 ounces) instant vanilla pudding mix
- 1 package (15 ounces) cream-filled sponge cakes
- 4 cups sliced fresh strawberries
- 1 carton (8 ounces) frozen whipped topping, thawed
- Additional strawberries, halved, optional

Direction

- Beat pudding mix and milk in a big bowl for 2 minutes. Allow to stand for 2 minutes till soft-set; reserve. Halve sponge cakes lengthwise; in a 13x9-inch ungreased dish, put filling side facing up. Scatter pudding over top.
- Set sliced strawberries on top of pudding. Scatter whipped topping on top of berries. Put cover and chill for a minimum of an hour prior slicing. Jazz up with strawberry halves if wished. Chill the rest.

Nutrition Information

- Calories: 215 calories
- Protein: 2g protein.
- Total Fat: 7g fat (4g saturated fat)
- Sodium: 256mg sodium
- Fiber: 1g fiber)
- Total Carbohydrate: 35g carbohydrate (30g sugars
- Cholesterol: 9mg cholesterol

320. Slow Cooker Fruit Compote

Serving: 18 servings. | Prep: 10mins | Cook: 02hours00mins | Ready in:

Ingredients

- 2 cans (29 ounces each) sliced peaches, drained
- 2 cans (29 ounces each) pear halves, drained and sliced
- 1 can (20 ounces) pineapple chunks, drained
- 1 can (15-1/4 ounces) apricot halves, drained and sliced
- 1 can (21 ounces) cherry pie filling

Direction

- In a 5-qt. slow cooker, mix apricots, pineapple, pears and peaches. Use pie filling to put on top. Cook with a cover on high till heated through, or for 2 hours. Serve with a slotted spoon.

Nutrition Information

- Calories: 190 calories
- Protein: 1g protein.
- Total Fat: 0 fat (0 saturated fat)
- Sodium: 18mg sodium
- Fiber: 3g fiber)
- Total Carbohydrate: 48g carbohydrate (34g sugars
- Cholesterol: 0 cholesterol

321. Snack Attack Fudge

Serving: about 2-1/2 pounds. | Prep: 5mins | Cook: 5mins | Ready in:

Ingredients

- 1 teaspoon butter
- 1 can (14 ounces) sweetened condensed milk
- 2 cups (12 ounces) milk chocolate chips
- 1 cup (6 ounces) semisweet chocolate chips
- 1 cup miniature pretzels, coarsley crushed
- 1/2 cup crushed ridged potato chips
- 1/2 cup Beer Nuts
- 1 teaspoon vanilla extract

Direction

- Line foil over a 9-inch square pan. Butter the foil; put to one side.
- In a large microwaveable bowl, combine chocolate chips and milk. Microwave without covering for 1 minute on high power; stir well. Cook until chocolate chips are melted, for 30 seconds to 1 minute longer, stirring every 30 seconds. Mix in vanilla, Beer Nuts, potato chips and pretzels.
- Pour into the prepared pan. Chill, covered until set, for 2 hours. Remove fudge from the pan using foil. Carefully take off the foil.

Divide fudge into squares, about 1 inch. Preserve in an airtight container.

Nutrition Information

- Calories:
- Protein:
- Total Fat:
- Sodium:
- Fiber:
- Total Carbohydrate:
- Cholesterol:

322. Snickers Cookies

Serving: about 2 dozen. | Prep: 10mins | Cook: 10mins | Ready in:

Ingredients

- 1 tube refrigerated chocolate chip cookie dough
- 24 to 28 miniature Snickers candy bars

Direction

- Cut dough into slices with a thickness of 1/4 inch, then arrange on each slice with a candy bar and wrap the dough around it. Put on grease-free baking sheets with 2 inches apart. Bake at 350 degrees until browned slightly, about 8 to 10 minutes. Transfer to wire racks to cool.

Nutrition Information

- Calories: 123 calories
- Protein: 2g protein.
- Total Fat: 5g fat (2g saturated fat)
- Sodium: 59mg sodium
- Fiber: 0 fiber)
- Total Carbohydrate: 17g carbohydrate (4g sugars
- Cholesterol: 6mg cholesterol

323. Snowman Cutouts

Serving: 2 snowmen. | Prep: 35mins | Cook: 10mins | Ready in:

Ingredients

- 1 tube (16-1/2 ounces) refrigerated sugar cookie dough
- 1/2 cup all-purpose flour
- 1/2 teaspoon almond extract
- 1 can (16 ounces) vanilla frosting
- Food coloring of your choice

Direction

- Allow the dough to sit for 5-10 minutes at room temperature until tender. Whisk extract, flour, and cookie dough together in a small bowl until blended.
- Roll the dough out on a lightly floured surface until the thickness is 1/4-inch. Cut out 2 circles with a floured 4 1/2-inch round cookie cutter. Continue with 3-inch and 3 1/2-inch round cookie cutters. Cut out two 2 1/4-inch carrots, four 1 3/4-inch mittens, and six 1-inch circles.
- On waxed paper, draw a pipe with 1 3/4-inch height and 3 1/4-inch width and a top hat with 2 1/2-inch height and 3 1/2-inch width; cut out. If needed, roll the dough scraps again. Cut out 2 pipes and 2 hats with patterns.
- Remove the pieces to oil-coated cookie sheets. Bake at 350° until turning light brown around the edges, 6-11 minutes. Transfer to wire racks to fully cool.
- Tint the frosting as you like; frost onto the cookie pieces. Allow to sit until set. Put in an airtight container to store.

Nutrition Information

- Calories: 183 calories
- Total Fat: 8g fat (2g saturated fat)
- Sodium: 91mg sodium

- Fiber: 0 fiber)
- Total Carbohydrate: 26g carbohydrate (18g sugars
- Cholesterol: 0 cholesterol
- Protein: 1g protein.

324. Snowshoe Cookies

Serving: 6 servings. | Prep: 20mins | Cook: 0mins | Ready in:

Ingredients

- 12 Nutter Butter peanut butter sandwich cookies
- 1/3 cup semisweet chocolate chips, melted
- 12 miniature marshmallows
- 12 pretzel sticks

Direction

- Arrange the cookies on wire rack on top of a big waxed paper piece. Drizzle cookies with chocolate in crisscross design to make snowshoes. Rest till chocolate hardens. Thread one marshmallow on an end of every stick of pretzel for ski poles. Serve a pair of snowshoes and a set of poles together.

Nutrition Information

- Calories: 191 calories
- Total Fat: 7g fat (2g saturated fat)
- Sodium: 521mg sodium
- Fiber: 2g fiber)
- Total Carbohydrate: 30g carbohydrate (8g sugars
- Cholesterol: 0 cholesterol
- Protein: 4g protein.

325. Snowy Cherry Trifles

Serving: 4 servings. | Prep: 15mins | Cook: 0mins | Ready in:

Ingredients

- 4 ounces cream cheese, softened
- 1/4 cup sugar
- 2 tablespoons milk
- 1-3/4 cups whipped topping
- 4 cups cubed angel food cake
- 1 cup cherry pie filling
- 1/4 teaspoon almond extract

Direction

- Beat sugar and cream cheese till fluffy in a big bowl. Add milk; beat till smooth. Fold cake cubes and whipped topping in.
- Put in solo serving dishes. Mix almond extract and pie filling; put on cake mixture. Refrigerate till serving.

Nutrition Information

- Calories: 432 calories
- Cholesterol: 32mg cholesterol
- Protein: 5g protein.
- Total Fat: 16g fat (12g saturated fat)
- Sodium: 433mg sodium
- Fiber: 1g fiber)
- Total Carbohydrate: 65g carbohydrate (53g sugars

326. Soft Raisin Cookies

Serving: 2 dozen. | Prep: 10mins | Cook: 10mins | Ready in:

Ingredients

- 1 package (9 ounces) yellow cake mix
- 1 cup quick-cooking oats
- 6 tablespoons unsweetened applesauce

- 1/4 cup egg substitute
- 2 tablespoons butter, melted
- 1/2 teaspoon apple pie spice
- 1/2 cup raisins

Direction

- Beat together the first six ingredients in a large bowl; beat till incorporated. Stir raisins into the mix.
- Drop tablespoonfuls of the mixture 2 in. apart onto baking sheets sprayed using cooking spray. Bake till the edges are lightly browned at 375° for about 10-12 minutes. Let it cool down for about 5 minutes, then take out to wire racks to cool thoroughly.

Nutrition Information

- Calories: 126 calories
- Protein: 2g protein. Diabetic Exchanges: 1-1/2 starch
- Total Fat: 3g fat (0 saturated fat)
- Sodium: 166mg sodium
- Fiber: 0 fiber)
- Total Carbohydrate: 22g carbohydrate (0 sugars
- Cholesterol: 0 cholesterol

327. Spiced Rum Nut Brittle

Serving: about 1 pound. | Prep: 25mins | Cook: 0mins | Ready in:

Ingredients

- 1 cup sugar
- 1/2 cup light corn syrup
- 1/2 cup chopped cashews
- 1/2 cup chopped pecans
- 1 teaspoon butter
- 1/2 teaspoon ground cinnamon
- 1/4 teaspoon cayenne pepper
- 1/8 teaspoon salt
- Pinch ground nutmeg
- 1 teaspoon baking soda
- 1/2 teaspoon rum extract
- 1/2 teaspoon vanilla extract

Direction

- Grease a 15x10x1-inch0 pan with butter; put aside.
- Mix together the sugar and corn syrup in a 2-quart microwave-safe bowl. Microwave on high, with no cover, for 3 minutes; stir. Microwave for another 2-1/2 minutes. Stir the nutmeg, pecans, butter, cinnamon, cayenne, salt and cashews into the mixture.
- Microwave on high, with no cover, until mixture has a light amber color, for about 2 minutes (the mixture will get very hot). Stir baking soda and extracts quickly into the mixture till foamy and light. Pour into the prepared pan right away; use a metal spatula to spread the mixture. Let it cool down fully. Crack into pieces. For storage, keep in an airtight container.

Nutrition Information

- Calories: 263 calories
- Protein: 2g protein.
- Total Fat: 9g fat (2g saturated fat)
- Sodium: 267mg sodium
- Fiber: 1g fiber)
- Total Carbohydrate: 46g carbohydrate (43g sugars
- Cholesterol: 1mg cholesterol

328. Spiderweb Cheesecake

Serving: 6-8 servings. | Prep: 30mins | Cook: 0mins | Ready in:

Ingredients

- 1 envelope unflavored gelatin
- 1/4 cup cold water

- 2 packages (8 ounces each) cream cheese, softened
- 1/2 cup sugar
- 1/2 cup heavy whipping cream
- 1 teaspoon vanilla extract
- 1 chocolate crumb crust (8 or 9 inches)
- 2 tablespoons semisweet chocolate chips
- 1 tablespoon butter

Direction

- Add gelatin over water in a small saucepan and let it rest for about 60 seconds. Heat the gelatin and mix until its completely melted. Take off heat and let it cool a little. Mix in a bowl sugar and cream cheese until turns smooth. Slowly add vanilla, cream and the gelatin mixture, and blend it until smooth. Gently pour it over the crust.
- Dissolve the butter and chocolate chips in a microwave; stir it until smooth. Place it into a heavy-duty zip lock bag and cut a tiny hole in its corner. On the center of the cheesecake, draw a circle of chocolate and pipe evenly a 1/2-in. apart thin concentric circles over the filling. Starting from the center, slowly pull a toothpick through the circles toward the outer edge and then clean the toothpick. Repeat the steps to make a web pattern. Seal it with a cover before placing it in the refrigerator for 2 or more hours before slicing it.

Nutrition Information

- Calories:
- Sodium:
- Fiber:
- Total Carbohydrate:
- Cholesterol:
- Protein:
- Total Fat:

329. Strawberries With Chocolate Cream Filling

Serving: 3 dozen. | Prep: 30mins | Cook: 0mins | Ready in:

Ingredients

- 1-1/2 ounces semisweet chocolate, grated, divided
- 1 package (8 ounces) cream cheese, softened
- 1 teaspoon vanilla extract
- 1 cup whipped topping
- 18 large fresh strawberries, halved

Direction

- Set 2 tablespoons of chocolate aside for later. Melt the rest of the chocolate in a microwave; stir chocolate until consistency is smooth. Allow chocolate to cool.
- Beat vanilla and cream cheese together in a small bowl until consistency is smooth. Add the melted chocolate and continue to beat. Add 1 tablespoon of grated chocolate and whipped toppings; fold. Snip a hole on the edge of a food-safe plastic bag or the tip of a pastry bag. Insert the #21-star pastry tip to the pastry bag. Transfer the cream cheese mixture into the bag.
- Arrange the strawberries cut side up on a serving platter. Pipe the mixture on the strawberries and sprinkle reserved grated chocolate. Leftovers can be refrigerated.

Nutrition Information

- Calories:
- Sodium:
- Fiber:
- Total Carbohydrate:
- Cholesterol:
- Protein:
- Total Fat:

330. Strawberry Cheesecake Pops

Serving: 9 pops. | Prep: 15mins | Cook: 0mins | Ready in:

Ingredients

- 2 cups 2% milk
- 1/2 cup heavy whipping cream
- 1 package (3.4 ounces) instant cheesecake or vanilla pudding mix
- 2 tablespoons strawberry drink mix
- 1 cup chopped fresh strawberries
- Fresh mint leaves and quartered fresh strawberries
- 9 Popsicle sticks

Direction

- In a blender, process drink mix, pudding mix, cream and milk, covered until blended. Let stand till soft-set or for 5 minutes; mix strawberries in.
- In a muffin pan, put foil-lined muffin cups. Fill every liner using 1/3 cup strawberry mixture. Use a strawberry and mint leaves to garnish. Use foil to cover pan. Insert sticks in the center of every cup; freeze. Peel liners off; serve.

Nutrition Information

- Calories: 120 calories
- Sodium: 184mg sodium
- Fiber: 0 fiber)
- Total Carbohydrate: 15g carbohydrate (12g sugars
- Cholesterol: 23mg cholesterol
- Protein: 2g protein.
- Total Fat: 6g fat (4g saturated fat)

331. Strawberry Dream Pie

Serving: 8 | Prep: 15mins | Cook: | Ready in:

Ingredients

- 1 (8 ounce) package cream cheese, softened
- 1/3 cup strawberry preserves
- 1 1/2 cups frozen whipped topping, thawed
- 1 (9 inch) prepared graham cracker crust
- 1 cup fresh strawberries
- 2 teaspoons white sugar
- 2 teaspoons grenadine syrup

Direction

- Combine strawberry preserves and cream cheese in a bowl. Fold in the whipped topping. Transfer the mixture into the prepared pie crust then set aside.
- Put grenadine syrup, sugar, and strawberries in a food processor or blender then turn the machine on to blend till slightly chunky. Spread on the cream cheese mixture. Put in the fridge for at least 2 hours to allow the mixture to chill before serving time.

Nutrition Information

- Calories: 340 calories;
- Total Fat: 20.8
- Sodium: 258
- Total Carbohydrate: 36.3
- Cholesterol: 31
- Protein: 3.7

332. Strawberry Lemon Trifle

Serving: 14 servings. | Prep: 20mins | Cook: 0mins | Ready in:

Ingredients

- 4 ounces fat-free cream cheese, softened
- 1 cup fat-free vanilla yogurt
- 2 cups fat-free milk
- 1 package (3.4 ounces) instant lemon pudding mix
- 2 teaspoons grated lemon zest

- 2-1/2 cups sliced fresh strawberries, divided
- 1 tablespoon white grape juice or water
- 1 prepared angel food cake (8 to 10 ounces)

Direction

- Beat yogurt and cream cheese in big bowl. Add lemon zest, dry pudding mix and milk; beat till smooth. Process grape juice and 1/2 cup strawberries till blended in blender.
- Tear cake to 1-in. cubes; put 1/3 in 3-qt. serving bowl/trifle bowl. Put 1/3 pudding mixture then 1/2 leftover strawberries over. Drizzle 1/2 strawberry sauce; repeat. Put leftover cake then pudding mixture over. Cover; refrigerate for a minimum of 2 hours.

Nutrition Information

- Calories: 0g saturated fat (0 sugars
- Cholesterol: 1/2 fruit.
- Total Fat: 0 fiber). Diabetic Exchanges: 2 starch

333. Strawberry Pound Cake Dessert

Serving: 4 servings. | Prep: 10mins | Cook: 0mins | Ready in:

Ingredients

- 1 loaf (10-3/4 ounces) frozen pound cake, thawed
- 2 containers (16 ounces each) frozen sweetened sliced strawberries, thawed and drained
- 1-1/2 cups whipped topping

Direction

- Cut cake to eight pieces. Prepare four serving plates and put one cake slice on each. Decorate with a half cup of strawberries, three tablespoons of whipped cream and add leftover slice of cake on each plate. Serve with whipped cream and the rest of the strawberries.

Nutrition Information

- Calories: 580 calories
- Cholesterol: 109mg cholesterol
- Protein: 6g protein.
- Total Fat: 18g fat (11g saturated fat)
- Sodium: 284mg sodium
- Fiber: 5g fiber)
- Total Carbohydrate: 103g carbohydrate (78g sugars

334. Strawberry Shortcake Ice Cream

Serving: 5 servings. | Prep: 10mins | Cook: 0mins | Ready in:

Ingredients

- 1 pint strawberry ice cream, softened
- 1/2 cup sliced fresh strawberries
- 1/4 cup marshmallow creme
- 2 slices frozen pound cake (3/4 inch thick), cubed

Direction

- Mix marshmallow crème, strawberries and ice cream till blended in a bowl. Fold very gently in cake cubes. Immediately serve.

Nutrition Information

- Calories: 169 calories
- Total Fat: 7g fat (4g saturated fat)
- Sodium: 84mg sodium
- Fiber: 0 fiber)
- Total Carbohydrate: 26g carbohydrate (7g sugars
- Cholesterol: 42mg cholesterol

- Protein: 2g protein.

335. Strawberry Sundae Cups

Serving: 2 servings. | Prep: 15mins | Cook: 0mins | Ready in:

Ingredients

- 4 ounces bittersweet chocolate, chopped
- 2 scoops strawberry ice cream
- Whipped cream in a can

Direction

- Melt 3-oz. of chocolate in a microwave, then stir until smooth. Brush evenly the inside of 2 foil muffin cup liners with the chocolate. Freeze until set, about 10 minutes. Do the brushing and freezing steps in the same manner 2 times more.
- Melt leftover chocolate and move to a small resealable plastic bag. In the corner of bag, cut a small hole, then pipe on waxed paper with 2 heart shapes. Freeze until they are set.
- Just before serving, peel liners off the chocolate cups carefully and throw away. Fill ice cream into cups. Use chocolate hearts and whipped cream to decorate.

Nutrition Information

- Calories: 198 calories
- Protein: 3g protein.
- Total Fat: 12g fat (6g saturated fat)
- Sodium: 40mg sodium
- Fiber: 1g fiber)
- Total Carbohydrate: 25g carbohydrate (5g sugars
- Cholesterol: 19mg cholesterol

336. Strawberry Sundae Sauce

Serving: 8 cups. | Prep: 15mins | Cook: 10mins | Ready in:

Ingredients

- 2 quarts fresh strawberries
- 6 cups sugar
- 1 pouch (3 ounces) liquid fruit pectin
- 1/3 cup chocolate syrup
- 1/3 cup raspberry liqueur, optional
- Vanilla ice cream

Direction

- Rinse and crush strawberries, measure out sufficient mashed berries to have 4 cups. Mix sugar and strawberries in Dutch oven. Let come to full rolling boil on high heat, mixing continuously. Mix in pectin. Boil for an additional of 1 minute, mixing continuously. Take off from heat. Mix in liqueur if wished and syrup. Scoop off froth.
- Put into freezer containers or jars, keeping a half-in space above. Cool for an hour to room temperature. Place cover and rest overnight or till firm. Chill for up till 3 weeks or freeze for up till a year. Serve together with ice cream.

Nutrition Information

- Calories: 174 calories
- Cholesterol: 0 cholesterol
- Protein: 0 protein.
- Total Fat: 0 fat (0 saturated fat)
- Sodium: 3mg sodium
- Fiber: 1g fiber)
- Total Carbohydrate: 43g carbohydrate (42g sugars

337. Strawberry Tart

Serving: 6-8 servings. | Prep: 20mins | Cook: 10mins | Ready in:

Ingredients

- 1 sheet refrigerated pie pastry
- 3 ounces German sweet chocolate, melted
- 2 packages (8 ounces each) cream cheese, softened
- 3 tablespoons heavy whipping cream
- 2 teaspoons vanilla extract
- 1-3/4 cups confectioners' sugar
- 2-1/2 cups sliced fresh strawberries
- 1/4 cup red currant jelly

Direction

- Press the pastry up the sides and onto bottom of an unoiled 9-inch fluted tart pan with the removable bottom. Put on the baking sheet. Bake for 10 to 12 mins at 450°, until golden brown. Place on wire rack to cool.
- Spread bottom of the crust with the melted chocolate. Place in the refrigerator until almost set, about 5 to 10 mins. In the meantime, beat vanilla, cream cheese and cream in a large bowl until smooth. Beat in the confectioners' sugar gradually. Spread over the chocolate layer.
- Place the strawberries over the filling and brush with the jelly. Place in the refrigerator for at least 120 mins. Discard the sides of pan to serve.

Nutrition Information

- Calories: 432 calories
- Total Carbohydrate: 57g carbohydrate (41g sugars
- Cholesterol: 44mg cholesterol
- Protein: 4g protein.
- Total Fat: 22g fat (12g saturated fat)
- Sodium: 187mg sodium
- Fiber: 1g fiber)

338. Strawberry Topped Yogurt Pie

Serving: 8 servings. | Prep: 10mins | Cook: 0mins | Ready in:

Ingredients

- 1 package (8 ounces) cream cheese, softened
- 2/3 cup plain yogurt
- 1/3 cup nonfat dry milk powder
- 1/3 cup honey
- 1 graham cracker crust (9 inches)
- 2 cups diced fresh strawberries
- Orange peel strips, optional

Direction

- Beat together honey, milk powder, yogurt and cream cheese in a bowl, then scoop the mixture into crust. Cover and freeze for a maximum of 1 month. Take out of the freezer about a half-hour prior to serving. Put strawberries on top then use orange peel to decorate if wanted.

Nutrition Information

- Calories: 194 calories
- Sodium: 272mg sodium
- Fiber: 1g fiber)
- Total Carbohydrate: 33g carbohydrate (0 sugars
- Cholesterol: 3mg cholesterol
- Protein: 8g protein. Diabetic Exchanges: 2 starch
- Total Fat: 4g fat (0 saturated fat)

339. Streusel Coffee Cake Mix

Serving: 9 servings per batch. | Prep: 10mins | Cook: 0mins | Ready in:

Ingredients

- COFFEE CAKE MIX:
- 4-1/2 cups all-purpose flour
- 2-1/4 cups sugar
- 2 tablespoons baking powder
- 1-1/2 teaspoons salt
- STREUSEL MIX:
- 3/4 cup packed brown sugar
- 3 tablespoons all-purpose flour
- 1 tablespoon ground cinnamon
- 1/4 teaspoon ground nutmeg
- 1-1/2 cups chopped pecans
- ADDITIONAL INGREDIENTS:
- 1 egg, beaten
- 1/2 cup milk
- 1/4 cup vegetable oil
- 1 tablespoon butter, melted

Direction

- Blend coffee cake mix ingredients together in a large bowl; put aside. Mix the first 4 streusel ingredients, followed by pecans. Preserve both mixes in different airtight containers in a cool and dry place for a maximum period of 6 months. The expected outcome should be 3 batches (2 1/4 cups of streusel and 6 cups of cake mix).
- Mix oil, milk, egg and 2 cups of cake mix in a bowl to make coffee cake. Transfer to a 9" square baking pan coated with cooking spray. Mix butter and three-fourths cup of streusel mix together; add onto the batter. Bake for 25 to 30 minutes at 375 degrees until a toothpick slid into the middle comes out with no batter streaks. Serve while still warm.

Nutrition Information

- Calories: 294 calories
- Protein: 4g protein.
- Total Fat: 13g fat (2g saturated fat)
- Sodium: 250mg sodium
- Fiber: 1g fiber)
- Total Carbohydrate: 41g carbohydrate (23g sugars
- Cholesterol: 29mg cholesterol

340. Sunshine Cupcakes

Serving: 24 | Prep: 30mins | Cook: | Ready in:

Ingredients

- Cupcakes
- 1 cup egg whites (7 to 9 large)
- ¾ cup sifted cake flour
- 1 cup sugar (see Tip)
- 2 teaspoons vanilla
- 1 teaspoon cream of tartar
- 3 egg yolks
- Halved or quartered fresh strawberries (optional)
- Orange and/or lemon peel strips (optional)
- Lemon Fluff
- ½ 8-ounce container frozen light-whipped dessert topping, thawed
- ½ teaspoon finely shredded lemon peel
- 1 tablespoon lemon juice

Direction

- Let the egg whites stand in a huge bowl at room temperature for half an hour. In the meantime, sift 1/2 cup of sugar and cake flour 3 times. Use the paper bake cups to line 24 2 1/2-inches muffin cups; put aside.
- Set the oven to 375°F for preheating. Add the cream of tartar and vanilla to the egg whites. Use an electric mixer to beat the mixture at high speed until it forms soft peaks that can curl the tips. Add the remaining 1/2 cup of sugar gradually, whisking well until it forms stiff peaks, also, tips will stand straight. Sift 1/4 of the flour mixture over the egg white mixture, folding the mixture carefully. Do the same procedure of sifting and folding using the remaining flour mixture, adding 1/4 of the flour mixture at a time. Pour half of the egg white mixture into separate bowl; put them aside.

- Beat the egg yolks in a medium bowl using the electric mixer with a speed of high for 5 minutes until lemon-colored and thick. Fold the egg yolk mixture into one portion of the egg white mixture. Pour dollops of white and yellow batters into the paper bake cups alternately. Make sure that the cups are filled 2/3 full. Use a narrow metal spatula or knife to cut through the batter.
- Bake them for 10-12 minutes until the cupcakes will spring back when touched lightly near the middle. Remove them from the cups and let them cool completely on a wire rack.
- Fold 1/2 of the 8-oz container frozen light whipped dessert topping (thawed) in a medium bowl together with 1 tbsp. of lemon juice and 1/2 tsp. of the finely shredded lemon peel until just blended.
- Frost cupcakes with Lemon Fluff. Garnish them with orange and/or lemon peel strips and raspberries if desired. Place the cupcakes inside the fridge.

Nutrition Information

- Calories: 72 calories;
- Total Carbohydrate: 14
- Sugar: 9
- Protein: 2
- Sodium: 18
- Fiber: 0
- Cholesterol: 23
- Total Fat: 1
- Saturated Fat: 1

341. Surprise Cookie Pops

Serving: 1 dozen. | Prep: 10mins | Cook: 15mins | Ready in:

Ingredients

- 2 Milky Way candy bars (2.05 ounces each)
- 12 Popsicle sticks
- 1 tube (18 ounces) refrigerated chocolate chip cookie dough

Direction

- Slice widthwise each candy bar into six pieces; pierce into each a Popsicle stick. Divide cookie dough into 12 pieces. Flatten the dough; wrap each piece around per candy bar, shaping a ball.
- On the ungreased baking sheets, position the balls 3-inch apart. Bake at 350° for about 13-15 minutes, or up to lightly browned. Let cool for 3 minutes before transferring to wire racks.

Nutrition Information

- Calories: 418 calories
- Sodium: 201mg sodium
- Fiber: 1g fiber)
- Total Carbohydrate: 59g carbohydrate (40g sugars
- Cholesterol: 22mg cholesterol
- Protein: 4g protein.
- Total Fat: 19g fat (6g saturated fat)

342. Sweet Fruit Slush

Serving: 6-8 servings. | Prep: 20mins | Cook: 0mins | Ready in:

Ingredients

- 3 cups water
- 1 cup sugar
- 1 can (20 ounces) crushed pineapple, undrained
- 1 can (6 ounces) frozen orange juice concentrate, thawed
- 1 medium ripe peach, chopped or 2/3 cup sliced frozen peaches, thawed and chopped

Direction

- Boil water and sugar in a large saucepan over medium heat. Remove from the heat. Let it cool for 10 minutes.
- Add the peach, orange juice concentrate, and pineapple and stir thoroughly. Transfer the mixture into a freezer container, freeze for at least 12 hours or overnight (this can stay frozen for up to 3 months). Take it out of the freezer 1 hour before serving.

Nutrition Information

- Calories: 191 calories
- Protein: 1g protein.
- Total Fat: 0 fat (0 saturated fat)
- Sodium: 2mg sodium
- Fiber: 1g fiber)
- Total Carbohydrate: 49g carbohydrate (47g sugars
- Cholesterol: 0 cholesterol

343. Sweet Tooth Treats

Serving: 2-1/2 dozen. | Prep: 20mins | Cook: 5mins | Ready in:

Ingredients

- 1 cup peanut butter
- 1/2 cup light corn syrup
- 1/2 cup confectioners' sugar
- 1/4 cup sweetened shredded coconut
- 2 cups Cheerios
- 1 cup (6 ounces) semisweet chocolate chips
- 1 tablespoon shortening

Direction

- Mix the coconut, sugar, corn syrup and peanut butter in a big bowl until combined. Mix in the cereal. Form into balls of 1-1/2 inches.
- Melt the shortening and chocolate chips in a microwave; mix until smooth. Dip the balls in chocolate halfway; let excess drip off. Put onto the baking sheets lined with waxed paper; allow to stand until set.

Nutrition Information

- Calories: 232 calories
- Total Carbohydrate: 26g carbohydrate (18g sugars
- Cholesterol: 0 cholesterol
- Protein: 5g protein.
- Total Fat: 14g fat (5g saturated fat)
- Sodium: 135mg sodium
- Fiber: 2g fiber)

344. Thick Chocolate Pudding

Serving: 4 servings. | Prep: 5mins | Cook: 10mins | Ready in:

Ingredients

- 1/3 cup sugar
- 1/4 cup baking cocoa
- 3 tablespoons cornstarch
- 1/8 teaspoon salt
- 2 cups milk
- 1 teaspoon vanilla extract
- Whipped topping, optional

Direction

- Mix together the first 4 ingredients in a microwaveable bowl of 1 quart. Mix in milk until the mixture is smooth. Heat in the microwave on high without covering for 2 minutes and whisk. Keep heating in the microwave until the mixture becomes thick, 3 to 5 minutes more, whisking every minute. Mix in vanilla. Divide into individual serving dishes and let cool. Chill in the refrigerator. Spread whipped topping on top to decorate (optional).

Nutrition Information

- Calories: 180 calories
- Fiber: 1g fiber)
- Total Carbohydrate: 31g carbohydrate (22g sugars
- Cholesterol: 17mg cholesterol
- Protein: 5g protein.
- Total Fat: 5g fat (3g saturated fat)
- Sodium: 134mg sodium

345. Three Fruit Dump Cake

Serving: 6-8 servings,. | Prep: 5mins | Cook: 45mins | Ready in:

Ingredients

- 1 can (21 ounces) apple pie filling
- 1 can (15-1/4 ounces) sliced pears, drained
- 1 can (15-1/4 ounces) sliced peaches, drained
- 1 package (9 ounces) yellow cake mix
- 1/4 cup butter, cut into 1/8-inch pieces

Direction

- Mix together peaches, pears and pie filling in a big bowl, then scoop into an 8-inch square baking dish coated with grease. Use cake mix to sprinkle over and dot with butter.
- Bake at 350 degrees until golden brown, about 45 to 50 minutes. Serve warm.

Nutrition Information

- Calories: 313 calories
- Total Fat: 9g fat (5g saturated fat)
- Sodium: 300mg sodium
- Fiber: 2g fiber)
- Total Carbohydrate: 58g carbohydrate (41g sugars
- Cholesterol: 15mg cholesterol
- Protein: 2g protein.

346. Three Fruit Frozen Yogurt

Serving: 1-1/2 quarts. | Prep: 15mins | Cook: 0mins | Ready in:

Ingredients

- 2 medium ripe bananas
- 1 package (10 ounces) frozen sweetened sliced strawberries, thawed and drained
- 1 can (8 ounces) crushed pineapple, drained
- 3/4 cup (6 ounces) strawberry yogurt
- 1/2 cup sugar
- 1 carton (8 ounces) frozen whipped topping, thawed

Direction

- Mash strawberries and bananas together in a big bowl. Stir in sugar, yogurt and pineapple, then fold in whipped topping. Cover and freeze until the mixture is firm. You can freeze for a maximum of one month.

Nutrition Information

- Calories: 151 calories
- Protein: 1g protein.
- Total Fat: 3g fat (3g saturated fat)
- Sodium: 9mg sodium
- Fiber: 1g fiber)
- Total Carbohydrate: 29g carbohydrate (24g sugars
- Cholesterol: 1mg cholesterol

347. Toffee Ice Cream Pie

Serving: 8 servings. | Prep: 20mins | Cook: 5mins | Ready in:

Ingredients

- 1 quart vanilla ice cream, softened
- 1 Heath candy bar (1.4 ounces), crushed

- 1 chocolate crumb crust (8 inches)
- CHOCOLATE SAUCE:
- 1 cup (6 ounces) semisweet chocolate chips
- 1/4 cup butter, cubed
- 1 cup confectioners' sugar
- 1 can (5 ounces) evaporated milk
- 1 teaspoon vanilla extract

Direction

- Mix crushed candy and ice cream in a big bowl. Spread onto crust. Freeze, covered, till firm.
- Melt butter and chocolate chips on medium low heat in a small saucepan. Add evaporated milk and confectioners' sugar. Stir and cook till thickened for 4-5 minutes. Take off heat. Mix vanilla in. Slice pie to slices. Drizzle sauce on.

Nutrition Information

- Calories: 496 calories
- Fiber: 2g fiber)
- Total Carbohydrate: 63g carbohydrate (49g sugars
- Cholesterol: 51mg cholesterol
- Protein: 6g protein.
- Total Fat: 27g fat (14g saturated fat)
- Sodium: 226mg sodium

348. Toffee Oat Cookies

Serving: about 4 dozen. | Prep: 15mins | Cook: 10mins | Ready in:

Ingredients

- 3/4 cup butter, softened
- 1 cup packed brown sugar
- 3/4 cup sugar
- 2 eggs
- 3 teaspoons vanilla extract
- 2-1/4 cups all-purpose flour
- 2-1/4 cups old-fashioned oats
- 1 teaspoon baking soda
- 1 teaspoon baking powder
- 1/2 teaspoon salt
- 1 package English toffee bits (10 ounces) or almond brickle chips (7-1/2 ounces)

Direction

- Cream sugars and butter in a large bowl until fluffy and light. Put in eggs, one by one, beating thoroughly between additions. Beat vanilla into the mixture. Mix together salt, baking powder, baking soda, oats and flour; slowly add into creamed mixture and combine well. Mix in toffee bits.
- Drop rounded tablespoonfuls of batter onto ungreased baking sheets, keeping a 2-inch distance away from each other. Bake at 375 degrees until cookies are golden brown or 10 to 12 minutes. Allow to cool in pans for 60 seconds, then transfer to wire racks until thoroughly cool.

Nutrition Information

- Calories: 250 calories
- Cholesterol: 37mg cholesterol
- Protein: 3g protein.
- Total Fat: 11g fat (5g saturated fat)
- Sodium: 252mg sodium
- Fiber: 1g fiber)
- Total Carbohydrate: 36g carbohydrate (22g sugars

349. Toffee Peanut Clusters

Serving: 5 dozen. | Prep: 30mins | Cook: 0mins | Ready in:

Ingredients

- 1-1/2 pounds milk chocolate candy coating, coarsely chopped
- 1 jar (16 ounces) dry roasted peanuts

- 1 package (8 ounces) milk chocolate English toffee bits

Direction

- Put candy coating in a microwave, melt the candy coating and stir it till becomes smooth. Mix in toffee bits and peanuts. Line baking sheets by waxed paper and use the toffee mixture to make rounded tablespoonful drops on the baking sheets. Allow the drops to sit till they are set. Keep in an airtight container.

Nutrition Information

- Calories: 123 calories
- Protein: 2g protein. Diabetic Exchanges: 1-1/2 fat
- Total Fat: 8g fat (4g saturated fat)
- Sodium: 78mg sodium
- Fiber: 1g fiber)
- Total Carbohydrate: 11g carbohydrate (9g sugars
- Cholesterol: 3mg cholesterol

350. Triple Chip Cookies

Serving: about 2-1/2 dozen. | Prep: 15mins | Cook: 10mins | Ready in:

Ingredients

- 1 tube (16-1/2 ounces) refrigerated peanut butter cookie dough
- 1 cup coarsely crushed potato chips
- 1/2 cup butterscotch chips
- 1/2 cup swirled milk chocolate and peanut butter chips

Direction

- Soften the cookie dough by letting it stand for 5-10 minutes at room temperature. In a large bowl, combine the chips and cookie dough.
- Drop by tablespoonfuls of dough onto ungreased baking sheets 2 in. apart. Bake at 350° until light brown or 10-12 minutes. Transfer to wire racks. Keep in an airtight container.

Nutrition Information

- Calories:
- Fiber:
- Total Carbohydrate:
- Cholesterol:
- Protein:
- Total Fat:
- Sodium:

351. Tropical Fruit Cream Pie

Serving: 6-8 servings. | Prep: 10mins | Cook: 0mins | Ready in:

Ingredients

- 2 cups cold 2% milk
- 1/2 teaspoon coconut extract
- 1 package (3.4 ounces) instant vanilla pudding mix
- 1 can (15-1/4 ounces) mixed tropical fruit, drained
- 1/2 cup sweetened shredded coconut, toasted
- 1 graham cracker crust (9 inches)

Direction

- Beat pudding mix, extract, and milk in a large mixing bowl for 2 minutes. Allow to sit until soft-set, about 2 minutes. Fold in coconut and fruit. Spread over the crust. Chill until ready to serve.

Nutrition Information

- Calories: 0
- Total Carbohydrate: 42 g carbohydrate

- Cholesterol: 8 mg cholesterol
- Protein: 3 g protein.
- Total Fat: 10 g fat (5 g saturated fat)
- Sodium: 293 mg sodium
- Fiber: 2 g fiber

352. Tropical Island Dessert

Serving: 12-16 servings. | Prep: 30mins | Cook: 0mins | Ready in:

Ingredients

- 3 packages (3 ounces each) berry blue gelatin
- 2 cups boiling water
- 2-1/2 cups cold water
- 4 tablespoons fish-shaped gummy candies, divided
- 2 cups cold milk
- 1 package (3.4 ounces) instant vanilla pudding mix
- 1 medium lime
- 2 cinnamon sticks
- 1 round wooden toothpick
- 2 tablespoons graham cracker crumbs
- 6 whole allspice
- 1 disposable cup (2-ounce size)
- Fresh blueberries and additional gummy candies, optional

Direction

- Dissolve gelatin in boiling water in a bowl. Mix in cold water. Add into a 6-cup ring mold greased with cooking spray. Put in 2 tablespoons of gummy candies. Allow to chill for 60 mins. Mix in the rest of candies. Allow to chill until set, about 1-2 hours.
- Whisk pudding and milk together in a bowl. Cover up and let chill until ready to use.
- To create palm tree leaves, cut lime into two; remove and throw away the pulp. On a cutting board, arrange lime halves with cut side down. Sketch five leaves with a pencil from bottom up to top on each half. Cut out the leaves, leaving the middle intact; create little cuts to form a palm leaf look. To make tree bases, place the disposable cup upside down; make two small slits in the bottom. For tree trunks, put a cinnamon stick in each slits. Break toothpick into two. Add the pointed ends into the middle of lime halves; add the broken ends into cinnamon sticks.
- Unmold the gelatin to place on a serving platter of 12 inches. Put cup in the middle of gelatin ring. With a spoon, add vanilla pudding over cup, filling middle of the ring. For sand, sprinkle with graham cracker crumbs. For coconuts, arrange allspice at the tree bases (remove the allspice before serving). If desired, garnish with more gummy fish and blueberries.

Nutrition Information

- Calories: 78 calories
- Sodium: 118mg sodium
- Fiber: 0 fiber)
- Total Carbohydrate: 16g carbohydrate (14g sugars
- Cholesterol: 4mg cholesterol
- Protein: 2g protein.
- Total Fat: 1g fat (1g saturated fat)

353. Vanilla Cake With Raspberries

Serving: 4 servings. | Prep: 5mins | Cook: 0mins | Ready in:

Ingredients

- 1 package (19.6 ounces) frozen vanilla layer cake
- 3/4 cup fresh raspberries
- 3/4 cup (6 ounces) raspberry yogurt

Direction

- Split the cake into two then put the other half in the freezer. Rest the other half at a room temperature. Slice the cake into eight pieces and put the four slices on a dessert platter. Drizzle with raspberries. Add the remaining four slices. Casually add some yogurt.

Nutrition Information

- Calories: 610 calories
- Protein: 8g protein.
- Total Fat: 23g fat (6g saturated fat)
- Sodium: 287mg sodium
- Fiber: 5g fiber)
- Total Carbohydrate: 21g carbohydrate (68g sugars
- Cholesterol: 55mg cholesterol

354. Vanilla Chip Dessert

Serving: 15 servings. | Prep: 25mins | Cook: 5mins | Ready in:

Ingredients

- 3 cups crushed vanilla wafers (about 90 wafers)
- 1/2 cup butter, melted
- 3 tablespoons brown sugar
- 1 package (10 to 12 ounces) white baking chips
- 2 packages (8 ounces each) cream cheese, softened
- 2 cups (16 ounces) sour cream
- 1 carton (8 ounces) frozen whipped topping, thawed
- Chocolate ice cream topping, optional

Direction

- Mix butter, brown sugar and wafer crumbs in a big bowl and flatten it on a greased 13x9-inch baking pan. Put it in the oven and bake for 5 to 8 minutes or until it turned light brown at 350°F. Let it cool.
- On the other hand, melt white chips in a microwave and mix until smooth. Allow it to cool.
- In a separate big bowl, beat sour cream and cream cheese together until smooth, and put in melted chips. Blend well and fold in.
- Pour the mixture over the prebaked crust, cover and chill until set or for 2 hours. Sprinkle some chocolate toppings (optional).

Nutrition Information

- Calories:
- Protein:
- Total Fat:
- Sodium:
- Fiber:
- Total Carbohydrate:
- Cholesterol:

355. Vanilla White Chocolate Mousse

Serving: 4 servings. | Prep: 10mins | Cook: 10mins | Ready in:

Ingredients

- 1-1/4 cups heavy whipping cream, divided
- 2 tablespoons sugar
- 2 large egg yolks
- 7 ounces white baking chocolate, chopped
- 2 vanilla beans
- Toasted sliced almonds, optional

Direction

- Cook sugar and 1/4 cup cream in small saucepan on medium heat till bubbles form around pan's sides.
- Whisk small amount hot mixture into egg yolks in small bowl; put all back in pan, constantly whisking. Cook on low heat, constantly mixing, till thermometer reads

minimum 160° and thick just enough so it coats metal spoon; don't boil. Take off heat immediately; mix chocolate in till smooth.

- Lengthwise, split vanilla beans; scrape seeds from center into chocolate mixture using sharp knife's tip then mix. Put in big bowl; cool for 10 minutes.
- Beat leftover cream till soft peaks form in small bowl; fold into chocolate mixture. Put in 4 dessert dishes; refrigerate 1 hour before serving, covered. Sprinkle with almonds if desired.

Nutrition Information

- Calories: 559 calories
- Cholesterol: 195mg cholesterol
- Protein: 6g protein.
- Total Fat: 44g fat (29g saturated fat)
- Sodium: 68mg sodium
- Fiber: 0 fiber)
- Total Carbohydrate: 41g carbohydrate (40g sugars

356. Versatile Oat Mix

Serving: 6-8 servings. | Prep: 15mins | Cook: 15mins | Ready in:

Ingredients

- 3 cups all-purpose flour
- 1 cup packed brown sugar
- 1/2 cup sugar
- 3-1/2 teaspoons baking powder
- 1-1/2 teaspoons salt
- 1-1/2 cups shortening
- 3 cups quick-cooking oats
- ADDITIONAL INGREDIENTS FOR OAT PANCAKES:
- 1 egg, lightly beaten
- 1 cup water
- ADDITIONAL INGREDIENTS FOR OATMEAL MUFFINS:
- 1 egg, lightly beaten
- 2/3 cup milk
- ADDITIONAL INGREDIENTS FOR PEACH CRISP:
- 1/4 cup packed brown sugar
- 1 can (21 ounces) peach pie filling
- Ice cream or whipped topping, optional

Direction

- Mix together salt, baking powder, sugars and flour in a big bowl. Slice in shortening until the mixture like fine crumbs, then stir in oats. Keep in an airtight containers in a cool and dry area for a maximum of 6 months. Produce: 9 cups (but the quantity of batches will be different depending on the used recipe).
- For pancakes: In a bowl, mix together water, egg and 1 1/2 cups of oat mix. Allow to stand about 5 minutes. Put on a hot griddle that lightly greased with 1/4 cupfuls of batter. Turn when top forms bubbles and cook until the other side turn golden brown. Produce: 10 pancakes.
- For muffins: In a bowl, mix together milk, egg and 3 cups of oat mix. Fill the mixture into muffin cups lined with paper, until 2/3 full. Bake at 400 degrees until a toothpick exits clean, about 15 to 20 minutes. Allow to cool about 5 minutes before transferring to wire rack. Serve warm. Produce: 1 dozen.
- For peach crisp: In a bowl, mix well together brown sugar and 2 cups of oat mix. Pat 1 1/4 cups of the mixture into an 8-inch square baking pan that greased, then spread pie filling over. Sprinkle with leftover oat mixture and bake at 375 degrees until browned slightly, about a half hour. Serve warm together with whipped topping or ice cream, if you want.

Nutrition Information

- Calories: 330 calories
- Fiber: 2g fiber)
- Total Carbohydrate: 38g carbohydrate (16g sugars

- Cholesterol: 64mg cholesterol
- Protein: 6g protein.
- Total Fat: 17g fat (4g saturated fat)
- Sodium: 271mg sodium

357. Very Berry Bruschetta

Serving: 6 servings. | Prep: 25mins | Cook: 0mins | Ready in:

Ingredients

- 1 carton (8 ounces) spreadable strawberry cream cheese
- 6 tablespoons orange juice
- 1 teaspoon grated orange zest
- 2 cups sliced fresh strawberries
- 1 cup each fresh blueberries, blackberries and raspberries
- 6 slices pound cake
- Whipped cream in a can

Direction

- Whisk the orange juice, zest and cream cheese till incorporated in a small bowl. Put together the berries in a big bowl. Put a slice of cake on every of six dessert plates; atop with cream cheese mixture and berries. Jazz up with whipped cream.

Nutrition Information

- Calories: 291 calories
- Fiber: 4g fiber)
- Total Carbohydrate: 34g carbohydrate (14g sugars
- Cholesterol: 96mg cholesterol
- Protein: 4g protein.
- Total Fat: 17g fat (11g saturated fat)
- Sodium: 238mg sodium

358. Very Berry Pie

Serving: 8 servings. | Prep: 15mins | Cook: 0mins | Ready in:

Ingredients

- 1-3/4 cups reduced-fat whipped topping, divided
- 1 reduced-fat graham cracker crust (8 inches)
- 1 cup fresh raspberries
- 1 cup fresh blueberries
- Sugar substitute equivalent to 1 tablespoon sugar
- 1 cup cold fat-free milk
- 1 package (1 ounce) sugar-free instant white chocolate pudding mix

Direction

- Spread over the crust with 1/4 cup of the whipped topping. Mix the sugar substitute and berries; then scoop over the topping with 1 cup.
- Beat the pudding mix and milk in a bowl for 2 minutes (the mixture will become thick). Scoop over the berries carefully. Spread the rest of the whipped topping over. Add the remaining berries on top. Chill in the fridge until set, for 45 minutes.

Nutrition Information

- Calories: 214 calories
- Protein: 2g protein. Diabetic Exchanges: 1-1/2 fruit
- Total Fat: 5g fat (3g saturated fat)
- Sodium: 259mg sodium
- Fiber: 2g fiber)
- Total Carbohydrate: 39g carbohydrate (23g sugars
- Cholesterol: 1mg cholesterol

359. Warm Fruit Compote With Cream Cheese Topping

Serving: 6 servings. | Prep: 15mins | Cook: 0mins | Ready in:

Ingredients

- 1/4 cup packed brown sugar
- 1 teaspoon cornstarch
- 1/4 cup water
- 1/4 cup thawed orange juice concentrate
- 2 tablespoons butter
- 1 can (20 ounces) pineapple chunks, drained
- 1 can (15-1/4 ounces) sliced pears, drained and halved
- 1 can (15 ounces) mandarin oranges, drained
- TOPPING:
- 3 ounces cream cheese, softened
- 1 tablespoon sugar
- 1 tablespoon thawed orange juice concentrate

Direction

- Combine cornstarch and brown sugar in a large saucepan. Stir in orange juice concentrate and water until consistency is smooth. Add butter in. Bring to a boil and cook while stirring until thickened, about 2 minutes. Lower the heat. Add fruit and heat it through.
- Beat the ingredients for the topping in a small bowl until smooth. Serve with the fruit.

Nutrition Information

- Calories: 263 calories
- Total Fat: 9g fat (5g saturated fat)
- Sodium: 94mg sodium
- Fiber: 1g fiber)
- Total Carbohydrate: 45g carbohydrate (43g sugars
- Cholesterol: 26mg cholesterol
- Protein: 3g protein.

360. Warm Peach Dessert

Serving: 2 servings. | Prep: 30mins | Cook: 0mins | Ready in:

Ingredients

- 2 cans (one 15-1/4 ounces, one 8-1/2 ounces) sliced peaches, drained
- 2 teaspoons cornstarch
- 2 tablespoons graham cracker crumbs
- 1/8 teaspoon ground cinnamon
- Dash ground nutmeg
- 2 teaspoons butter, melted

Direction

- Drain peaches, saving 1/2 cup syrup. Arrange peaches in an oiled 1-quart baking dish. Combine reserved peach syrup and cornstarch in a small saucepan until smooth. Heat to a boil; stir and cook until thickened, about 1 minute. Spread over peaches.
- Mix together nutmeg, cinnamon and graham cracker crumbs; mix in butter. Drizzle over peaches. Bake at 350 degrees without cover, till the topping is slightly browned, about 10-15 minutes.

Nutrition Information

- Calories: 227 calories
- Sodium: 75mg sodium
- Fiber: 2g fiber)
- Total Carbohydrate: 49g carbohydrate (42g sugars
- Cholesterol: 0 cholesterol
- Protein: 0 protein.
- Total Fat: 3g fat (0 saturated fat)

361. White Almond No Bake Cookies

Serving: about 3-1/2 dozen. | Prep: 25mins | Cook: 5mins | Ready in:

Ingredients

- 2 cups sugar
- 1/2 cup butter, cubed
- 1/2 cup 2% milk
- 1 cup white baking chips
- 1/2 teaspoon almond extract
- 3 cups old-fashioned oats
- 1 cup dried cherries or dried cranberries, optional

Direction

- In the big saucepan, mix the milk, butter and sugar. Cook and stir on medium heat till the butter melts and the sugar dissolves. Take out of the heat. Stir in the extract and baking chips till smooth. Put in the oats, and if you want, cherries; stir till coated.
- Drop by rounded tablespoonfuls to the baking sheets which are lined with waxed paper. Keep refrigerated for roughly half an hour till set. Keep stored in the airtight container in the fridge.

Nutrition Information

- Calories: 101 calories
- Protein: 1g protein.
- Total Fat: 4g fat (2g saturated fat)
- Sodium: 23mg sodium
- Fiber: 1g fiber)
- Total Carbohydrate: 16g carbohydrate (12g sugars
- Cholesterol: 7mg cholesterol

362. White Chocolate Berry Parfaits

Serving: 4 servings. | Prep: 15mins | Cook: 0mins | Ready in:

Ingredients

- 1 package (3.3 ounces) instant white chocolate pudding mix
- 1 cup sliced fresh strawberries
- 1/2 cup Oreo cookie crumbs
- 1/2 cup whipped topping

Direction

- Assemble pudding following the package instructions.
- Scoop pudding; 1/4 cup each, into 4 parfait glasses. Arrange cookie crumbs and half of the strawberries on top of the pudding. Repeat layering once more. Top with whipped topping. Store in refrigerator to chill before serving.

Nutrition Information

- Calories: 308 calories
- Fiber: 2g fiber)
- Total Carbohydrate: 50g carbohydrate (42g sugars
- Cholesterol: 12mg cholesterol
- Protein: 5g protein.
- Total Fat: 10g fat (5g saturated fat)
- Sodium: 553mg sodium

363. Whoopie Cookies

Serving: about 1-1/2 dozen. | Prep: 20mins | Cook: 10mins | Ready in:

Ingredients

- 1 package devil's food cake mix (regular size)
- 1/4 cup butter, softened

- 2 large eggs
- 1 jar (7 ounces) marshmallow creme
- 4 ounces cream cheese, softened

Direction

- Beat butter and cake mix together in a big bowl until well-mixed. Beat in eggs then form the mixture into 1 inch balls. Put on ungreased baking sheets with 2 inches apart.
- Bake at 350 degrees until tops become cracked, about 7 to 9 minutes. Allow to cool about 2 minutes before transferring to wire racks to fully cool.
- Beat together cream cheese and marshmallow crème in a big bowl until mixed but (avoid over-beating). Spread on the bottoms of half of cookies with the filling, then put leftover cookies on top. Refrigerate until filling has set, about 1 to 2 hours.

Nutrition Information

- Calories: 152 calories
- Total Carbohydrate: 25g carbohydrate (16g sugars
- Cholesterol: 28mg cholesterol
- Protein: 2g protein.
- Total Fat: 5g fat (3g saturated fat)
- Sodium: 206mg sodium
- Fiber: 1g fiber)

364. Wonton Kisses

Serving: 2 dozen. | Prep: 15mins | Cook: 10mins | Ready in:

Ingredients

- 24 milk chocolate kisses
- 24 wonton wrappers
- Oil for frying
- Confectioners' sugar

Direction

- In the center of a wonton wrapper, place a chocolate kiss. (Use a damp paper towel to keep remaining wrappers covered till ready to use.) Use water to moisten edges; fold opposite corners together over candy kiss and pinch to seal. Repeat.
- Heat 1 inch of oil in an electric skillet to 375°. Fry wontons for approximately two and a half minutes till they have golden brown color, turning once. Place on paper towels to drain. Dust with confectioners' sugar.

Nutrition Information

- Calories: 58 calories
- Total Carbohydrate: 7g carbohydrate (2g sugars
- Cholesterol: 2mg cholesterol
- Protein: 1g protein.
- Total Fat: 3g fat (1g saturated fat)
- Sodium: 50mg sodium
- Fiber: 0 fiber)

365. Yummy Chocolate Double Chip Cookies

Serving: 2-1/2 dozen. | Prep: 15mins | Cook: 10mins | Ready in:

Ingredients

- 1/2 cup butter, softened
- 3/4 cup packed brown sugar
- 1 egg
- 1 teaspoon vanilla extract
- 1-1/4 cups all-purpose flour
- 1/2 teaspoon baking soda
- 1/2 teaspoon salt
- 2/3 cup semisweet chocolate chips
- 1/3 cup butterscotch chips

Direction

- Cream together butter and brown sugar in a large bowl till fluffy and light. Beat egg and vanilla into the mixture. Mix together the salt, baking soda and flour; add them gradually into the creamed mixture and combine thoroughly. Stir the chocolate and butterscotch chips into the mixture.
- Drop rounded tablespoonfuls of the dough 2 in. apart onto greased baking sheets. Bake to a golden brown at 350° or for 10-12 minutes (the tops will feel soft to touch). Let them cool down for 3 minutes, then transfer to wire racks to cool thoroughly. Keep in an airtight container.

Nutrition Information

- Calories: 101 calories
- Fiber: 0 fiber)
- Total Carbohydrate: 14g carbohydrate (7g sugars
- Cholesterol: 15mg cholesterol
- Protein: 1g protein.
- Total Fat: 5g fat (3g saturated fat)
- Sodium: 89mg sodium

Index

T

Conclusion

Thank you again for downloading this book!

I hope you enjoyed reading about my book!

If you enjoyed this book, please take the time to share your thoughts and post a review on Amazon. It'd be greatly appreciated!

Write me an honest review about the book – I truly value your opinion and thoughts and I will incorporate them into my next book, which is already underway.

Thank you!

If you have any questions, **feel free to contact at:** *publishing@crumblerecipes.com*

Wilma Walker

crumblerecipes.com

Printed in Great Britain
by Amazon

73990175R00102